PAULA MARAIS

A NUCLEAR FAMILY

A novel of mental illness, marriage and murder

A NUCLEAR FAMILY

By Paula Marais

Logogog

Copyright © 2021 Paula Marais
First published in 2021 by Logogog Press
Cover design by Kara Peters
ISBN 978-0-620-94606-3 (printed book)
ISBN 978-0-620-94607-0 (e-book)

This is a work of fiction. Names, characters, businesses,
places, events and incidents are either the products of the
author's imagination or used in a fictitious manner. Any
resemblance to actual persons, living or dead, actual events
or actual places is purely coincidental.

~For Jed, with love~

A NUCLEAR FAMILY

By Paula Marais

"I sat on the padded bench, his naked back once more before my eyes, the wind scouring the deck, and thought of the strange transitions from enchantment to disenchantment and back again that moved through human affairs like cloudbanks, sometimes portentous and grey and sometimes mere distant inscrutable shapes that blotted out the sun for a while and then just as carelessly revealed it again."

Rachel Cusk ~ *Outline*

~PART I~

Cutting loose

Five minutes later would have been too late. Thank God for her forgotten laptop on the dining room table. And the fact she'd realised she'd left it there and turned her car around. Dropping her keys on the kitchen counter, she saw his schoolbag hanging neatly on his 'Albert' hook. Alice felt an unexpected feeling of disquiet creeping into her gut. *Why was he still here?*

'Bert?' she called.

There was no reply and she wondered, not for the first time, how well she actually knew her child. To think he'd bunk school, knowing for sure that she wouldn't have noticed, made her blood boil. But it just wasn't like him, which made her feel suddenly more anxious than irate.

'Albert!' she called.

No reply.

She marched down the passageway to his bedroom; the door was tightly shut, and when she pushed it, found that it was locked from the inside. She beat hard on the door.

Bang! Bang!

No reply.

Albert was an unusual boy, but he was generally more defiant that disobedient. Until today, of course: missing school.

Alice banged one more time and when she again got no response, exited the house to peer in through Albert's window. And it was then that she saw him, his prepubescent body hanging from the light fitting by his scrawny neck. His eyes bulging. A rope of sorts – perhaps the belt of a dressing gown – holding him. Alice screamed. If she had not heard herself, she would not have believed a scream like that could come from her. But it also pushed a huge surge of adrenaline into her body. When the window pane tumbled before her like a jagged waterfall, she barely noticed the shards of glass burying themselves into her flesh. She tossed the garden chair she'd seized to shatter the window, her feet light upon her crystal carpet.

She couldn't reach his neck. But she did register where Albert's scratching fingers had tried to untie the tightening noose. And so she held him, lifting his whole body to ease the pressure where the life had begun to leave him.

'I've got you,' she said. But how to free him without letting him go? She needed help. Then she glanced around frantically and realised the stool where Albert had been standing was lying at his feet.

'I'm going to have to release you,' Alice told her son. 'Just for a second.' He shook his head wildly. 'I need to cut you loose.' But it was less than a second and his feet were back on the stool that had set him swinging. Alice saw Albert's nail clippers lying next to his bed and used these to hack at the noose. It may have taken only a few moments, but it felt like hours. Shredded material nicked and ripped to reveal a neck ringed by a welt of crimson. He had a pulse, thank God, and he was breathing. She placed her child on the bed, her own breath echoing in her head. 'I'm calling an ambulance,' she told him. 'But I'm coming back. I love you.'

And when the siren finally wailed increasingly loudly as it came down the road, it was the sweetest sound she'd ever heard.

Settling

In the beginning, or the beginning of them as a family, Alice had had certain expectations. Bruce was going to be a wonderful father. People liked him. He was sporty. He loved kids. He enjoyed team games. Unfortunately she had not realised that a love for the outdoors and certain qualities of extroversion did not necessarily make a good dad. From the moment Albert was born, Bruce complained about the lack of sleep. He moved immediately into the spare room, leaving her with her little bundle who howled most of the night. Had she had another child to compare Albert to, she might have thought the overly active baby was unusual. But she did not. Because she was inexperienced, she also did not realise that the way Albert spoke full sentences by seven months and could recite all the capitals across the globe by three and a half was not mere fluke. Albert was a challenge. Lithe and energetic, he was hard to exhaust. Bruce thought himself remarkably clever to teach Albert how to turn on the remote for the television and tune into CBeebies. That way, when the little mite exited his bed at five in the morning, he could entertain himself for hours and they got to lie in. Except that what Bruce wanted to do in that time was not what Alice was after. He wanted wild, passionate bonking and equally passionate kissing (preferably with raunchy commentary in between). She wanted an uninterrupted sleep. They fought about it more than she cared to admit. It felt to her that where Albert ended Bruce began and she was left with nothing of herself. When, for instance, had she last read a full book? Or sat on the loo without either Bruce or Albert walking in? At least Bruce didn't expect to sit in her lap, but she wouldn't put it past him. It was like living with two toddlers, not one. How was it then that two years later, they would find themselves adopting? It wasn't that she ever wished she could send Enjoy back, especially after the tragedies the poor girl had suffered. It's just that, well, Alice was further reduced. And then the dog. A Jack Russell, Malawi, with short legs and a bad temper, that dug up her garden and howled if there was thunder, which didn't happen often, that was true. But still …

She didn't have much time to think about her choices but when she did, Alice thought that perhaps she'd settled too young. Too inexperienced. Despite being a competent draftsman (draftsperson?), she wished she had studied further, not followed her future husband across the country where he did his postgraduate studies in electrical engineering. And then, of course, his scholarship to the US, where she was not allowed to work and so spent much of her time doing various courses on the internet, which added up to something but nothing (interior decorating; fabric design; furniture restoration; paint effects; découpage). And it wasn't that she didn't enjoy their time in the States. They'd considered living there, after all, and not coming back. But the thought of raising a family without a support network had drawn them home − that and the consulting position Bruce had secured in green energy, which wasn't even the rage then. But now, now Bruce's company was doing so well "people were throwing their credit cards at him", as he so tactfully put it. Their house was already completely off the grid. *Why give those corrupting bastards a chance to have a hold on us* − which was especially useful, as the dam levels sank lower and lower and people were flushing their toilets with buckets of grey water saved from the bath (while their own grey-water system had been doing this automatically for several years). From anybody's viewpoint, they had a good life. They hadn't lost parents yet, although hers were far away living in Edinburgh (so much for family support), and his mother, Janet, now remarried to a professor of audiology, spent a great deal of time travelling with him to medical conferences. A retired tour operator, she had very little interest in being at home, or spending time with their children. The message was clear. She'd done her time and it had been a burden. As soon as Bruce and his brother were out of the house, she'd dumped their father − a quickie divorce, during which she pretty much gave him everything and told him not to contact her − and went to teach English in Japan. The TEFL course she'd been doing had been a preparation for this exit. Bruce's father, an unassuming and rather grey financial director of an insurance firm, had not seen any of it coming. Janet had always been moody, even flighty. Prone to giddy excitement and wallowing self-pity. But it appeared, this time, that things were different. Bruce and his brother Gabriel had been left to pick up the shattered pieces of their wrecked family, while their mother cheerfully waved from the airport, blowing enthusiastic kisses as she went through customs. That first exit, she'd apparently not returned for two years; not even for Christmas.

12

It was not really surprising, then, that neither Bruce nor Gabriel wanted their mother, or her new husband, around. Though Alice did not know them very well, and didn't particularly like Janet, she did like Janet's husband with his booming laugh, affable manner and ability to speak to children. Bruce's father, Albert, after whom their son was named according to tradition, had only become greyer, working long hours, drinking expensive wine before bed (a bottle a night, on average) and very occasionally dating women much younger than him, none of whom ever lasted. Albert (senior) infrequently invited them to Kelvin Grove for Sunday lunch and a game of tennis. It wasn't a completely dispiriting affair. Albert also attempted levity, but his in-between-relationship loneliness was almost palpable and made Alice pity him. When he looked at her across the table, she sometimes had a sense of looking at her own husband twenty years on, which gave her a disheartening sense of foreboding. Would she make Bruce that unhappy too? It wasn't as if she was about to jump on a plane and leave her family behind, but when she thought about it, she could almost understand Janet's actions. Not, of course, that she'd ever admit it. Freedom was something she'd never really experienced. She'd met Bruce very young, at fifteen, at a swimming gala, where she was serving hotdogs to raise money for the SPCA. He was already in Matric, captain of the swimming team and insatiably hungry. After the fifth hotdog, which he'd bought shirtless, dazzling her with his tanned chest and manly arms, she was already smitten. Bruce had helped her carry the trestle table to her mother's car, lifting it in with one hand while he grinned at her. In those first moments of their meeting, she'd hoped he'd ask for more than her name, but he hadn't. Nevertheless, she knew where he went to school and made it her business to attend every gala after that. She was gratified, at least, that when he saw her again, he remembered her name. It was a sweet meeting, as she recalled it, and he touched her shoulder, a moment she can still recall with such clarity that she wonders now if perhaps it had become more in her head than it actually ever was. The jolt to her shoulder. The smile. His casual mention of a movie, if she was interested. It was called *Dances with Wolves* and there was a crowd of kids. It wasn't *a date*, as such, but she'd dressed and prepared for it like it was. Her mother dropped her at Cavendish and walked with her to the cinema.

'I'm fine, Mom,' she'd said, trying to slip away with as little fuss as possible.

'I'd like to see who you're going to be with,' her mother said, the Scottish burr still obvious after twenty years in South Africa.

When Bruce appeared from the ticket booth, he saw her and waved, walking casually over. 'I bought all the tickets,' he said. 'So we could sit together. Hello, Mrs Macdonald.'

Alice's mother smiled. 'What time, darling?'

And when she'd left, Bruce tapped on Alice's arm. 'Follow me, the other guys are there already.'

She followed him nervously. Going to a girls-only school had transformed boys into strange unknowable beings. Her little brother Jake didn't count. But Bruce's friends weren't only boys, and a few of the girls she knew by sight. They nodded at each other. It wasn't nearly as intimidating as she expected it would be. When the lights turned off and the music started, she was almost relaxed. Bruce was next to her, holding a huge carton of popcorn, which crunched grittily between his teeth. On the other side was a boy whose name she did not know but later learnt was Bruce's best friend Martini. (This nickname was some weird corruption of Oliver to olive to the drink – men's nicknames were strange.) It was hard to concentrate, however, knowing that Bruce was sitting next to her, and being a person who usually filled empty air with chatter, she found her own silence unnerving. When Bruce offered her some popcorn, she took it gratefully, appreciating the distraction of the cracking kernels. Later, she would remember very little about the movie. The Civil War, some Indians (Native Americans?), beautiful scenery, a love story. Mainly it was the first time that Bruce slipped his hand into hers, squeezing it so gently that she almost wondered if it was really happening. And when the movie finished and he let her go, she thought she might have imagined it, that, except for the gentle heat from her palms. They went afterwards to the Spur and drank cream soda floats. They were sweet and filling, and she wished she was sharing hers because it was just too much for her. She wondered if she would look like a killjoy if she didn't finish it. The conversation flowed around her and she knew she was quiet. Quieter than she'd ever been. How was she supposed to make an impression on Bruce when she couldn't even speak? And why could she think of nothing useful to say? She spooned ice cream from the float into her mouth. The saccharinity was cloying. She needed to pee, and how was she going to get past all these people she didn't know when she was sitting at the end of the bench? Shifting a little, she glanced at Bruce but he seemed oblivious, laughing with his friends about some prank they'd pulled at school. Something to do with marbles that she didn't think all that hilarious. She took a decision. Nothing of any use to her was going to happen at this table. It was enough for one night. She was making no impression on anyone in this state, and she didn't foresee that changing soon.

She patted Bruce on the arm.

'I'm sorry, but I have to go,' she said softly when he turned to her.

He blanched. 'Hey, it's still early.'

'I know but–' The fact was she couldn't think of an excuse. She was bored? Left out? Hoping for something more than this cluster of inane chatter? Needing more attention? She picked up her handbag. 'Sorry, guys, I need to slide along. Won't disturb you for long.'

Bruce stood up quickly. 'Seriously? Let me walk you at least.'

One of the girls in the group glared at Alice, making her feel vaguely powerful.

'You sure?'

He nodded.

'Let me just dash to the loo.' She hated how that sounded, but the truth was, she was fairly desperate.

When she exited the ladies, Bruce was already waiting at the entrance to the Spur. He looked caught off guard.

'Not your vibe?' he said idly as he walked her towards the exit where her mother was going to collect her.

'It's not that.'

'No?'

'I'm just a bit shy. Not good in … crowds.' She thought how pathetic she sounded. If she wanted to put Bruce off, she was certainly doing a good job.

But he seemed unperturbed. 'So, if I were to say, let's go and sit somewhere on our own, you might be keen?'

She smiled at him. 'I think your friends will miss you. Candice, was that her name, was already giving me daggers.'

'Cands does that with everyone she doesn't know. A bit, well, protective.'

'She likes you.'

He shrugged. 'Just friends, Alice.' And without any further discussion, he slipped his fingers between hers.

***

Bruce was her first and only. She suspected, when she was feeling morose, that she was not *his* first and only. His first perhaps, but not the latter. It was the comments he sometimes made. 'I didn't sleep with her,' when referring to an ex, when Alice was supposed to have been the only person he'd had sex with. It had certainly been true when they first crossed *that* threshold. If this was worth saying, then there had to be a reason to say it. Defending the indefensible. After all, they'd been together since that movie night. No break-ups, no drama. They'd even survived the long-distance year when he had been studying in Bloemfontein. She'd been at UCT, in her first years of architecture. And then the sudden move to the US, giving up her own career for a life with Bruce. Did she regret it? Occasionally. She felt like she'd merged her life with his without giving real thought to what *she* actually wanted. She felt she was somehow worth more than what she amounted to. A mother. A wife. An interior decorator/draftsperson. A daughter and daughter-in-law. A sister. And her family, it turned out, was not what she'd hoped for. For one thing, her own childhood had been stress-free, loving parents in a loving marriage. Financial stability. An older sister, Claire, who was a bit wild, but settled eventually (the dramas later were irrelevant; Alice wasn't living at home anymore). Jake, her little brother. The problem was that she and Bruce had different perspectives on just about everything. Discipline: she was lenient; he was dictatorial. Money: she was casual; he was miserly. Sex: she was restrained; he was uninhibited. Children: she gave too much; he gave too little. Time: she had none of her own; he protected his, doing whatever he wanted, whenever he wanted. The only thing that seemed to align for them was their love for each other. So while they disagreed, there was always that one inevitable truth – whatever happened, it was them against the world. Well, that is certainly what she thought, until Albert tipped the world off its axis.

What would I do without you?

Albert was a very, very lucky boy. That's what the doctor said as she stood in the corridor, while the nurses adjusted Albert's drip. She looked at the man in front of her, noticing his thin upper lip, the slightly sagging left eye, his thinning hair. His irises were a strange green, like algae, and she could barely force herself to look away. She realised she was shaking. As always, she'd skipped breakfast and now her sugar levels had completely dropped. It was the shock, too, of course. She watched the doctor's lips move, but she couldn't absorb any more of what he was saying. Her son. Hanging. Albert. She lifted her hand to halt the doctor's flow but he didn't notice. Referring to his notes, he commented on the lacerations at Albert's neck.

'Superficial,' he said. 'From his fingernails.'

'But the pipes? Why all those pipes?'

'As I said, unfortunately he showed poor clinical status and required immediate intubation, resuscitation and assisted ventilation. He'll be in intensive care for at least a few days.'

'Oh, God.'

'But the good news is there is no injury to his spine and aggressive treatment at this point is your son's best chance of recovery with no neurological damage. Of course we'll have to test for that. The signs, however, are good.'

Alice ran her fingers through her hair. She felt wispy. Faint. 'Have you heard from my husband?' she asked. 'I asked the nurse to call him. I left my phone–'

He shrugged. 'I don't know.'

'And the psychiatrist? Is she coming?'

'Booked up most of the morning. She'll come when she can. Albert's safe now. We've sedated him. And of course with the intubation …'

17

Alice checked her watch. Enjoy was going to be finished school at one. Alice always fetched her. And now what? She couldn't leave, of course. Albert had to know she was here. Right here waiting for him.

'Is there a problem, Mrs Louw?

'You mean apart from the fact that my son tried to–?'

He nodded sympathetically. 'Of course.'

'My daughter needs to be fetched from school soon. She worries if I'm late and I can't leave the hospital right now.'

The doctor looked at watch. 'A friend?'

'Yes but I don't have my flaming phone.'

'OK,' he said, pulling his own phone out his pocket. 'You need to call the school reception, don't you think? Tell them what happened. Maybe her teacher can stay with her until you or your husband can get there.'

'Thank you,' she said softly.

Like most school receptionists, this one was efficient and sympathetic. She took down the number for the hospital, asked who Enjoy's best friend was. Within twenty minutes, Alice's daughter was having a sleepover at Charlotte's with no idea of the reasons. It was a sleepover. In the middle of the week! Why ask questions?

But in another twenty minutes, Gillian swooped in. Her crazy hair tied up in a ponytail on her head, her gym clothes still slightly damp at her chest and back. She was breathing heavily, her cheeks pink, a sheen of perspiration over her forehead.

'Christ, Alice, why didn't you call me? I had to hear it from Nadia!'

She should have guessed that Charlotte's mom couldn't keep her mouth shut. But this time she was strangely grateful for Nadia's garrulousness and indiscretion.

Gillian grasped Alice in a firm hug making no excuses for her wet shirt. 'Fuck, girl,' Gillian said. 'Fuckity-fuck.'

For the first time since Alice had found Albert she allowed herself to let go. At first she was laughing, but then the tears began to run heavily down her cheeks. Gillian only held her harder. Though they'd only been friends for five years, since their sons had met at playschool, she felt closer to Gillian sometimes than she ever had with her friends from university.

'He was just hanging there, Gill, like a slaughtered animal on a hook.'

'But you got him, babe. You got him.'

'I don't understand what's happening here. This morning he was chirpy, you know. Talking about their Cape castle project. Like a normal day. Any other day. What did I miss?'

'I don't know, doll. I don't have a fucking clue. Kids! Own world. Own minds. Now where the hell is that husband of yours?'

Gillian found Bruce's number. Pushed call, then handed Alice the phone. 'Call him. Or is he going to weasel out of fatherhood today of all days too?'

'Gill!'

'Yeah, yeah. He's in meetings. Can't be reached during the day. Heard it. Heard it a thousand times.'

Alice lifted the phone to her ear. Voicemail. What a surprise. She spoke clearly though: 'Angel, you need to come to Vincent Pallotti. It's urgent. Please call me on Gill's number. I left my phone behind at home.'

Gillian took the phone back. 'We need coffee. Double shot. Or can I see Albert?'

'The doctors have knocked him out. He's fast asleep. He's attached to all these machines.'

'Alright. That means they're helping him. That's good, right? I'll dash down and get some caffeine. Want something to eat too?'

'I feel like throwing up.'

'So that's a no? Really babe, you should line your tummy. Who knows when you'll eat next? I'll get you something delish. You won't be able to resist it.'

***

It isn't the same, she finds, as having a kid in the hospital for appendicitis. A broken arm. Grommets. How many times has she commented on Facebook, seeing a friend's child in some hospital bed? *Get better soon, Ayyaan! So sorry to hear about your arm, Luthando. Brave girl, Sophie.* Now she's ashamed. Ashamed of what her son has tried to do. Protective that if people find out, they'll think differently of him. Which of course, they will. She's guilty. Doubting. Incredibly lonely. Gillian has been in every day. Sometimes more than once. But Gillian has two living, breathing, stable kids. And Alice is terrified to admit, even to herself, that she is jealous of this. Albert's headmaster has come to the hospital. He's a self-important, rotund man, with sagging jowls and overly flushed cheeks. He sits with her outside the hospital room and tells her that Albert's teachers are very shocked. What can they do to help?

'We need to keep this private,' she says, almost desperately. 'The other children in his class can't find out. He's already an outcast. This isn't going to do him any favours.'

'Of course,' he says. 'But you'll need to explain his absence somehow. The kids are already asking. You know how they are.'

She nods. Alice does know. And this is perhaps why they're in this mess in the first place. This year, now that she thinks back, Albert has been different. More withdrawn. But he's almost a teenager. She was quite a lot like him, needing time alone. Except that she used to read. He plays his piano, or codes on his laptop. And she knew he only had a few friends. But he did have friends. Aaron. And Michael. Joshua. They couldn't visit him here. And she didn't want them to either. Instead they've been FaceTiming.

'Mrs Louw?'

'I'm sorry. Let's just tell them he's been sick in hospital. They don't need to know more. It's up to Albert to decide what to say, after all.'

He nods. 'He's a bright boy. His class teacher says they will collect his work. And when he's ready …'

'I don't know when that will be,' she says, the tension in her voice evident.

'No pressure. No pressure at all. We're here for your family.'

But if he is here where is Bruce? Wasn't he part of this family?

That first day, when Bruce had finally retrieved her message, it was after five. Gillian had left and Alice was sitting alone. Despite Gillian's attempts to tempt her with carrot cake, Alice had felt too raw to eat. She'd have welcomed a G&T or a glass of red wine. Something to calm her jangled nerves. She'd called Enjoy after Gillian had retrieved her cell phone from the kitchen where she'd forgotten it. The brightness in her voice sounded fake, but Enjoy didn't seem to notice.

'So I'll fetch you from school tomorrow, darling.'

'Mmmhmmm.'

'You're okay?'

'Mom, Charlotte says I need to come. Nadia's made popcorn.'

'Right. You done your homework?'

'Charlotte says we'll do it after popcorn.'

'Don't forget now, Joy. You know how Mrs Challenger says you need to practise every day.'

'Yup. Can I go now, Mom?' A whine.

Alice started to speak but the telephone call was already cut. She thought that she should be glad not to have to worry about one child tonight. The phone rang almost immediately and this time it was Bruce.

'I called Gill. Like you said. She said you had your phone now. What's up?'

'She didn't tell you?'

'No. She said I should speak to you.'

When she explained how she'd found Albert, there was a silence on the other end of the line. It was so quiet, she thought she'd been crying on the phone into a void.

'Bruce? Bruce, are you there?'

20

'Jesus,' she finally heard. 'What the fuck was he thinking?'

Her heart pounded. Rather than sympathy, she heard exasperation. Like Albert had done it again. Whatever 'it' was.

'Are you coming?' she said.

'Is he awake? I have two meetings still; is anything going to change between now and an hour and a half's time?'

She hesitated. 'Well, I guess not.'

'Then I'll come after that. I'll bring you some dinner. A Woolies meal or something.'

Alice was quiet.

'Alice?'

'I found him, Bruce. He could have died.'

'I'm sorry, love. But you did find him. All's well that ends well. Listen, I've got to go. I'm chairing the next meeting. We'll talk properly later. Chin up.'

***

It was well after seven by the time Bruce arrived. She could hear his voice down the corridor long before he actually peered through the doorway. Rather than the Woolworths lasagne she'd been expecting, he was carrying her favourite sushi in a takeaway and chocolate milk and a pile of computer magazines for Albert. His backpack was slung loosely over his left arm.

He leant over to kiss her, and looked across at the sleeping boy.

'How's he doing?'

'The doctors say physically he's looking alright. It's the emotional side that's going to need taking care of.'

He nodded. 'You must be starving. Here, let me unpack this. I thought you might need a treat after the day you've had. I'm sorry I couldn't get here sooner.'

It was good to hear that. Not for the first time that day, she blocked out what they might have been doing tonight if she hadn't got home when she did. And throughout her time here, she'd been facing it without her husband.

Bruce opened his bag, extracting a bottle of white wine, a corkscrew and two glasses wrapped in tea towels.

'And for you, my love, only the best.'

Alice smiled, sipping the wine gratefully. 'You're going to get us into trouble,' she said, rather glad this time that he rarely followed the rules.

'Well, I'm not feeding it to Albert. Christ. I think we need this. It's not every day that your son does something this bloody stupid.'

'Bruce!'

'What? He's fast asleep. And what is so very wrong with his life that he would act in this way? Roof over his head. Loving parents. An adoring younger sister. Two bloody Russian dwarf hamsters, which I never wanted in the first place.'

'You don't understand,' she said.

'No, I do bloody not.'

'You're going to have to try, though. Clearly we're making mistakes. We need to do better.'

Bruce snorted, sipped his wine. 'Let's eat; I'm starving. I can't think clearly without something in my stomach.'

They ate quietly. Tuna nigiri. Fashion sandwiches with salmon skin. California rolls. But today they didn't taste like anything to her. She could have been chomping on cardboard. Despite the wine, her mouth was dry. But the wine tasted acidic.

***

Alice slept that night on a La-Z-Boy recliner. One parent per patient and it wasn't like Bruce could fall asleep there. He was much too tall.

'It'll be fine, love. I'll come through at six and bring you coffee.'

Fine for him, she thought, a little viciously. Their conversation had been desultory. It seemed that he'd rather avoid the real topic than address it head on.

When Albert woke for a few minutes, he saw them both and smiled weakly.

Alice pulled his hand into hers, squeezed it gently. But Bruce sat in the chair next to the bed, hesitating before he moved and patted Albert on the cheek.

'So we'll get you home soon, buddy. You'll be right as rain.'

Alice had an urge to slap him. This wasn't a rugby injury that just needed bones to knit. Muscles to rest. Bruce was always a doer, rather than a feeler. That hadn't changed. So why did it anger her so much that he couldn't even begin to talk about the emotional undercurrent?

Yet Albert wasn't in the mood to talk anyway. He was groggy from the sedatives. And his throat was sore. He closed his eyes again after acknowledging them.

When Bruce started jiggling his car keys from hand to hand, Alice knew he was preparing to head home. To escape. And even though his presence was making her nerves jangle, she didn't want him to go. To leave her alone in this ward with sick children and questions and nurses

22

shouting to each other down the passage. And a child who'd tried to hang himself in his bedroom, for what reasons she still had no idea.

'You're leaving?' she finally said. 'I've been here all day and you're leaving?'

'Darling, I can stay if you like. But Malawi needs to be fed. And what about the rodents? We can't have them die on us and make the situation worse than it already is. Albert will be devastated.'

His words sounded logical but it was a bit like after she'd given birth, when suddenly all his meetings seemed to coalesce in the same week. She'd spent a good deal of her time in hospital on her own or with her mother, who hadn't yet returned to Edinburgh. He was never comfortable in medical settings but, not for the first time, she thought that was too bloody bad. Who was?

'I'm scared,' she said then. 'How did we even get here?'

Bruce's face clouded. 'I don't know.'

'I mean, this morning he seemed upbeat. And yesterday he spent most of the afternoon working on his castle model. He seemed to be enjoying it. What is wrong with us that we didn't even notice something was wrong?'

'It can't just be from one moment, Alice. Or one day. A decision like this doesn't just happen overnight.'

'So we need to think back, then. Don't we?'

'He's always been a bit, well, odd. Not a boy who fits in easily. Maybe he's been bullied or something. We're not going to solve this tonight, love. Let's just get him home.'

'Home? Where he's so safe and can do it again?'

'You're distressed. I get that. So am I. But I think we're just going to have to take this one step at a time.' Bruce leant forward, put his arms around her and kissed her lightly on the head. 'We'll do what it takes, I promise you that.'

Alice wiped the tear from her cheeks. Bruce lifted her chin with his fingers. 'We've got this, love. One step at a time.'

***

In-patient care was a possibility, but the waiting list at the Red Cross's Therapeutic Learning Centre was ridiculous. Albert was too young to be admitted into a psychiatric hospital or clinic – they all seemed to cater for teens rather than children Albert's age, and private hospitals like Vincent Pallotti did not want him in their wards once he was physically recovered. Something about insurance or whatever. Alice never found out. It wasn't like they could tie him down or watch him like a psychiatric patient needed to be watched. Alice had always been rather a self-sufficient person. She'd needed to be; married to Bruce who had a range of hobbies that kept him busy. But she'd never felt more alone than she did now. She found herself trawling the Internet for facts on suicide attempts in children. These only made her more depressed. That Albert was a boy in a high-risk age group did not give her comfort. She even read that suicide, like whooping cough or measles, could actually be contagious. Who'd want to spend time with her son? Her crazy son who'd hanged himself in his bedroom?

Once Bruce had left the second morning, Gillian brought Albert a *Car* magazine, and her a second cup of coffee. Alice attempted a brightness she couldn't quite communicate to her eyes and Gillian, razor sharp as always, told her she needed to go home for a rest.

'You go for a bit,' she said. 'I'll watch him. Have a shower. Close your eyes for an hour.' She patted her handbag. 'I have my trusty laptop, and I can work from here.'

'I can't expect that!' Alice protested.

'Listen, babe. You know me. I don't do what I don't want to do. That's why Frank left me and I don't regret it for one moment. But that's another story. Anyway, I don't have to fetch Joshua until four. He's got cricket.' Gillian took Alice's hand. 'I don't want to be rude, but you look like hell. I, on the other hand, am looking fresh and delicious. I might find myself a lovely doctor to play with … Go home.'

And Alice laughed, for the first time since this had all happened. 'What would I do without you?' she said.

***

Walking back into the house was like one of those black-and-white movies, where you could see every frame. Replaying yesterday, except while her actions were exactly the same: clicking open the garage, driving in, unlocking the side door, entering the scullery, keys on the kitchen counter, her footsteps on the tiles … everything was different. Her life had become someone else's in the space of twenty-four hours. She felt out of her own body, like she'd burst from it and was trying to stuff herself back inside her skin. Except that she didn't fit anymore. Her heart was so swollen and sore; she felt the blood rushing in and leaving. Her fingertips were cold. Her toes hurt. Her head pounded.

Alice kicked off her shoes, hearing them clunk down somewhere. Then she began to unbutton her shirt. She slipped off her skirt, her knickers, her bra. She was standing naked in the kitchen and she felt absolutely nothing. Not even cold. How something in her could have died in such a short space of time seemed impossible to her. She walked through the house, her heart juddering as she passed Albert's room. The door was unlocked now, swung open like a hungry mouth. She'd have to fetch Enjoy after school. Amazingly, despite what had happened, life went on relentlessly.

In their bedroom, she saw that Bruce had left the bed unmade, a half cup of coffee or tea on the bedside table. Next to the bed in a half-hearted pile, his clothes from yesterday. She looked at them, these things just lying there, waiting for her to tidy. Alice tried to reason with herself. He'd left early, to be with her. So what if this mess was what he'd left behind? It wasn't life-threatening. Despite this, though, she had the urge to shatter the mug and leave Bruce to pick up the shards. The shards of her life. Then she looked away. Marched into the bathroom. Turning on the shower as hot as it would go. Maybe she could scald herself back to normality.

Looking for signs

They found a place at the Therapeutic Learning Centre for Albert. Physically, his recovery was remarkably good. The welts at his neck disappeared. His brain was unaffected, or at least they thought so. He hardly verbalised enough for them to properly tell. Sitting on the edge of his bed in hospital those first few days, the psychiatrist had spoken softly to him. Alice herself had been banished. She couldn't believe it. Always an attentive, perhaps overly attentive, mother she was forced to sit around the corner while her son explained to a complete stranger why he'd decided life *with* their family, *in* their family, was no longer worth living. Gillian had told her not to take it so personally, and if she hadn't been so furious, Alice would have laughed. Not take it personally? This was her son! This was her life too. She'd clenched her teeth tightly together and ground in her molars. She could almost feel the dust. But Gillian had seen her face and touched her lightly on the arm. 'That's not what I meant, exactly,' she said. 'I meant more that it's in his head and that you couldn't have done any more for him. I just don't want you to feel that this is your fault.'

'But who do I blame then, Gill, who?'

'Okay, let's put it this way. Say Albert got meningitis. Who would be at fault?'

'Nobody!'

'Exactly. You need to think about it like that.'

If only it were that simple but it certainly was one way of looking at it. The biggest heartache these days was flicking back through her child's short life and looking for the signs. And the problem is, there were many. More than she cared to consider. For one thing Albert's supreme intelligence isolated him. He faced complex intellectual subjects without the accompanying emotional backup. He understood in his brain, but not in his heart. For another, the sleeplessness. For weeks Albert had been complaining that he couldn't sleep. He woke up exhausted, dark circles under his eyes so he emerged from his room zombie-like. She'd been giving him Rescue Remedy. Then she'd phoned their GP to discuss melatonin. She'd told her that Albert needed to come in. But each time Alice had tried to set up an appointment, something had happened. Enjoy's school concert. Albert's coding session. Bruce's squash tournament that he insisted they watch, even though Albert hated squash, Enjoy yawned throughout and Alice thought about how much better she could be using her time.

She realised now she'd put Bruce's bloody squash above her son's health. His sleep. What was she even thinking? And then, his growing isolation at school. Though he had his friends, he struggled on the playground, unable to join little groups of boys without rejection. They found him ungainly, slow, and frequently, useless. He'd got in the car one day and not spoken throughout the journey home. Once there, he'd climbed into his bed, in full school uniform, shoes included and put the duvet over his head. She could hear him sobbing and he wouldn't let her near. Each time she approached, he would scream at her. JUST GO AWAY. LEAVE ME ALONE.

She didn't know what to do, and Enjoy, whose worried face peeked around the corner, slipped her little hand into Alice's as though she was frightened. And when the little girl had tried to comfort her brother he'd pushed her away so hard she'd hit her head. Of course that had made Alice angry. She'd shouted. Ripped the blanket off her son and demanded he apologise. So what could have been a moment of love and comfort turned out to be a stand-off. When it was two minutes before five, Alice found herself pouring a stiff gin and nursing a headache of astronomic proportions. Her one child in a ball in his bed. The other sitting in front of the TV with a confused look on her face.

Bruce's return home had not helped things. He chivvied them all together and told them they were a miserable lot. Pulling Albert out of his bed, he *strongly encouraged* him to have something to eat. He put Enjoy on his lap and tickled her, her loud shrieks giving Alice an even bigger thud in her head than before. Eventually, when Albert was allowed to retreat back to his room and she sat on the edge of his bed, he was finally able to tell her in a very small voice that he'd tried to join a soccer game on the field. When he approached, the boys told him that there was no more space for him. But when Callum, who was the school's equivalent of Bruce throughout his own academic career, came along, they accepted him without question.

As Albert cried, the snot and tears running freely, she'd held him close. In her mind she pictured the slow and painful assassination of those horrible little fuckers (she only used words like that in her head) and tried desperately to think how to make it better. Except she knew immediately that she couldn't and the next day she would be sending her son back to yet another round of rejection.

Bruce told her that Albert would have to toughen up. Boys will be boys.

'You mean boys will be arseholes?'

'I tell you what,' Bruce had said. 'I'll chat to Phil. Get him to ask Nate to try include Albert.'

She'd nodded knowing that was about as likely as an elephant on Table Mountain. Nate was kind but rather thoughtless. But it was the best they could do.

'He's going to have to learn to fight his own battles, love,' Bruce told her.

And even though she knew this was true, her heart was hurting. She wanted to fight the battles for him.

***

At the Learning Centre, Albert initially had a bed in the common room where there was a TV. It was an old TV and connected to an equally ancient DVD player. In the evenings, the kids – only seven of them, got to choose a movie. They were a mixed bunch from different social groups and backgrounds. If feeling isolated was a difficulty at school, the feeling was even more intense here. Most of the kids suffered from severe ADHD or issues affecting their schoolwork. Albert had never had that problem. He sailed through every test, regardless of the subject and now he was stuck in a classroom with kids who struggled to spell. For the first time in his life, however, he was king. Because he was the one who could spell, who could multiply. He helped one of the girls sitting next to him. Laila was two years older but her education, beset by difficulties, had left her struggling with subject matter Albert had long since tackled.

It made him feel important.

Laila adored him.

Alice, on the other hand, who was not allowed to visit for the first week while he was being assessed by the psychiatrists, bit off all her carefully manicured nails. Her hair became lank. Her sleep patterns were as disturbed as Albert's had been before his attempt. She missed her son like an amputated appendage. Her heart throbbed. She was afraid to admit it to herself, but the only reason she actually ever managed to sleep was when she drank too much. Most mornings she woke up with a headache. And though she'd forgiven her beautiful boy, it was very, very hard to wipe the

28

slate of her mind clean. The day he'd been admitted he'd not wanted to go. Instead he wanted to *just go home. I'm fine now. Really.*

But having interviewed him for hours, the psychiatrist was not so sure.

'It really is best we admit him. He's very likely a danger to himself and we won't be able to assess that out-patient. You're lucky, really. A place in the ward rarely opens up. This is an opportunity you won't get again if you don't take it now.'

Alice had tried to weigh the word 'lucky' against what she was being offered. It felt remarkably unbalanced. But Bruce made the decision without consulting further.

'Then we'll take it.'

'Bruce–'

He looked at her, his expression unreadable. 'We'll take it.'

And then that day. The admission. A look in her child's eyes she'd never seen before. 'Don't leave me here, Mom. Please Mommy, please.'

'Darling, we'll visit. Often. We'll phone. We want to get you better.'

'I want to go home.'

'You're not safe at home.'

His voice was higher. Squeaky. 'I want to go with you, Mom. I'm fine now Mom. Really.'

And Alice had looked at Dr Gibson for reassurance, Alice's arms almost reaching despite her, to pick up her child and cart him off, even though his head reached her shoulders and there was very little likelihood she could lift him. But Albert sensed her hesitation. It was obvious. He grabbed onto her hand and began to squeeze. It hurt. It hurt a lot. It felt like he was cracking her digits, grinding them down. She winced. Bruce moved forward, trying to detach her. But now Albert was hanging on like a leech. He was connected to her, and no amount of coaxing was going to remove him.

'You're hurting your mother, Albert,' Bruce said, his voice firm but raised. There was an edge to it. The hysteria, it seemed, was catching.

Dr Gibson was the only calm person in the room. 'I think it's time for you to go, Alice. Say goodbye to Albert. You can phone him tonight at seven. Every night at seven. We'll take very good care of him.'

But how was that even possible? Wasn't that her job?

Alice tried to pull herself free. But it was looking into her son's eyes that shocked her. Her beautiful boy was long gone, replaced by a – how could she even describe it? His eyes were glazed, the lenses closed like thick theatre curtains, hiding him somewhere inside his head. She tugged at her hands and Bruce, now taking over forcibly, unclenched their child's claws.

Albert was screaming. Shrieking.

'Leave me, Dad! Let me go!'

'Come, Alice. Bruce. I think you need to go.' Dr Gibson was still calm but now her words were firm. Commanding.

'You're an evil bitch! An evil bitch! I hate you!' Albert screeched at Alice.

It felt like he'd hit her. Although he was no longer clamped to her and the pain had subsided, the words were worse than any physical hurt. She'd never heard him use words like that ever before. Never mind against her. She stood. Bruce pulled her roughly, then stepped in front of her as Albert tried to pummel her. The psychiatric nurses yanked Albert back. Held him in an expert lock. Albert breathed heavily. Wet-dog whimpering.

Alice moved towards the door, the psychiatrist's hand at her elbow. She tried to meet her child's eyes without exposing her own extreme hurt.

'I love you, Albert,' she said, her voice surprisingly steady. 'I'll phone you at seven. I promise.'

The nurses had let Albert go. He stood there, just for a moment, then began to charge forward again, his elbows caught neatly again by the nurses.

'I want to say goodbye!' Albert said. 'I want to hug my mother!'

He was crying now. The tears coursing down his cheeks, as he sobbed. The psychiatrist hesitated a moment, then nodded.

And for the first time in her life, Alice was afraid of her son. As he barrelled towards her, she wasn't sure if he was going to hit or embrace her.

She felt simultaneously disloyal and hopeful. But mostly she was terrified. The action seemed to go in slow motion, the closer he came, the more she hesitated …

And then he hugged her, his snot-coated face drenching her shirt. The relief rose like a tide.

But how to delete all those minutes from her head? They'd felt like hours. Years.

They'd never be the same again.

~PART II~

Part of this family

Enjoy leant against the wall. It had taken Alice years to master Enjoy's hair, but now she prided herself on her ability to do all sorts of braids. So much so that Enjoy's friends, many of whom had straight hair with no personality at all, lined up for a chance for get one of Enjoy's many styles done. Now Enjoy was painting a welcome-home banner. It was a little skew, the left-hand side noticeably wider than the right, and it was more girly than Albert might like. But Enjoy was so determined to do it on her own for her brother that Alice had let her be. Albert would appreciate it for what it was. Though he and Enjoy fought a great deal, when it came down to it, they loved each other.

The last three months had been hard. Wednesday visits with Albert had been regular, and usually uneventful. They played Trivial Pursuit or did puzzles. Bruce would come around five and play soccer or tennis with Albert on the weed-tangled concrete outside. Sometimes the psychologist, a wiry man with thick spectacles and a goatee, would pop his head around and when Alice asked him pointed questions, he would always answer with a non-answer.

His most common refrain was, 'I'll take it back to the team and let you know.'

'Can Albert bring a radio in? He'd like to listen to the news?'

'I'll take it back to the team and let you know.'

'Is there any way we could make his schoolwork a little more challenging?'

'I'll take it back to the team and let you know.'

'Can Albert go for a run around the Common if his dad runs with him and brings him back straight away?'

'I'll take it back to the team and let you know.'

In her more rebellious moments, she pictured his wife, a much more rounded and passionate woman, engaging him in a moment of ecstasy and asking him to touch her, just there, only to have him whisper, confused, 'I'll take it back to the team and let you know'.

It was her equivalent of doing a speech to a huge audience and imagining everybody naked.

Alice was struck by the slowness of everything at the unit. Between visits, nothing much seemed to have happened. Gradually, they were introducing medication to assist with Albert's severe mood swings. When explaining their family history, these moods had come up.

Albert's inability to be happy, to see things positively, to respond in an enthusiastic way. His laziness and his messy dumping of his belongings all over the house. His defiance, especially towards authority figures, and most particularly his father. How he struggled to understand other people's personal space, and that, inevitably, on the playground, he would be involved in some kind of bust-up. He was always the common thread. And it hadn't mattered how much she and Bruce had tried to coach him to be kind (it's better to be kind than right), their efforts had been largely wasted.

There was, of course, also his relationship with his sister. Though Enjoy was only six months younger than he was, he knew her weaknesses and her adoption was the biggest one of all. The first time he had come home for a weekend – pick up on Friday, delivery on Sunday by five – for example, he'd had her in tears.

As Alice had walked into the playroom to check on them, she could hear his strident voice commenting, 'You're such a pain. I don't know why we don't just send you back. You don't belong here. You're not even part of this family!'

Alice had felt herself go so hot that she'd had to hold onto the back of the couch to rein herself in. She was aware, now more than ever, how fragile their family was. She'd been told not to leave Albert alone due to his very high risk of suicide, but now she was almost tempted to kill him. Enjoy had her faults, like anybody (a bit of a whiner, too casual about gift receiving, obsessed with her clothes matching even if this meant washing something specifically for her) but she was kind. That could not be disputed and the very idea of almost losing Albert had put her in a tailspin. She adored Albert and now he was doing his best to crush her.

'Albert,' Alice said sharply. 'What did you just say to your sister?'

'Nothing.'

'I heard you.'

'Well, why are you asking me then?'

'I want you to apologise right now.'

'But–'

'Albert!'

'Sorry, Joy.'

His voice sounded thin. Reedy. Not even robust enough to be properly heard but Alice didn't have the energy to push it.

'Now let's all try to get along. Okay? You're only here for the weekend, darling, and your family needs you to be kind. You're not the only one struggling here.'

Another weekend visit had involved Albert trying to burn down a holiday cottage they'd booked using a candle he'd lit with the braai fire. When she'd come out the cottage bearing a salad, she'd watched, almost unbelieving, the snaking flame up the edge of the thatch, and Albert biting his lip in concentration as though conducting his latest, most successful scientific experiment. She'd shrieked, dropped the salad, her feet covered with lettuce, her legs with tomato seeds. The singeing had been minor, in the end, but Alice's nerves were so jangled that she'd demanded they go home. Bruce, however, laconic, had commented that he would be damned if the little terrorist was going to ruin his entire weekend yet again.

'Yet again?' Alice said, confused.

'You mean, the cancelled fishing trip, dinner debacle and shrieking babysitter don't count?'

In the end, they had stayed. But while Bruce dozed outside under the trees, a beer next to him and the bees humming loudly up in the trees, she'd sat resentfully, one eye on Albert, waiting for him to stir up more trouble. She wanted to blame the medication. But thinking back, there were many things about her son that had been different. The medication just seemed to be intensifying certain elements of his nature. The rebelliousness most of all.

Back at the unit, in the weekend report she'd mentioned all of this, yet nothing seemed to come of it. She'd been assured that there was an adjustment period. It would get better.

Albert would get better.

Despite this, when he was finally ready for out-patient release (supposedly better), she was hopeful. It had been weeks without major incident and they were ready now to put Albert back into school, equipped with certain self-management skills taught to him by his psychologist and medication that he took regularly. His moods had been much more stable, and his psychologist had been convinced by Albert's assurances he was ready to leave. Alice had not been so sure, but trusting the man's judgment, Alice began to prepare. She visited the school, warned them of signs to look out for. She met with Albert's teacher and explained his need to escape – how the school had agreed, if necessary, for her to fetch him early if he needed to come home. To take him to the school psychologist who would call her. She'd talked to parents of friends. Asked them to visit with their children, to try and reintegrate him. All of this while attempting not to label him a lunatic with certain risky behaviours. He'd been through a terrible depression. He was a young boy with hormones beginning to pump. Albert would never be the same child from months before, because now he was the boy who'd lived through an in-patient programme in a children's psychiatric ward. Something that Bruce had insisted they keep secret as much as possible. And perhaps that was the start of the rot. If she couldn't talk about it, how was she going to avoid the pressure building inside her?

She couldn't promise that she herself wasn't going to explode.

Rough edges

Thank fuck his office wasn't at home. When he packed his laptop into his boot, it was as good as packing a suitcase for a flight somewhere very far away. He wasn't like Alice. Alice the highly sensitive person who claimed she could physically feel people's emotions. They hit her like waves, she said. And then she absorbed them, startled, wary.

She wasn't exactly easy to be around. She had this hare-in-the-headlights look about her, like she wasn't sure how to get off the damn pathway. Any moment now and she'd be mown down. Flattened like road kill.

He hated to see her like this. Even more he hated his weasel of a son who'd brought their family to its knees. Of course he also loved Albert, surely that went without saying?

His flesh and blood.

He remembered when Albert had emerged from his hiatus inside Alice, the slightly yellow yelping creature, almost too small to be believed. How his heart had filled, first with love, and then with terror. What the hell was he supposed to do with him? How to hold him? Move him? Communicate with him? Alice saying, 'Isn't he gorgeous?' And him thinking, *he looks a bit like a rat. With a fat face. A yellow rat with a fat face.*

Sometimes he thought about Enjoy's arrival as a special blessing. He didn't have to go through all that shit again. Nappies. Bottles. Mewling all night. Breast feeding wife with sore nipples. Distraction.

He had another kid. The factory was closed immediately. Sore, swollen balls but the alternative was not his idea of a good time either. No more nippers needed. And she had such a lovely nature. She didn't look like him. Obviously. But she was more like him than Albert was. Sporty. (Tennis. Running. Hockey.) Not particularly het up about things. They

36

liked to do the Park Run on the Common once a week, with Malawi, who spent a lot more time doubling back and sniffing arses than actual exercise.

And Enjoy laughed a lot. Joy worked hard. She wasn't afraid to unpack the dishwasher, clean up, do her homework.

Trouble-free.

When Albert had been in that loony bin, Bruce had tried to be on board about it. The problem was; after the first few weeks he wasn't sure it was entirely necessary. After the suicide attempt, he'd told Alice that they could manage on their own. A psych ward for a kid? Ridiculous. Take him home. Explain the rules. Deal. Get some professional help from the comfort of their own home. If that was even necessary. The kid needed a boot up the backside. A trick like that. But then the advice of the psychological team seemed logical. Helpful. Advised. It was only on Week Four that he'd begun to think it was all bollocks.

For three months their entire worlds revolved around this crazy, attention-seeking child. Most of the time he was tempted just to say, 'Listen, you little jerk. Can you stop thinking about yourself for just one small minute and think about what this is doing to your mother?'

Alice was obsessed.

Every night at exactly seven she would phone. Comfort him. Treat him like the little prince he had become. Prince Albert the Demanding. She bought puzzles and Trivial Pursuit. Science experiments. DVDs for him to watch with the other inmates – or whatever they were called. Weird little kids all of them. Glassy eyes and high-pitched little voices stabbing into his skull.

He hated going into that place. For one thing, he didn't really get the rules. It wasn't like a game of squash or tennis. Scoring and then someone wins. Nobody there seemed to be winning anything. The place was interminable. Boring. And he couldn't do or decide anything for his own son. The interviews with the psychologist. God. In the end, he said he wasn't going back again until they put an action plan in place. They needed milestones. Measurements. Actual solutions. Not pussyfooting around like ballet dancers trying not to take up real space.

Bruce kicked a ball outside with Albert. Limp-wristed little twit couldn't even return the blasted thing. Give him his due, though. He did try. And Bruce could see how pleased Albert was that he'd come. Waiting at the front gate, a happy smile on his face. So why not go home with Bruce? Break him out of that hellhole? He discussed it with Alice. More than once.

'He's a suicide risk, Bruce. I can't watch him every second of the day. What happens if he does something when I'm not looking?'

It wasn't like Albert hadn't tried again either. Tying one of the computer cords from the office around his neck, where the bruises were still healing. Caught in the nick of time by one of the nurses.

And then Alice. Alice sobbing herself to sleep in their bed wondering what she'd done wrong. It was hopeless. Never in his life had Bruce felt out of his depth like this. But the touchy-feely space they now operated in was as uncharted to him as the Alaskan wilderness. Nameless glaciers dotting treacherously all over their life. He felt everything sliding out of control like melting ice.

So he did what he always did when he was stressed.

He exercised.

First thing in the morning. Gym session or a run on the mountain. Evenings: squash, tennis, swimming, touch rugby, cycling. Usually, if he timed it right, he would be home for dinner without having more than half an hour with the kids. Shag before bed. By Saturday, he was physically done, except for the shagging. Never tired of that. And Enjoy's Park Run. Sunday, walk on the beach with the kids, if they could muster enough enthusiasm. At least Malawi was always keen. Tail wagging with expectation as they picked up the lead. And Enjoy didn't usually protest. She was amenable in every way that Albert was not.

The psych stay went on and on. The whole palaver was interminable. It was like their whole world had stopped. And he could feel Alice withdrawing. In their entire marriage, this had never happened before. Usually they were a good team. An excellent team. But everything was out of kilter and he blamed Albert.

When he'd first seen Alice all those years ago, he'd been enchanted. It wasn't at the gala, as she always told people when asked about how they met. Bruce had seen her before that at a school art fair. His mother, who was on the school board, always made him and his father attend – yearly penance for her having to work for money as a travel agent instead of dabbling in her own painting career at home. (The arguments about this were legendary.)

Alice was one of the school's star pupils. Her name had come up more than once at the dinner table at home – in particular a self-portrait, which she'd done entirely in shades of red. But his mother had never mentioned her prettiness. The frosting of freckles of her button nose, her intense grey-blue eyes, and neat butt. Everything about Alice was put together, then. That was one of the things that attracted him to her. She radiated organisation. Her life was on track and he wanted that; to be on her trajectory. As she stood at her painting on that evening chatting to a girl he never saw again, he'd been uncomfortably self-conscious. Too much so to approach her. But Cape Town was a small place. He'd see her again. He'd make sure of it.

He did.

The swimming gala, the 'casual' invitation. And when she'd tried to make her escape at the Spur, he wasn't going to let her go. She was his now and nothing was going to change that. He wooed her like he'd never wooed anyone before or since. But he knew that something in her had been crumbling since they'd been together. While his star had risen, hers had started to dip. The balance was out. Bruce didn't want to leave Alice behind when he'd been accepted for the scholarship in the States. And rather than let her complete her architectural degree and date long distance, he'd put the pressure on. She had to come with him. They loved each other! They were meant to be together!

Alice's parents had not been happy about it. They made that extremely clear. Of course, it was extremely difficult to say now whether they would have survived the time apart in order for her to complete her own studies. But he knew that sometimes, when she sat completing a rather boring draft, she wished she was creating something timeless. A skyscraper or a crazy house perched on the edge of a seacliff – like the one they'd seen on TV made almost entirely out of Boeing parts. Something individual.

Instead they'd got married. His business had taken off. Flown. The children. She was happy before. He thought. But this thing with Albert was exposing all the rough edges of their lives together.

So coming home from the office was not what it used to be. Alice looked frenzied. The dinner was made, the kids clean. But she was distant. And when he tried to reach for her, she pulled away – like it was his fault that things had gone so wrong. He didn't know what to say or how to react. The wall she was building around herself was getting more impenetrable by the day, and he didn't know how to break it.

So he didn't. He ran more. Cycled more. Played more squash. At least then he knew what the rules were.

Unhinged

Today was going to be a good day. After months of tears and heartache, she was finally going to rediscover her own life and send Albert back into the world, safe and ready to fight. When she looked out of the window, the sky was heavy. But she knew it wouldn't rain. Despite being well into June, there was little chance the drought was going to lift. She had Bruce to thank, however, for the fact that this was not affecting their family like it was affecting Gillian's. Last week when Gillian had popped in, she told about her most recent purchase: three buckets and three plastic tubs to put in their showers to catch the water for flushing the toilet. Gillian had sighed. 'This is one of the rare occasions I miss Frank. He may have been crap at everything else, but at least he could have set up a grey-water system.'

'I'll chat to Bruce.'

'Oh, girl, you have enough on your plate. Now tell me about Albert's plans for next week.'

Gillian could hear Albert down the hall. He and Enjoy attended different schools, yet they used to ride their bikes together and splinter off at their respective destinations. She used to think it would be good for Enjoy to have Albert to take care of her on the busy roads but this morning she was thinking that Enjoy would be the one in a supervisory role.

For one thing, she'd have to ensure that Albert actually *went* to school.

Alice sighed. Despite Bruce's assurances that it was best to return to the old routines, she wasn't so sure. To let her son go to school and possibly not actually go was not a sensible, motherly decision. The last time he'd bunked he'd tried to kill himself.

It put things in perspective.

So despite Bruce's cajoling, she picked up her keys. 'Kids! New plan. I'll drop you both off this morning. I have a meeting near the schools.'

Albert sloped into the kitchen. His tie was askew, his shoes unlaced. His complexion pallid and grey. He did not at all look like a boy who was ready for school. The 'team' had agreed to bridge him. He didn't need to be in class long. It was all about acclimatising to people. Crowds set him off these days, causing severe anxiety and often triggering actions he himself couldn't explain. Last time they'd had visitors, he'd punched Enjoy in the stomach. Another occasion he'd climbed out the window and shimmied up onto the roof, unable to climb back down.

Alice gulped. 'You look smart, Bertie.' She used a nickname she hadn't for years and he grimaced at her. But she continued bravely. 'You excited to see Josh and Aaron?'

He shrugged. But rather than focus on this, Alice noticed the quiver of his nose. His rapid blinking.

Albert was terrified.

She held out her hand to him. 'It's going to be fine, bud. And if you're not managing, you can come home.'

He nodded, pulling his hand back and crossing his arms over his chest. 'Can we just get this over with, please?'

She nodded. Collected her handbag from a chair. 'Joy! You coming?'

Enjoy ran into the room, her book bag slung over her shoulder. She glanced at Albert, a slight expression of unease crossing her face, before disappearing imperceptibly. Alice thought then that she was probably projecting.

They all climbed into her Audi, Albert slamming the door. Rather than react, Alice chose simply to turn on the car. Lately she'd discovered that it was often better just to keep quiet about certain acts of wilfulness. Clothes dumped in the entrance hall. Half-drunk glasses of juice all over the house. Loud music that made the walls reverberate. If she could endure it, she would get a few moments of 'peace' before yet another storm.

When they reached Enjoy's school, she peeled out, a half-wave as she made her way over the pedestrian crossing. Alice turned to look at Albert. His teeth were clenched and he was fiddling with the radio, jumping from station to station in a frenzied cacophony. Instead of shouting, she put her hand gently on his. He dropped his hand from the dial and when he looked at her, she knew the fear in his eyes was real. Her heart sunk. This wasn't going to be easy. Maybe Bruce, who could distance himself from emotion, should have done this. It wouldn't have hurt him so much.

Alice turned on the indicator, pulled into the parking spot opposite the school. Boys trailed along the road at a snail's pace. Unclipping her safety belt, Alice made as if to get out the car.

'No,' Albert said.

'I thought I'd just walk you in the gate, darling. Just see you safely in.'

'No,' Albert repeated. He tugged at his bag. Pushing open the door with one foot, he slid out the car.

'Will you at least kiss me goodbye?'

'Mom!' he whined. 'Just leave it. I'll see you at ten thirty in reception.'

'Albert …'

He looked at her.

'Take care, boy. And remember how much we love you.'

He nodded. And though, before, she would simply have driven away, now she could not. She sat, inert, in her seat, watching the little boy dissolve into a sea of grey and blue, and feeling an increasing sense of dread in the pit of her stomach. When the gates closed and the bell rang, she was still sitting there, wondering how much more could go wrong.

***

Albert lasted two days. Each day, Alice and his teacher, Emma – thank God for Emma – WhatsApped each other.

- He's here. Don't worry.
- Does he seem OK?
- He's quiet. But I'll keep him close. I've put Aaron next to him.
- THANK YOU SO MUCH .

Alice's work was suffering. She had all these deadlines for plans she was supposed to be drafting, colour charts she was meant to be drawing up, samples she had to collect. But she couldn't get her mind right. Albert filled her brain like a tumour, and it was all she could do to force herself to eat. Over the last few months she'd lost weight. Enough weight for people to comment in the flippant way people do.

'Wow Alice, you look spectacular. What's your secret?' (*My son tried to commit suicide twice; he's in a psych ward.*)

She'd shrug. 'Lucky with my metabolism, I guess.' Meanwhile she could see the varnish peeling from her nails, her eyebrows growing bushy. Self-care was the last thing on her mind right now. Especially since Bruce seemed to be spending less and less time at home. Alice had a feeling he was avoiding them. Their family was crumbling and she didn't know what to do about it.

Nevertheless, Alice resolved that though she couldn't control Bruce, she could try to take back her own routines. Her morning gym sessions, which she'd long since committed herself to, had recently fallen by the wayside. But there was no reason not to start again. So she was on the treadmill with sweat pouring down her back and between her breasts when her phone rang. The music was so loud in the gym that at first she didn't hear it. As she reached for it, it stopped. Then the second ring, and she could see instantly it was from the school. She hesitated for only a millisecond, fearing that her life was about to change, yet again. Then she picked up.

'Hello, Alice speaking.'

'Alice? It's Emma. Albert's teacher.'

'Yes? Emma?' she said, feeling faint. She pushed the red emergency button and climbed off the exercise machine.

'Firstly, I want to assure you, Alice, that Albert is safe.' Emma's voice betrayed the calm message.

'Safe?'

'Yes. But you need to come and get him.'

Alice felt like she was choking. 'Oh God, what happened?'

'We found him in the boy's bathroom. He … he had a Stanley knife.'

'A blade?'

'Luckily it wasn't sharp. The wounds are superficial. Nothing serious, Alice. We stopped him in time. But he needs to go home. Perhaps you might, um, arrange an appointment with his psychiatrist?'

'Wounds?' Alice realised she sounded mentally deficient.

'Alice? Alice are you okay? He's bandaged up. Quite fine. Alice? Do you think you can drive?'

'Of course,' she said faintly. 'Thank you for calling. I'm on my way.'

***

The decision to keep Albert home was not a hard one for Alice. But Bruce wasn't so sure. After all, this Albert wasn't the easy, delighted two-year old they once knew. Now his moods swung like a pendulum but with nothing of its regularity. Alice found herself dispensing pills with the efficiency of a trained pharmacist. The wide-eyed glazed look of a hyper state − what she'd taken to calling it − was dealt with swiftly. Yet Bruce, who refused to attend any of the medical meetings as 'Alice seemed to be on top of it' consistently commented on how Alice was 'overmedicating their son'. She couldn't win. She worried continually about Albert's sleep, or lack thereof, since the less he slept the more out of control he became. The melatonin only worked for a few weeks. As Dr Gibson had said, 'Melatonin regulates the sleep and body clock. It tells your brain when it's time to sleep. But, unfortunately, it doesn't increase your need for sleep or the drive to sleep.' She wondered what the point of taking it actually was then. Nevertheless, she spent many mornings lining up the pills and packing them in dispensers marked with the days of the week. Clearly, whoever had produced them had no idea how many pills a child like Albert would need to take. They often didn't even fit.

Since Albert slept so little at night, she found him drowsing off a great deal of the day. But, following the advice of people she trusted (Emma, the psychiatrist, Gillian), she set up a homeschooling programme. She joined a homeschooling support group. She even bought textbooks and enrolled Albert in a syllabus that would allow him to write exams at the end of the year.

He was a difficult age, on the cusp of high school, which meant he'd have to have *something* to use for applications. Not that she ever mentioned that to him. He had enough to worry about. What she had not accounted for, was how much they were going to clash. While Alice was amenable, she was a perfectionist. Albert was highly strung and very lazy. Each day would result in a battle of wills that drained her so badly, she lost colour. Every evening she felt like she'd been to war. Her body hurt. She cried herself to sleep. And Bruce, who still did enough exercise for a small rugby league, was hardly ever there to take some of the slack. Enjoy, never the demanding one, became whiny and commented how Alice 'always spends more time with Albert'.

When Bruce came home, the conversations were always the same. Alice's dreadful day. Bruce's neglectful sympathy and then inappropriate advice. 'You need to be firmer with him, Liss. Give him a smack.'

'He's eleven, Bruce. And you know how I feel about hitting.'

'Well, for fuck's sake. Can you not at least try? What you're currently doing is obviously not working.'

Against her better judgment, the next time Albert let fly at her, she hit him with a wooden spoon, which snapped. Both of them ended up crying.

'I'm not doing that again, Bruce. It's just not my style.'

He shrugged, unconcerned, she thought. But how could she be sure? They hardly spoke, really spoke, these days. And her loneliness was so intense, she found herself crying as she drove to fetch Enjoy from school. The music was loud enough to drown out her sobs, but she could see the expressions of people alongside her in the traffic. Without a doubt, she looked unhinged. Purple-black rings under her eyes. Uncombed or unwashed hair, depending on the day. A shabby tracksuit. And once, much to her shame, her winter pyjamas.

It was Enjoy who finally put her foot down. Thank God.

'Mommy, I think I'll just meet you at the car when you fetch me. Otherwise I'll just ride my bike.'

'What do you mean?'

44

'I think you should just wait in the car and I'll come to you when the bell rings. Or I should ride to and from school every day.'

Alice glanced at Enjoy, who refused to meet her eyes. 'What's going on, Joy?'

Her daughter shrugged. 'Nothing.'

'You want to go for a milkshake and talk about it?'

'No!'

'No? But you love chocolate milkshakes.'

'No thanks, Mom. Let's just go home.'

Was she imagining it, or did her daughter just roll her eyes at her? Alice turned her car onto the road from the school exit. She could feel her daughter's emotions. Tight. Unnerved.

'What aren't you telling me, Joy?'

'I said it was nothing! NOTHING! Okay?'

The click, click, click of the indicator. 'Alright,' Alice acquiesced.

They drove in silence, all the way home, with Alice too uneasy to turn the radio on. She'd need to get to the bottom of this but she had a horrible feeling her daughter was disowning her.

The roost

So he hired Leo. Enough of a shaggy, unkempt wife and distressed daughter embarrassed by said wife. Not to mention the crazy antics of his weird son who seems to have been getting weirder by the day. When he came home, he wanted peace. He wanted calm. He did not want tears, and whining and the evil eye because he chose to look after himself and do a little exercise to keep fit.

For Christ's sake, he worked his arse off. He was entitled to some time off. And it was obvious that despite Alice having a full-time nanny on board, she was simply not capable of managing the family tyrant on her own. They were all tiptoeing around each other while he ruled the roost. BRUCE'S ROOST. Fuck it. After Joy told him her friends had started calling Alice 'the old hag in PJs', something clearly had to give. So he logged onto mytutor.co.za and scrolled through the list. Since Albert's recent delight in taking off his clothing in public, clearly they'd need an oke. And a fit one at that. To chase him. Of course, he came home with his solution in place and told Alice what was happening, so he was expecting delight. Relief. But she just looked at him, and said, 'You know you could spend more time with him. Half the reason he's so unstable is you're never here. You're just palming off your responsibilities on someone else.'

He tried not to grind his teeth too hard and looked at her. 'Christ, Alice. I'm giving you a break. How about a bit of gratitude?'

All he got was her back. Without another word, she went down the passage, locked the bathroom door. Shower water noises. Enjoy studied her father from her corner of the couch and shrugged.

'Maybe you should have talked to her first, Dad,' she said. Wise-arse.

'I don't know why,' he retorted. 'These days I'm in the dog box whether I talk or not.'

Another shrug.

But he'd had enough and whether Alice liked it or she didn't. Leo was going to be a fixture for the foreseeable future. It was going to cost a bomb and he'd already signed on the dotted line. The least his wife could do was get her hair done and sort out her cuticles. And maybe, just maybe, attempt a smile on that miserable face. Shit. Was that so much to ask?

But then he calmed himself down, tried to be reasonable. Alice had had a terrible time, and frankly, she'd taken the worst of the slack. He walked down the passage, knocked on the bathroom door. The shower was already off so there was no way she couldn't hear him. Despite this, there was a deafening silence.

'Liss?'

'What?' she barked.

'Can I come in?'

He could hear her moving about, a door closing. Then she padded to the door, opened it up. Her hair was towel dried, hanging at her shoulders, her towel wrapped around her. She looked at him, her grey-blue eyes reddened from crying. Despite that, she still looked beautiful to him.

He walked towards her, putting his arms around her still-damp body. 'I don't understand what I've done wrong,' he said truthfully. 'But I'm sorry I've upset you.'

She bit her lip. But she didn't pull away, which was a good sign.

'You can't just make executive decisions, Bruce,' she said. 'Especially when it comes to our children.'

'What do you mean?'

'You've hired some guy I've never even met to be in our home. To watch our child. What do you even know about him?'

'I've interviewed him over the phone. He sounds nice. He sounds educated. And reasonable. Good head on his shoulders. Psychology background.'

'But you didn't even ask me. You didn't even discuss it! You've basically just told me that I'm not good enough. That I'm not doing a good enough job.'

Bruce was genuinely flabbergasted. 'When did I say that?'

Alice pulled away. 'You've fired me from my job of homeschooling Albert. That's what you've done.'

'Have I? I thought I was giving you your life back.'

'Albert is my life! And so are you, but lately it seems that you don't want to even be here. You're never at home. You don't engage with the kids.'

'I do! I was just talking to Enjoy right now.'

Alice started to laugh. But it wasn't a joyous giggle. It was mocking, and unrecognisable. It made his temples throb.

'Whatever, Bruce.'

'I don't like the way you're talking to me,' Bruce said.

'I don't like you deciding about our family without my involvement.'

'Got it,' he said icily. 'So where does that leave us?'

'You tell me.' Alice dropped her towel, started to dress, her back to him.

'Why don't we just try it for a month? If it doesn't work out, it doesn't work. We're done with him.'

'Do I even have an option?'

'Try it, Alice. Take some time for yourself.'

'Like you've been doing? I'm the only reason this family's still together.'

'That's bullshit and you know it.'

Alice slipped a coral T-shirt over her head. 'Fine. But you get to tell Albert all about your special plan. Might involve you in a ten-minute conversation. You can ... bond.'

Fuck you, he thought, but he kept his expression neutral, a monumental effort of will, before he replied. 'I wouldn't have it any other way. It's about time someone was firmer with him.'

'Proving my point, yet again,' said Alice, stalking out the room like a pissed-off cat.

The plaster

Alice buzzed open the gate. He was wearing a cap that masked his face, Adidas trainers, jeans and a leather jacket.

'Leo?' she said, a little suspiciously. She didn't like that she couldn't see his eyes. Malawi yapped frantically at his heels, then jumped around him. She growled, baring her teeth. It was obvious Malawi was as suspicious as Alice was. For the first time in a long while, Alice appreciated her cantankerous dog.

But he smiled, stepped forward. 'Yes. Are you Mrs Louw?'

His handshake was firm. He had nice, clean hands. Well, at least he seemed older than she expected. Mid, maybe late twenties rather than an eighteen-year-old recruit with no sense.

'Come in.'

He followed her into the lounge. 'You have a lovely home,' he said. It was trite, yes, but he sounded sincere.

'Thanks. Please sit. I thought we should chat a bit, before you get started. Albert is in his room. I'll introduce you in a moment.'

'I'm looking forward to meeting him.'

Gosh. Such nice manners. She could only assume this couldn't last. She watched as Leo leant forward to give Malawi a tickle. Putty in his hands. Well, she didn't bite him, at least. The growling continued, until the dog flopped over, exposing her rounded belly. They sat a moment. Silence not quite uncomfortable, but getting there quickly.

Leo took off his hat. He had a mop of curly black hair, deep blue eyes. A slightly beaked nose. He studied her, and she noticed that he seemed less disturbed by the quiet than she did. He smiled slightly, now patting Malawi's silky brown ears.

'You like dogs?' she said, more to fill the emptiness than because she cared.

'I used to have a rescue Dachshund. Not very manly, I know, but he was very portable.'

She nodded. 'Cute. Right, Leo. Let's cut to the chase. My husband hired you without consulting me. I knew nothing about you until yesterday.'

'Oh.' His face showed no reaction.

'I'm not convinced you should even be here. But my husband has insisted that ...' She raised her fingers drawing some inverted commas into the air. '... *I need a break.*'

He said nothing, but he blinked a bit faster.

'I don't know, really, why I have to have a stranger in my home. Even an educated stranger like yourself. Yes, I've seen your CV. The bottom line, however, is that I'm going to have to put up with it. But you should know I'm not happy about it.'

'Right.'

'I'm not blaming you, of course. But it is inexplicable to me how we're going to manage this ... situation. Do you have any ideas?'

'I'll try keep a low profile, Mrs Louw.'

'Oh God. Call me Alice. I'm not my mother-in-law.' Although *she* wasn't a Louw anymore, she recalled.

'Alice, then.'

'It's just that ... these last few months have been particularly hard. Albert's illness. Our lives are different now. But it is the new normal and I feel my family should be adjusting to this, not bringing in a temporary plaster that's just going to get ripped off.'

Leo leant forward, his hands in his lap. 'Just so I'm clear on your analogy, Alice. Am I the plaster?'

His expression was neutral, but there was a slight smile playing at the corner of his lips. It should have made her irritated, but instead it was like untying the knot in a swollen balloon. Her frustration and anger began the slow process of deflating.

She laughed.

'Well, I guess that's enough of that. Now to meet your charge.' She stood up to call down the passage. 'Albert! Albert! You can come through now.'

Keeping things going

He parked at the building site, thinking back to when the children were little. Then, they would accompany him, and play in the building sand, while he inspected the grey-water tanks or consulted with clients about water-saving taps and shower roses. Both Enjoy and Albert loved to come with him. They would take beer-can boxes and slide down the sand heaps as if it were snow. By the time they came home, the kids would be covered in sand from head to toe and Alice would stand in mock-anger, her arms crossed over her breasts. She would tell Enjoy and Albert to strip to their undies in the garage before hosing them down in the outside shower that Bruce had installed because he liked to bathe under the stars.

Those days, he recalled, were *good*. But it was easier to be in the midst of good times without appreciating them for what they were, than to be in the hell they were now experiencing and escape it.

Enjoy, who was sitting next to Bruce in the SUV, wouldn't dream of getting her new top dirty. It came from Cotton On (he only knew this because she'd dragged him there) and was one of those ones with sequins that could be flapped either way so the heart on the front was either red or blue. She was proud of it. Had been nagging for one just like it for weeks. And Bruce, seeing this as an easy win, was not hard to convince. If only it were as easy to make Alice happy. Enjoy leant forward, a quizzical expression on her face.

'What are we waiting for, Dad?'

'I've got a meeting, honey. But my colleagues don't seem to be here yet.'

His friend Martini had set this up. Bruce had been reluctant at first, but what the hell. It was only a meeting. Half an hour of his time. And Enjoy would be just fine reading in the car until he finished. She grinned at him.

'I want to do a soccer party for my birthday,' she said. And he smiled. He wondered sometimes if this was really what she wanted or if she was trying to keep him on her side. Albert, the useless little wimp that he was, would be more likely to organise a fucking chess championship. Oh, he would win it, of that Bruce had no doubt, but chess? For fuck's sake.

Bruce got out the vehicle, stretched. His back hurt from yesterday's squash match with Martini, when he'd suggested this meeting. Tight muscles. He didn't used to get this kind of ache post-match. But he wasn't a spring chicken anymore.

'You stay here, Joy,' he said. 'And lock the doors.'

Another car had arrived. A black Land Rover with tinted windows. You couldn't see a thing inside. For some unfathomable reason, Bruce's stomach knotted. Then the men exited. The taller one was black, with a very short haircut. Nearly completely shaved. Stocky and broad-shouldered. Silver Rolex watch. Stylishly casual with a plaid button-down shirt tucked into designer jeans. Oval-shaped wire-rimmed glasses, with a tortoise-shell effect.

The other was Asian. Chinese, perhaps, although Bruce couldn't really tell. Wide face. A flattish nose and dark, black eyes. Protruding incisors. Straight shoulder-length black hair. His clothes, however, were his distinguishing characteristic. Suave suit, probably expensive. A bright crimson tie. And patent leather shoes totally inappropriate for a building site. It made Bruce sneer slightly, until he collected himself. Rearranged his face.

He wondered why they were meeting here instead of a coffee shop, which would have been more appropriate. The first man shook his hand, firm but not forceful.

'I'm Senzo Nyembe. We spoke over the phone.'

Bruce nodded. A nice private-school boy. Currently advantaged with his fancy car and his excellent connections. He knew this from Martini.

The second man moved forward. There was something about him that made Bruce flinch slightly, but he shook the pale limp hand, careful not to break it. It was dry, soft. Like a girl's.

'And this is my business partner, Mr Hing.'

'Shall we?' Bruce said, indicating the first gate. I'm assuming you'll need to get an idea of specs.'

'Who's in the car?' Nyembe said, tilting his head towards Bruce's SUV.

'My daughter, Enjoy. I've just fetched her from school.'

'Daughter?' Hing looked at the dark head, dark skin. Squinted slightly.

'Yes,' said Bruce, not feeling that he owed an explanation. 'My daughter. This way please.'

The site was only recently laid out, the foundations indicated with string. There were to be twelve properties. Overpriced houses: 'family homes in a security complex'. That always added on a few mill. But the big ticket item was off-the-grid living, right in the Southern Suburbs. No reliance whatsoever on the City, except to flush the shit; literally. It was Bruce's brainchild, but of course, he had investors. All forcing him to cut costs. Cut corners, he thought a lot of the time.

But that's what brought Nyembe and Hing to him. Cheap but quality imports of all the key stuff. Solar panels. MPPT charge controllers. Invertors. Cable, connectors, mountings. Nickel-iron batteries. Then water-harvesting solutions: rain, grey, black. Condensers, possibly. Energy-efficient lighting. He'd thought of everything. But everything was chewing up his profit margins and that didn't look pretty.

He walked slightly ahead of the two men. They didn't say much. It seemed to him that he didn't really have all that much to show them. The positions for the tanks. Where the walls would be constructed. 'Walls', really, as they were to be giant rainwater catchers separating the houses. His idea of dual-space management, DSM, as he'd termed it.

'Obviously,' Bruce said. 'I have a complete list of specs, which I would need to supply you with. And the plans, of course, which I have in CAD.'

Mr Hing nodded. He cleared his throat, then hacked a huge globule of phlegm on the dry sand. Bruce tried to look away, but found himself mesmerised by the quivering mucus.

Seemingly unperturbed, Nyembe looked at Bruce. 'So this is how it works, Bruce. I'm the oil of the operation. Hing secures the stuff in China. Exactly to your specifications. Of course, there are issues to overcome. The biggest one being import duty, customs officials throwing their weight around. But that is where I come in. I smooth the way. Keep things going.'

Bruce didn't have to be a genius to read between the lines. *Keep things going.* How, he wondered, did Nyembe achieve this? Bruce loved making a buck as much as the next guy but he wasn't into screwing SARS unless he could do it legitimately. He wasn't squeaky clean. Who was these days? But he had to ask.

'So how do you do this?'

'Do what?' Nyembe blinked his dark eyes, inscrutable behind his spectacles.

'Keep things going?'

'Contacts.' Nyembe touched his finger to his nose. 'Let's just say, it's all about *who* you know, not *what* you know.'

'Right. But what about securing some of the items in South Africa? Broad-based black empowerment and all that?'

Nyembe put his hands on his hips. 'I've got BEE written all over me,' he said, and laughed merrily.

Somehow Bruce wasn't reassured.

The shine in his eyes

Albert approached Leo as warily as she had. He didn't say anything as he stepped down the passage, his bare feet light on the carpet.

'Shake hands,' Alice hissed, just audibly.

And Albert did.

The silence was weighty but once again Leo showed his mettle. He stood very quietly, waiting for Albert to speak. Alice thought this interesting. Usually it is the adults who attempt to fill the quiet, like the responsibility for carrying a conversation is more related to age than it is about having something to say. She'd noticed that with some men too. Those men regarded their conversation as more important, more valid, than what she had to talk about. Especially now that she'd started homeschooling and it had dominated her life.

Her entire self-image was crumbling. The former architecture student, once top of her class, was now a middle-aged married woman who taught her suicidal kid from home. Sure, she still did some designs when she had spare time, but really her life had been overrun. The silence continued. And Alice couldn't take it any longer.

'Can I make you some tea?' she said. 'What about you, Albert, hot chocolate?'

Safely in the kitchen with the kettle boiling, she leant against counter. Her temples throbbed. If this was supposed to relieve her, she couldn't tell how. She picked the mugs up out of the cupboard above the kettle, extracted the sugar bowl. When she'd laid the tray and picked it up to take it through, she realised she still couldn't hear any indication of conversation. Aha, she thought, a little smugly, Bruce's plan backfiring on Day One. But as she emerged, she saw that Albert and Leo were engrossed with something. Their heads were so tightly together that she considered backing out and leaving them to it. Their hands were almost touching and

55

Albert's stringy hair fell forward so she couldn't see his expression. But the body language, well, that spoke so many words that her heart fluttered. Her son was happy. Such a temporary fragile state. Like a cracked eggshell.

She smiled.

'Your drinks, guys.'

Leo looked up. 'I hope you don't mind that I brought Rascal with me.'

'Rascal?'

'Leo has a pet rat! She's a girl! And she doesn't bite. She likes me, Mom. See?'

My God, she thought, trying to hide the look of horror that must have reached her eyes. This explained then, Malawi's uneasiness. She was resisting the rat, not the man. Boy?

'She's very clean, Mrs Louw. And very loving.'

'Alice,' she corrected absently.

'She sits in Leo's pocket, and she poops on demand. She's white and she has red eyes!'

'Wonderful?' she attempted.

Leo smiled. She wondered if he was mocking her, pleased by her obvious discomfort. 'I'm sorry, Mrs … Alice. It's just that your husband said that Albert likes animals.'

'I do,' Albert said excitedly. 'Does she do tricks too?'

'She does, but I don't think we should try them with your Jack Russell in the room, not sure she'll make it out–'

'Mom, please take Malawi away! I want to see the tricks.'

Alice stood, calling to the dog, which was still keeping a very wary eye on Rascal. Malawi refused to move, and eventually she had to pick her up, hauling her across to the garden. She thrust the yapping canine outside and closed the door, very firmly. Unhappy, the dog jumped so they could see her little head popping up at the window every now and again. She looked demented.

'Okay, Leo,' Albert said. 'She's safe now.'

The rat twitched its pink nose, its crimson eyes darting. Alice thought it (she?) looked evil, and stood far enough away not to touch it. The rodent paced their coffee table and she thought about how she would need to disinfect it. But Leo picked up the cap he'd taken off his head, and moved to the other end of the table. With a sharp whistle and a flick of his fingers, he called Rascal. With her head erect, Rascal turned, then galloped across the table springing into the air and landing neatly into the very centre of Leo's hat. Leo rewarded her with a little pellet from his pocket.

Albert laughed delightedly. 'Can I try?'

'Sure,' said Leo, passing him both the hat and the pellet.

Albert positioned himself at the other end of the table. He attempted a whistle, failed, but despite this, the white rat pounded her way back and flung herself into the hat. The grin on Albert's face was a sight to behold. Alice began to laugh.

'See, Leo, even Mom is impressed! What else can she do?'

'Have you got an empty cup?'

'Mom! An empty cup!' Albert was already in the kitchen. She could hear cupboards opening. A slam. Something toppling. Leo glanced at Alice. He had beautiful, penetrating eyes betraying a wisdom much older than his years. He smiled slightly, as the clumsy tween careened back into the room.

'Here! Here! Is this okay?'

'Perfect,' said Leo as he extracted a five-rand coin from his wallet. This time he put the coin on the table, the cup next to it. Clicking his tongue, he called Rascal, who approached inquisitively, her little whiskers alight with anticipation. Then without any further delay, the little creature hustled to the coin, picked it up between her paws, and dropped the coin into the cup. Alice found that she was laughing out loud. She'd never witnessed anything like it. But even better was the shine in her son's eyes. She hadn't seen *that* for months.

Windswept and rosy

Bruce threw his bag into the corner, kicked off his shoes. Then he marched to the fridge. Pulled out a beer. He was exhausted. Behind him, he could still hear Enjoy unpacking her school bag and hanging up her blazer on her hook. Alice was nowhere to be seen. Where the hell was she? And Albert? Little twerp.

He walked to the warming oven, pulled it open. But even before it was fully extended he knew there was nothing to eat in there.

For fuck's sake. Alice was barely working and now Leo was around, the least she could do was make him a decent dinner. Then Bruce noticed that Malawi wasn't yapping at his ankles. The only thing predictable about this house these days was his little yapper. He loved that dog. But getting old and crotchety. Like him, he thought ruefully. He needed to chill out. The meet with Nyembe and Hing had unsettled him. He felt the anxiety in the pit of his stomach and wished he didn't. On the face of it, there was nothing out of the ordinary. They'd gone to Forries, had a drink. (Hing had glugged down three beers within an hour but shown no sign of any effect.) Enjoy had seen one of her friends and disappeared while the men talked.

Nyembe had explained everything a little less cryptically. And Hing had produced several e-brochures on his iPad to show his products. Although Hing's English was stilted, it was obvious that he knew more than he was able to communicate. He even made suggestions on customising; ways to cut costs in a viable way. So why did Bruce still not feel it?

Then when Enjoy had come to him to complain of being tired, Nyembe's glance towards Bruce had made him feel uncomfortable. In retrospect, he should never have brought her along with him but it was just what happened. He'd come directly from the school run, which he almost never helped with. He'd made their excuses and left, promising another meeting.

Enjoy disappeared down the passage the moment they came home. She'd eaten a pizza at Forries, so dinner for her wasn't an issue. Bruce scrabbled in the fridge and found some steaks. He could do them on the gas and be eating in ten minutes. Then he heard a key in the lock and Alice, Albert and Malawi burst through, followed by whom he could only assume was Leo.

'Bruce!' Alice said. Her hair was windswept and her cheeks rosy. She was smiling, and he tried to recall when he'd last seen that expression of joy on her face.

Malawi jumped around Bruce on her hind legs like a little ballet dancer, then once he'd patted her silky head, she collapsed on the sofa. Albert, wary, didn't say anything, but stood next to Leo, who jiggled some keys in his pocket.

'This is Leo,' Alice said, unnecessarily. 'Leo, Bruce.'

'Nice to meet you, sir,' Leo said extending his hand. They shook.

'Are you staying, Leo? I was about to put some steaks on the braai.'

'Thank you, sir, but I best be off. We've been walking in Newlands Forest. I'm already late for my friends.'

'Of course.'

It seemed he couldn't leave fast enough as within seconds he was out the door without even so much as a backward glance.

'Something I said?' Bruce joked as the door closed after Leo. Albert's face turned glum almost immediately. 'Have you guys had fun?' Bruce asked.

'The doctor said Albert needs to get as much exercise as possible. For the serotonin.' Alice said this a bit defensively, and Bruce began to wonder what he was missing. But he was hungry and had little time or inclination to debate it further.

'Now, who's for steak?' he asked, watching Albert turn and slouch his way back down the passage. 'Albert! Albert! Come back here when I'm talking to you.'

A different story entirely

Leo was different from what she'd expected. For one thing, he wasn't a boy, with boy shoulders and boy face, boy naiveté. Rather, he seemed worldly. Wise, even. And even though she wanted to see him just as Albert's tutor, she realised he had a charisma that extended beyond that. She found this made her uncomfortable. She didn't know exactly how to treat him. Alice was at least twelve years older than he was and she knew he must think of her as old, ancient, even.

So when her stomach flipped as he walked in the door, she was ashamed of herself. And it wasn't just cartwheels of nervousness inside her; it was more than that. She was attracted to him in a way she hadn't felt since she'd first seen Bruce and *their* story had begun. But this was a different story entirely. And when she found herself primping in the mirror, applying lipstick when she was expecting him, she wanted to stop herself. He wasn't ringing the doorbell for her. This was about Albert. Albert's needs. But–

Since Albert's attempted suicide, Bruce had been different. Distant. It wasn't that he didn't want to make love to her – that hadn't changed, but he'd stopped talking. And while he connected through touch, she needed words. Words he wasn't giving her. She tried to raise topics but he was so disconnected that often he'd just grunt, leaving her sentences to float away like bubbles. And this made her feel terribly alone. Sarah, their nanny, had retreated completely. She didn't want to be involved and made that more than obvious. She wouldn't clean Albert's room if he was anywhere near it. Alice understood, but it didn't make it any more bearable. Her beautiful son had become some sort of monster that no one wanted to be around.

Usually a social couple, she and Bruce hadn't invited anyone around for weeks. It was just too difficult. They never knew what to expect from Albert. Last fight he'd had with Enjoy, he'd climbed on top of her and tried to choke her, leaving bruises on her neck. Unnerving. Horrible. They'd had to tranquilise him. And what do you say to a daughter whose brother is so unhinged that he doesn't remember attacking her?

But Leo. Leo was different from Bruce. He seemed softer, somehow, but not soft. He didn't allow Albert to talk back, while Alice did. She was too afraid of the consequences. She felt safer with Leo around. Once, he'd just looked at her, and when she'd broken his gaze, she still felt his eyes on her and they were filled with sympathy. She'd had to get up, run to bathroom and wipe the tears from her eyes. It was easier to be hard amongst hardness. But his tenderness was so unfamiliar to her that it made her feel vulnerable.

But here she was again, titivating in front of a mirror. She felt almost tempted to wipe away all the make-up but that would take more time than leaving it. She would need to greet Leo, it was only polite, but this had become a ridiculous pantomime to her. Hiding her attraction and acting like the mother she was. It would be easier to avoid him completely.

Leo was already sitting with Albert at his desk, from where he looked at her and smiled. His beautiful face lit up and she felt an unfamiliar, once forgotten twist inside her gut.

'What are you working on today?' she asked, business-like.

'The solar system,' Albert said. 'We're going to build a mobile.'

'You are?'

Leo smiled again. 'We thought it would be a good idea to see the planets in perspective. And get our hands a bit dirty.'

Alice nodded. 'Do you need anything?'

'If it's okay with you, we're going to pop out to buy what we need.'

'Well, we have a scrap box in the playroom. Perhaps you'll find something in there?'

He nodded. 'Thanks.'

'Well, I guess I'll be in my office. If you need me.'

'We won't,' Albert said firmly.

And Alice felt both dismissed and cut off. She realised she was going to have to find herself some work to do. Albert clearly didn't need her today.

Something else happening

The first time Alice opened the door, he was surprised how small she was. She couldn't have been much taller than five foot, and her doll-like proportions made her seem vulnerable. He thought she looked like Snow White with her dark hair and pale porcelain skin, but overwhelmingly he sensed her sadness. He'd known her and Albert for only two weeks and realised that she carried more in the family than she should, than her small frame should be able to manage. That first day, however, her dark hair had been tipped with grey, as though touched with a paintbrush. Surprisingly, he found he liked it; she reminded him of a skunk. That probably didn't seem all that complimentary, but actually he liked the look of skunks, and having never had the misfortune to smell one, had no real negative feelings about them. He thought they were cute. Like chipmunks. Or squirrels. Or his pet rat, Rascal, who'd brought out Alice's first smile. Her first laugh. And that was good, he thought. For her to laugh.

But despite this, Leo knew he needed to tiptoe around Alice. She didn't like him invading her home like this, and had made that clear. It made him consider her husband, Bruce, whom he had not met face to face until he'd already been tutoring Albert for two weeks. Bruce, who had hired somebody into their home without either meeting him in person or asking his wife what she'd thought. Leo decided that if ever married, he would try to be a better man. More democratic. Not that Bruce, at first, seemed unlikeable. He was cheery and even a little chummy. But he tried too hard as if he was trying to hide something more sinister below the surface. Alice didn't respond like Leo thought a wife should to his touch. When Bruce put his arm around Alice, Leo noticed that she flinched. To anyone else it might have been imperceptible, but Leo was one of five children and he was the only boy. He knew women, and he knew too that Alice was

62

unhappy. Unhappy beyond the crisis her family was going through in Albert.

It was Leo, then, who suggested that Alice join them for a walk in Newlands Forest. Leo who taught Albert to make tea and bring a laid tray to his mother's office (chocolate biscuits on the side). Leo who told Albert that he was more than old enough to unpack the dishwasher. And because Leo didn't generally raise his voice, or perhaps for some other unfathomable reason, Albert complied.

It wasn't easy teaching a boy like Albert, though. He couldn't concentrate for long periods, and when his mind became too active, he would begin swinging his legs on his chair, or spinning around as though on a merry-go-round. Or he would climb under the desk and hug Malawi. Then Leo couldn't see his face, his eyes. He couldn't see if Albert was even listening.

And the boy's hands were continually moving. Fingers clicking. Thumbs tapping. Digits beating drum beats on the desk.

The solar system was Leo's way to pull Albert back. Kinaesthetic learning, although he'd heard this was all bullshit. It didn't matter. Albert liked the cold feel of the clay, the pressure of the balls forming under his palms. He liked the calculations and the relativity: one planet sized up against another. It seemed to calm him, and from what Leo was beginning to gather, this was unusual. Albert freaked out over even very little things, although since it was early days, rarely with him. With Alice, however, it was a little different. He knew she was experiencing a different Albert, the terror of losing him to mental illness keeping her close. Too close. Smothering.

Once or twice, Leo noticed Alice hovering outside the door, as though considering whether to disturb them or not.

It was obvious Albert adored her, but their relationship was intense. Alice helicoptering around him because she'd failed him once, or so she seemed to believe.

'Alice?' Leo said, when she passed for the third time. 'Why don't you come in and see what Albert has made?'

Alice stood self-consciously at the door. 'I'm sorry. I don't want to barge in.'

'You're not.'

'No?'

Albert held up the mobile. The sun was painted in yellows, with darker patches alternating between the brighter oranges. It seemed to be made of papier-mâché and they'd even managed to insert a globe inside, so the sun was actually shining. The other planets were rendered in precise details: Uranus egg-blue and smooth; Mercury freckled grey; Venus mustard and cracking; a red-glowing Mars. Saturn was spectacular. Its rings were designed from an old CD, a foam ball, glue, paint and glitter. They'd googled it. But Leo had done his utmost to let Albert decide. Albert build. Albert manage. Another kid, perhaps, might have found this project childish, or daunting. But Albert was only too glad to be using his hands, rather than writing lengthy sentences. And Alice's delighted expression was enough to convince Leo that he'd done something right.

'It's wonderful!' she said, smiling broadly. 'Are you going to hang it up?'

Albert shrugged, losing interest in the project now it was complete.

'Albert?' Alice asked, and he turned his back on her, blocking her out.

Leo watched the interaction, feeling the tension in the room, but not understanding it. 'Do you have a ladder we can use, Albert?'

The boy nodded.

'Can you fetch it? Is it heavy?'

Albert left the room and when he returned, they could hear the metal of the ladder vibrating as he stepped down the corridor. But when he entered, he simply dumped the steps in the bedroom, turned and left.

'What's wrong?' Leo asked, bemused.

'It's Albert,' Alice said softly, as if that was explanation enough.

'Shall I go after him?'

'Let's hang it up. You've both made a lot of effort. There's already a hook we can use from a mosquito net we used to have before we installed the mozzie screens.'

Leo nodded and opened the ladder, balancing it carefully under the hook. He was about to climb up himself, when he found that Alice was already ahead of him. She ascended the ladder and now that he was close to her, his eyes in line with her tight arse and skirt shorter than he'd thought. Disconcerted, he tried to look away, but he was holding the ladder, and it was a view that suited him. Her toned legs, her slim thighs …

'Leo?' Alice said, making him start.

'Uh, yes?'

'Can you pass it up now?'

He leant over to the desk, lifting the mobile with one hand while trying to grip the ladder. It shook slightly but Alice seemed unconcerned. Leo got the impression that Alice was used to doing things for herself. As she hooked up the mobile, he saw the string he and Albert had set up to close the circuit (Topic 10, electric currents) and turn on the light of the sun was twisted upwards.

Still holding the ladder, he pointed it out.

'Okay,' Alice said. 'Got it.' She tugged gently and the sun turned on. Alice laughed delightedly. 'How clever!'

Leo had to admit, the mobile did look awesome. 'Albert!' he called. 'Come check this out!'

Alice began to descend the ladder. He was holding it tight but as she came down, she lost her balance. He found himself hanging onto her before she hit the floor. He was holding Alice in his arms, and he could smell her perfume, her hair tickling his nose. But the feeling of her. He knew he should let her go immediately, but he found she was leaning into him. The seconds passed, with neither of them pulling apart. And this is how Albert found them.

The boy's questioning look was enough to send them scattering.

'I fell off the ladder!' Alice said quickly. 'Thank goodness Leo caught me or we would have been on the way to the ER.'

Leo bowed slightly. 'Your knight, madam.'

'Whatever,' Albert said, looking up. 'That's really dope.'

'Magical!' Alice agreed. 'You've outdone yourselves.'

Relieved that Albert's focus had been taken up by the mobile, Leo looked at Alice. But she refused to meet his eyes. Instead she put her arm around Albert, almost turning her back.

'Right,' she said, letting her son go. 'I'll take the ladder back outside.'

'Let me do it,' Leo said.

'No, no. You guys carry on. I'm going outside anyway.' Alice picked up the ladder. While Albert had seemed to carry it effortlessly, Alice looked awkward. And when Leo moved forward to help her, she shook her head slightly.

Don't, her expression said. But when their eyes locked, it was like a key turning. Something opened inside him, and the slight trembling of her lip made him wonder if she was about to cry.

Or if something else had just happened inside her too.

Fixing it

Martini spent the weekends on a smallholding in Elgin. 'Smallholding' was Martini's term, but Bruce looked across the expansive area and thought it was big enough to be called a farm. They even had horses. Well, of course they did. Martini's wife Elaine was so horse mad it seemed unlikely she would ever live far from a ride.

Bruce looked towards Alice. She was sitting with Elaine, a glass of rosé in her hand. Alice wasn't normally a wine drinker. She preferred the hard tack, whisky especially. Elaine was talking, which wasn't unusual. Fuck, that woman could go on. And God help you if you asked about her health. She was the one person who would tell you. Every time you saw her she had a new disease. And whatever story you told, she could top. If you'd climbed Kili, she'd climbed Everest. If you'd swum two kays, she'd crossed the fucking Channel. Alice told him often enough that if you could get past that, you found beneath the layers a warm, kindly woman who would do anything for her friends. *Better than we could,* Bruce had retorted, sending them both into peals of malicious laughter.

But Martini had been a mate since school and that meant putting up with his horsey wife. As mind-numbing as that was. At least she was something sexy to look at, Bruce could certainly see the attraction there. Given half a chance …

Martini had lit a braai. Steaks marinated in a bright yellow bowl. Bruce's stomach roared. He'd done an early run with the boys. Malawi was keeping up still but the poor dog was getting old. Like him. He'd be forty-four next week. Alice said that wasn't old but he knew better. He could feel it in his fucking knees. Bend down and he creaked like an antique.

Martini stoked the coals. He was wearing an apron with Keep Calm and Braai emblazoned across it. Probably a good thing as he'd already spilt some sauce down the front. It dripped slowly, like lava. Martini's T-shirt strained against his pumped-up chest and biceps. He may well have been the runt in school, but now with his neatly trimmed beard and eyes with lashes so dark he looked like he was wearing eyeliner, he was a person you noticed. And, of course, his investment in some medical research start-up company had more than compensated for any lack of height he might have had. Because Martini and Elaine were loaded.

Martini studied Bruce thoughtfully. 'What's on your mind, bugger?'

Bruce grimaced. 'Oh, you know. The usual.'

Martini poked the coals. 'What the hell is the usual – wife, kids or work?'

'A little bit of everything, hey.'

'Well, Albert looks like a happier boy. Did you see him talking to the horses?'

Bruce grunted. 'We have this oke around; the one I hired? Lionel or whatever his name is. Costs a bomb but seems to have brought the kid a bit out of his shell. Doesn't seem about to top himself at every moment.'

'That must be a relief.'

'Yes and no. Every time I come home that guy is around. It's like I've adopted an extra family member I don't even want.'

'And what does Alice say about it?'

'She doesn't. I was the one who insisted on it. So it's not like I can carp on about it.'

Martini picked up a steak, tossed it on the grid. It sizzled and spat. 'Maybe it's temporary.'

'Who the fuck knows? My wife has that kid so pumped up on drugs, I'm surprised he can keep his eyes open. And when she forgets, he runs like a terrorist through the house. He threw a brick at Enjoy. For no reason whatsoever except that she'd pissed him off.'

'Ouch.'

'I try to talk to Alice about it and she gets all defensive. If the kid could just pull himself towards himself then we could get on with life the way it was.'

'You think so?' Martini's eyes darkened and for the first time, Bruce noticed that Martini was carrying some worries of his own.

'What's new on your side, anyway?' Bruce said. 'I'm tired of talking about my fucked-up life.'

'Oh, nothing too much. Bit of trouble with the missus.'

'Really?' Bruce tried not to sound too enthusiastic.

Maybe Martini wasn't such a wonderboy after all …

'I don't want to talk about it. It's kinda complicated. But I'm fixing it. How did the meeting go with Nyembe?'

Bruce watched Martini flip a steak. Too early, was his thought, but then Martini liked his steak so bloody it could walk off the plate.

'I don't know, mate. There's something a little off with those two. Rethinking a little. That Nyembe is shifty. Can't meet your eyes half the time.'

'Cultural, boytjie. Sign of respect. Don't be a prick.' Martini's barbed tone caught Bruce by surprise. 'Nyembe's going to save a heap of dough. Just get with the bloody programme. I mean it, don't be a *doos* and stuff this up.' Martini looked towards his wife, waving his lifter in the air to get her attention.

'Ten-minute warning!' he called, and she nodded, toasting him with her wine glass. Elaine stood, wrapping her thick woollen cardigan around her, and Alice followed her into the house. There was something different about his wife today. Her face had loosened, like she was happy. It was a nice change from the sourpuss he'd been facing since Albert's suicide attempt. It was definitely true what he'd heard: a family is only as happy as its unhappiest member. Misery was like a pandemic.

Elaine emerged carrying a huge bowl, a French loaf wrapped in brown paper tucked under her arm. Alice held a pile of plates, some cutlery balanced on top. It looked heavy but despite this Alice was laughing. It made Bruce smile.

Nevertheless, his thoughts returned to Nyembe and his Chinese sidekick. Despite what Martini said, suspicion still stuck in his gut.

The real stuff

She'd enjoyed the lunch with Martini and Elaine. And the kids had taken the horses out with Elaine after lunch. Now she had a further complication – Enjoy wanted to learn to ride. When the heck was she supposed to find the time to fit that in? She supposed she could take Enjoy while Leo watched Albert. But they'd have to drive to Noordhoek and then she would have to sit and wait until the lesson was done. She already had enough on her plate without that hassle.

Maybe she'd take a leaf from Bruce's book and hire someone without consulting *him*. She smiled to herself, feeling devilish. But she knew she wouldn't even if it was tempting. And her poor daughter didn't get anything these days – their world revolved around Albert to the point that even she was irritated by it.

The doorbell rang and Alice looked up. Albert was fast asleep as he often was when he'd had his lunchtime medication. Enjoy was playing squash. For once, Alice was actually in front of her computer doing some designs for a hotelier who'd insisted on waiting for her to clear her schedule, and now she was getting the job done. Unlike the hotelier, Alice wasn't particularly enthralled by French Provençal but that didn't matter. She would do as she was requested, and haul out the natural materials, suggest rough-staining or painting plaster walls and even engage in the folly that was unnecessary beams across a ceiling that would have done very nicely just the way it was. It was what she was being paid to do, and frankly, the work – any work – served as a distraction from what was her current strange life.

She stood up.

When she peered out the window near the front door, she could see Leo standing there with a hand blocking the sun from his face. Despite herself, her stomach tangled like kelp.

'Hello?' she called from the now-open doorway. 'Have I forgotten something?'

Leo shook his head and indicated for her to open up. She did.

'I'm sorry to disturb you,' Leo said. 'Is Albert here?'

'Well, he is but he's out cold. You know how he gets after his meds.'

'Oh. Yes. Of course.'

Leo's face scrunched up. And even then, he looked gorgeous. 'Was it urgent? Seeing Albert?'

'Not actually. I just found out about a mate of mine who's building a computer from scratch. I know how Albert loves that sort of sh—, I mean stuff. I wanted to ask him if he was keen to have a look some time.'

'And you didn't phone?' Alice hated her tone the moment she said it.

Leo looked stricken. 'I'm sorry, I was just driving past and it was a spur-of-the-moment idea. I just knew my little buddy would get a kick out of it. I wanted to see his face. The way it lights up.'

Alice smiled. 'You know? I was just about to make some coffee. The real stuff. Would you like a cup?'

The greyness between

It was stupid of course, to be drawn to Alice. Married. A mother. Clearly unhappy. But there was an intangible something that defined her. Leo had always been a sensitive boy. Attached to his mother in an extreme way; like a pea unable to be shelled from the pod. Eventually his mother had sent him to relatives in Florence, in Italy, to spend a holiday; an attempt, he later realised, to cleave him from his umbilical cord. He'd cried himself to sleep almost every night. He was sixteen. Too old to cry. And his pseudo-aunt (he thought she was actually his mother's second cousin), realising his homesickness, decided to feed him. He put on five kilograms that trip, which actually looked good on him. He'd always been far too thin.

But apart from the weight gain, Leo had also developed a talent for observation – both visual and auditory. Being the outcast and with very ungrammatical Italian, he'd been on the edge of every group. A David Attenborough observer of human, rather than animal, behaviour. It allowed him to learn to mimic certain body language, copy certain phrases. And as many experts on body language could have told him, people are attracted to others who unconsciously copy – not mock – their physical language. A language, Leo believed, that was far more honest. He was good at identifying a lie. And also the truth. The greyness that lay between was only really possible in the spoken word. Body language was never grey. Indistinct.

At the beginning of the holiday, he'd been unaware of the effect of his physical appearance on women. He'd seen girls look, but not in the way that might have indicated attraction. Rather it was curiosity. His clothes, his manner, clearly identified him as a stranger and a shy stranger at that. But then his 'aunt's' friend Pia had arrived for a holiday from America, her husband, Claude, in tow. The man was self-important – like Bruce – and

71

self-indulgent. He would talk ad infinitum about his work, his research, his life. And all the time he spoke, Leo was watching his flamboyant wife, a psychologist from Boston. She was like a pheasant. Multi-coloured, floaty. With a gravel-voice from years of smoking, when she had a chance to speak, she was also able, or so it seemed to Leo, to conjure words that painted visual masterpieces. Leo was fascinated by her and although she said nothing at first, once she cupped his teenage jaw and told him he was positively Davidian. He had no idea what she was talking about, and so she dragged him to the Galleria dell'Accademia. Standing below the enormous statue (seventeen foot she said, which meant nothing to him, coming from South Africa), he felt himself blush. Pure scarlet. The muscle and bone, the hairy stone genitalia; they were too intimate, too *real*. But it was there that she kissed him, her tongue darting into his mouth, sending pure heat down into his lungs, as though she was a hot fire-breathing dragon. And he was besotted.

Though he followed her around like a faithful puppy, it never came to more than that. This wasn't some torrid affair under the neglectful auspices of Claude. It was a moment. But it was enough to make him grow from a tearful boy into, not a man exactly, but a man-boy. With thoughts bigger than just returning to his mother and sisters, but rather his eye on a bigger prize of making a living one day out of *meaning* rather than simply *existing*. He didn't know exactly how or what he was going to do, but his ambitions gradually graduated to psychotherapy and art history. And this is what had brought him to Albert's doorstep. Because Bruce, as much as Leo distrusted him, was offering Leo a way to pay for his PhD practising simultaneously the craft that had chosen him in Florence.

But he hadn't counted on Alice. And sitting in the kitchen drinking a cup of freshly brewed coffee, he had the urge to grab hold of her hand and tell her that everything was going to be all right. She looked slightly tearful. And it wasn't the first time she'd seemed that way either. But instead they chit-chatted about – what was it? – French Provençal style and the plans she was drawing up for The Kirstenbosch, a hotel located nearby the botanical gardens. Gradually though, as they sat there, she seemed to grow within herself, taking on an assurance that must have existed, formed within her like a backbone, cell upon cell.

'I was going to be an architect,' she said lightly. 'More Frank Lloyd Wright than Le Corbusier.'

'Organic,' he said.

'Exactly!' she said, looking pleased. And surprised. 'Like bringing nature into the building itself. For one of my final projects – that is, before we moved to the US – I designed an entire house around an oak tree. It was magnificent.'

Leo smiled. He liked the way her face lit up, as though sunshine had suddenly beamed onto her features.

'I think I may still have the designs somewhere.'

'I'd love to see them.'

'You would? Really?'

'Absolutely!'

She stood up, unconsciously scratching her earlobe. 'I wonder where I put them.'

She walked over to the bookcase in the lounge, peered down into the cupboards below. While everything else in the house was neat, these appeared to hide a multitude of sins. Toys rolled out. And crafty stuff. Wrapping paper. Old files. Sticky tape. Photo frames? She sighed. Walked back to where Leo was sitting without even bothering to pick the debris up. She shrugged. Took back her position, deflated.

'But now,' she said, clouding over. 'Now I have my family and a very sick boy.'

'That doesn't mean you should give up on yourself. I could help you find the designs. We could clear that out together.'

Leo ruefully considered his offer. His mother would have been falling over herself with surprise. Her baby son offering to tidy. *Impossibile.*

'You're sweet,' she said, briefly reaching out to touch his hand. And when she did, he found himself reacting instinctively. He placed his other hand on top of hers so she couldn't take it away.

'I'm not *just* sweet,' he told her.

There was a momentary silence, a shift of something tectonic. The worried face of the woman in front of him softened, then reformed.

'I think I need a whisky,' she said, standing up. 'Are you even old enough to drink?'

Brace yourself

He left Martini's Constantia house feeling irritated. Bruce was a self-made man, not some wimp to be pushed about by his very slightly richer and possibly more powerful friend. Martini came from a long line of influencers. His father, some hotshot on the Johannesburg Stock Exchange was still frequently quoted – on and offline. And Martini had that knack of being able to transform opportunities into action: action-reaction, Ka-Ching. He expected Bruce to follow him around like some man-slave, lift, carry, produce. But Bruce had his own business. His own decisions to make. And now the fuckwit wanted him to go ahead with this BEE deal. There was a little pressure. To say the least. Bruce said he'd think about it, but actually he didn't want to. He didn't like Nyembe or that Hing individual, with his soft hands and creepy sallow skin, like some death mask. And now Martini had made him late for his squash match, and he just knew his brother Gabriel would be pissed off. He pulled into the parking lot, grabbed his racquet and rushed into WPCC. The door was wide open, and as he turned left, he could see Gabe banging a ball against the wall of a court, a sour look on his face.

'Merry Christmas,' Gabriel said, aiming the next ball at the glass. It thumped resoundingly. Bruce had been about to apologise, but fuck it. He was here, wasn't he?

Bruce dropped his bag on the steps, flung open the door and marched in. He returned Gabriel's serve with little trouble. Soon they were both lost in the dull slap of rubber against wall. Crosscourt. Backswing. Light on his feet, Bruce ran back to the intersection of the red lines, waiting to retrieve Gabriel's next shot. Bang. The ball flew hard into the back corner. One point to Bruce. Bruce took his time with his serve, from the left service box. But when his racquet came into contact with the ball, the rubber thudded resoundingly. Back and forth. They were evenly matched but

Bruce liked to put Gabriel on the defensive, volleying his next serve. Bruce often thought it was about rhythm, upsetting the opponent's sense of predictability. A bit like jazz. Pacing the shots differently. Whack! Whack-whack! Changing direction. Making the bugger run. Gabriel was panting, sweat pasting his balding head. Bruce won, but only narrowly. New game.

Bruce served a lob, aiming to land the ball in the back corner of the court, close to both the side walls and the dirty glass. He angled it nicely, the ball smacking the side wall in Gabriel's corner of the court. Gabriel jumped, trying to volley the ball before it smashed against the side. Missing that, he still tried to gallop across the corner to get to the back corner. He thumped into the wall, wincing. The ball idled. Bruce grinned. Not giving Gabriel even a chance to recover, he hit again. This time an underhand power serve. A backhand. Gabe returned the shot, but Bruce got into position quickly. They hadn't spoken, but the vicious cut of the squash racquet near Bruce's head brought the message home very clearly that Gabriel was still angry at him. He sulked like a woman. Too bad for him. *Pussy.* Bruce was dominating the centre of the court. Controlling the ball. Gabe glanced at him, his face now blood red.

'Ease off a bit, champ, I'm not getting any younger.'

'Can't keep up?'

'It's a game, Bruce. You know, for fun?' Gabriel leant over, breathing heavily. He held his hands to his hips as he sucked in air.

'I'm having fun,' Bruce said, grinning wolfishly. 'But don't worry. I'll give you the soft treatment.'

Gabriel looked at him. 'You know, Brucie, you used to be nice. I think I'm done for today.'

Bruce frowned. He wasn't good at reading people. Not like Alice was. Maybe he'd just pushed too hard.

'Oh come on, Monk, let's play. We don't even have to score. I could use the exercise.'

'Fine,' Gabriel said, standing up and moving back into position. 'Just stop using that bloody nickname. And don't be late next time.'

***

When Bruce drove into the garage it was just after seven. Hopefully he'd timed it late enough to miss the dinner fighting, and a meltdown or two. He saw, however, that a car was parked on the street. That Lionel guy. Fuck. He wanted a beer, to chow down dinner. Not an evening with the little people. He wanted Alice to rub his sore, swollen feet. A shag for pudding.

Bruce walked into the house, dropped his keys on the kitchen counter. The sounds of voices echoed down the passage. Unwillingly, he followed the noise. And there in the lounge, his family and the babysitter playing a raucous game of 30 Seconds. The shouting stopped as he walked into the room. Alice looked at him, a slightly glazed look on her face. *Was she drunk?*

'Darling,' she gushed. 'You're back.' She giggled.

Even Malawi hadn't bothered to get up to greet him. The traitorous dog lay with her legs in the air while the hired help tickled her belly. Slut. And as for his own children, neither Enjoy nor Albert had even bothered to acknowledge him. Lionel, nevertheless, stood up to shake his hand. He too had a drink in front of him. What the hell was this? Aftercare for students?

'I need a beer,' Bruce announced. 'Anyone need anything?'

'We're having whisky,' said Alice. 'Give Leo a top-up, please. And me.'

Leo?

'Haven't you had enough?'

'Oh no. We're just getting started. You're a drink or two behind, dear. Brace yourself.'

The irritation rose in his chest but he complied. He wasn't expecting a party at home but what did it really matter?

'Daddy, you can be on our team!' Enjoy said. 'Come sit with us.'

He nodded and sat down as Enjoy shifted up to make room for him.

'And go!' Albert shouted turning over the timer.

Bruce's wife was now standing opposite Leo attempting her first clue. 'Shaken not stirred!'

'James Bond?'

Alice nodded emphatically. 'Time of the year with lots of heart gifts and love tokens.'

'Valentine's Day!'

'Not Coke but–'

'Sprite?'

'Um, no. Same colour. Different make.'

'Pepsi!' shouted Leo.

'Paralympian who killed Reeva.'

'Oscar Pistorius!'

'Stretch of land along the sea. Transkei. Eastern Cape area.'

'Coffee Bay? Port St Johns?'

'No. No, more general!'

'Um … Wild Coast?'

'And finished!' Alice shouted enthusiastically. 'Well done, pard-ner!' They high-fived. Alice moved their playing token forward five.

Bruce felt his competitive juices begin to flow. He was good at this. And the kids seriously sucked. They were way behind. 'Our turn,' he told his children. 'Keep up, kids.'

He stood up.

'And go,' Alice said, turning over the timer.

Bruce studied the card. 'The rodent who lives in Disneyland.'

'Rodent?' Enjoy asked.

'Like a rat, but not a rat,' Albert explained.

'Mickey Mouse?'

'Yes!' Bruce air-punched. 'Band. They sing Mamma Mia.'

'What?'

'You know. The two chicks and two guys. From Sweden or Norway or something.'

Enjoy and Albert looked at each other, confusion on both their faces.

'Pass that clue and come back,' Alice suggested.

'Seriously?' Bruce said. 'Oh okay. Singer of Thriller. Black and White. Billie Jean.'

The blank stares of both children was enough to send him to the next clue. 'A painter. He cut off his own ear.'

'Vincent!' said Albert.

'Good enough,' said Alice. 'Next one.'

'Capital of Argentina.'

'Brazil!' shouted Enjoy.

'No.'

'Paris?'

'No!'

'Rio de Janeiro,' said Albert.

'No! For Christ's sake. What are these kids learning in school?'

'Bruce, just go back to the other questions.'

'But they don't know the bloody answers.'

'And, time,' said Leo.

Bruce felt the irritation welling. Two points! He glugged down the rest of his beer. Went to fetch another. As Alice and Leo danced through another card, he opened a new bottle. Another childish high five. His wife was seriously pissed and he didn't like it. He sat down on the couch, waiting for Albert to stand up.

'Now, boy,' he said. 'Be clear and clever about this. We're a long way behind.'

'No pressure,' muttered Albert under his breath, but not soft enough that Bruce didn't hear him.

Albert flipped over his card. 'Um. I'm not really sure what this is.'

'For Christ's sake,' Bruce said. 'Go onto the next one. And next time use that bloody brain of yours.'

Not like you

Alice wasn't as drunk as Bruce seemed to think she was. For the first time in months she was having fun. Real fun. Not the kind of fun she was supposed to be having – fake 'dates' with her husband while he griped about how much money she was spending on the psychiatrist, or why she was losing focus on her 'real' work (and all the time worried about what Albert was getting up to at home). As if raising a child to adulthood wasn't real work. But now she was sitting as Albert stuttered through one clue after the next. Ironically, he'd done fine without Bruce there. Not brilliantly, but fine. But now he stammered and struggled as though enduring the worst case of stage fright she'd ever seen.

'Okay, it's like … like … a long river. But it's, like, between two continents. And boats, um, boats can go through it.'

Alice watched Bruce. He was leaning forward as though this would help him hear better. His hands were on his knees. He craned his neck, a vein visibly pulsing.

'A strait?' Bruce said.

'Ocean?' Enjoy offered.

'Which continents is it between, boy? Spit it out!'

'Well, it's more like it connects two oceans.'

'This one is in South America. At the top.'

'Panama Canal!' shouted Bruce, thumping his hand hard down on his thigh.

'Good clue,' Leo said. 'You did that really well, Albert.'

'Get on with it!' Bruce said, glaring at Leo. 'No hijacking our time, mate.'

'A type of insect. It's a cartoon now.'

'Enjoy, I don't watch cartoons! Out with it,' Bruce instructed.

'A Bug's Life!' said Enjoy.

'No, she's striped,' said Albert.

'Bee Movie!'

'No.'

'And, time,' said Leo quietly.

'What the hell was it?' Bruce said.

'Maya the Bee.'

Bruce sighed heavily. Alice watched him sink back into his chair, irritation permeating from him like rancid body odour. Though he didn't say anything further, his bad mood had soured what could have been a pleasurable time.

'Why don't we call it a day?' Alice said. 'I'm starving. Leo, will you stay for dinner?'

Leo's drink was still half-full, but he was already standing. 'No thanks Alice. I think I should go. Give you all a bit of family time.' He looked across at Albert, who glowered stonily. 'I'll see you tomorrow, champ. You were great. Next time I'd like to be on your team, if you don't mind?'

A half-smile appeared on Albert's face. 'Sure.'

'I'll see you out,' said Alice.

'No,' her husband said. 'You organise some grub. I'll do it.'

Alice nodded, put her hand up in a half-wave. 'Thanks for coming, Leo. It really meant a lot to Albert.'

Leo looked at her a moment longer than perhaps was necessary. When he smiled, she could see he knew what she was actually saying. 'See you, Alice,' he said.

Alice went to the kitchen. She stared out the window, watching Bruce and Leo walk down the drive. She felt a tug of anger as she watched her husband lope his way to the road, the remote in his right hand. This had been the first happy evening she'd experienced in the months since Albert's suicide attempt and time in-patient at the psychiatric facility. But Bruce had ruined it. She was sick of his constant attitude. She was sick of *him*. Slapping some sandwiches together, she called the kids to sit at the counter. Neither child seemed too worried about the meal but once again it was Bruce who complained the moment the front door shut.

'You're kidding, right? This is dinner?'

At first, Alice said nothing. She bit into the cheese and tomato, trying to marshal herself.

'Alice. Don't you at least have something hot? This isn't like you!'

But the tension that had been building up in her the whole evening, for weeks, exploded. She stood up, pulled a pan out from the drawer under the sink, fired up the hob and poured some olive oil into the pan. Then she shredded his sandwich into tiny pieces with her fingers, the tomato breaking off in uneven clumps and ribbons. She cracked an egg, pouring the contents over the ragged sandwich remains. When the cheese was vaguely melted, the egg mostly cooked she shoved the shrapnel onto his plate.

'Dinner is served,' she said, banging the plate in front of him as the children looked on wide-eyed. 'Eat it while it's *hot*.'

A lot of trouble

Alice was not there the next morning when he got to the house. Albert opened the door and led him past Sarah who was cleaning the lounge, a vacuum cleaner fired up as she held its long handle to suck up the dirt. In the kitchen, he could see a few dishes still sitting in the sink – something he'd never seen in all the weeks he'd been tutoring Albert. Generally the house, and especially the kitchen, were both spotless. Sarah waved at him as he and Albert walked to his room, where his computer was already on.

'Where's your mom?' he asked.

Albert shrugged. 'Meeting, I think.'

'Will she be back later?'

He shrugged again. 'Dunno. She left my pills out. Even the ones for ten o'clock.'

Leo nodded. 'So, geography today. Scale and map-reading. Fancy taking a walk?'

They clipped on Malawi's harness and Leo carried a large sketchpad and a few pens and pencils. He wrote Alice a note, stuck it prominently on the fridge. GONE TO PARK. MAP SKILLS PRACTICE. He added a smiley face and regretted it immediately – it looked as childish as you could get. They got into his car. Malawi's nose stuck to the window of the back seat as she balanced on her hind legs. Albert climbed in next to Leo.

'You're quiet today, champ,' Leo said.

Albert didn't say anything, only confirming Leo's observation.

'You okay?'

Albert nodded.

'Anything you want to tell me? I promise, it's a safe space. I won't repeat anything you tell me.'

'Like a psychologist?'

'Or even better, like a friend.'

Albert sighed heavily, eyed him with his wide expressive eyes and said, 'Mom and Dad had a big fight.'

'Oh?' He tried to hide the thrill of hearing that. 'What about?'

'Dunno.' The boy shrugged.

'When did this happen?'

'Just after you left.'

'Well, Bert. If I were you, I'd park it. Adults have fights sometimes and they usually sort it out. For all you know, they could have made up when you were asleep.'

'Dad slept in Enjoy's room. On her spare bed. And this morning, they didn't greet each other.'

'Ah.'

They were both quiet and despite Leo's temptation to solve the issue with soothing words, he didn't. 'I tell you what. I can't fix that but we can get this geography done. Check this compass out. Isn't it cool?' He held it out, and as he expected, Albert reached for it, immediately touching the buttons and dials. 'We have to map out the park. So the important thing is to know where north is. Have a look if you can work that out. We'll then measure out the park using your strides as our unit of measurement. Instead of metres.'

Albert nodded but Leo could see he wasn't concentrating. Leo realised belatedly, too, that he'd left Albert's ten o'clock medication behind – something Alice had warned him never to forget. But he knew this couldn't take long, and the point was not a masterful map but an appreciation of the skills needed for map making. Scale. Distance. Direction. If things went a little off course, there was still time to get back. A half hour, maybe an hour late couldn't be too bad, surely?

'Okay, Bert, buddy,' Leo said. 'Let's mark up north on the paper and do a rough sketch of the shape of the park.'

Albert pointed vaguely north and scribbled it on the paper. He had the most terrible handwriting – he wrote as if he was trying to conserve paper, one letter on top of the other. Piled up like Pick-Up Sticks. Leo couldn't always tell certain letters apart. His zeros and sixes were so similar, that Leo usually had to guess.

'Try to be as neat as you can, so we can read it later.'

'Who cares about neatness?' Albert said. 'It's not going to change the world.'

'I don't think this map is going to change the world either,' Leo said, 'but we need to do it, so let's just get it done.'

'I've been thinking a lot about iPads,' Albert said, as if that were in any way related to what they were talking about.

'Oh?'

'Did you know the iPad Air 2 is getting a successor? The iPad 9.7. It's a medium-shelf model with 2048 x 1536 pixel retina display. It's got an Apple A9 chip!'

'Awesome, buddy, but let's get back to schoolwork.'

'The entry-level model is 32GB with Wifi. Up to ten hours surfing on one battery. It weighs just under 470 grams.'

'Sounds fantastic. But let's focus.'

'I am. I'm focused on the iPad 9.7. It's a good price. The base model is $397. Oleophobic coating. 8-megapixel rear camera. 1.2 megapixel front camera.'

'What the heck is oleophobic?'

'Any material that lacks an affinity to oils. It keeps fingerprint spots off the glass panel.'

'Right. Can we do geography now?'

'I'm not feeling it, Leo.'

'Feeling what? Crikey dude, we need to do this work.'

Leo watched as Albert's hands became more and more agitated. As he tried to make Albert walk and measure, the boy was kicking his slippers (yes, he'd refused to change them) into the dirt, whipping up clouds of dust, Malawi darting behind him. Albert was muttering under his breath, the words beginning to come out in gushes, rather than streams. Then his arms started to rotate, like he was trying to make himself fly. Looking into Albert's eyes, he saw how much they'd changed in the few minutes they'd been here at the park. His pupils were hugely dilated, so that his eyes looked almost completely black. And they were wide, completely transforming his expression.

'Albert, are you feeling alright?'

'What? I'm fine. Fine. Just a bit hot. Really hot.' He waved his arms even more, trying to fan himself.

'Let me help you take your jersey off.'

'I can do it,' Albert said. And with that he started to take all of his clothes off, in the middle of the park.

Horrified, Leo tried to stop him. 'Albert, Albert. You can't do that here, boy.'

'I want to be free!'

'Okay, but I think we should get in the car. You can be free in your garden at home.'

'I like it here. Can you hear the birds?'

'There are birds in your garden, Albert.'

The boy shot down the path, the shed clothing abandoned behind him.

'Damn it,' Leo muttered under his breath, and ran after Albert, who was surprisingly fast and agile. He didn't catch him nearly as quickly as he'd expected, but when he did, he had the awkward decision of how to hold him without touching any of the dangly bits.

'Put me down,' Albert shouted, as Leo decided to fireman's lift him over his shoulder. Albert beat him hard on his back, screaming.

Oh my God, Leo thought, how am I going to get this kid to the car? And where's the damn dog?

It was at this point, of course it was, that an old woman in a red beret and khaki woollen coat arrived at the scene, a beagle yanking the leash she held in front of her.

'What's going on here? Is this man trying to hurt you?' she asked Albert. 'Why are you naked?'

'Let me go!' screeched Albert.

The woman pulled a mobile phone from her pocket. 'I'm calling the police. And ADT. Put the boy down.'

But Leo, now a little desperate, knew that if he let Albert go he would lose him again. The kid would get even further from the car and that could be critical. 'Ma'am,' he said in the politest voice he could muster, 'the police are not the answer. Or ADT for that matter. I'm responsible for this boy. He's sick and he needs to get home to his mother.'

Now Albert began to kick and scream. 'Help me!' he screamed. 'Help me!' He bucked and twisted and it took all Leo's strength to keep holding him. Another dog walker arrived, a young woman with a ponytail touching her butt and a thin, narrow face and buck teeth. 'What the fuck?' Like a typical Millennial (Leo did not regard himself as one), she took out her phone and began to film a resisting Albert, and Leo trying to walk away with him.

'Please,' Leo said, the desperation in his voice almost palpable. 'Could you get his clothes?'

The old woman glared at him. Her face was attached to her phone, and she was repeating with mounting hysteria that a child molester was in Keurboom Park abducting a naked child. Then a grey-haired man arrived. He lifted the clothes with his walking stick, a bemused look on his face.

'You want these back, tyke?' he said gruffly.

But Albert continued to shout for his freedom. 'Help me! Let me go, asshole.'

This, of course, did not help.

'Can I have those, please?' Leo said. 'He took them off himself. He does this sometimes. Please. I need to get him to the car.'

The old man hesitated, then stood his ground. 'I'm not really sure I should give them to you. Evidence. Are you filming, young lady?'

She gave him a thumbs up, grinning, then glared at Leo. 'It's not like he wants to go with you, sicko.'

Then Leo heard the sirens. *Oh God. Oh God.*

Brakes screeched. Doors slammed.

The cops ran from the vehicle, the rolls of encased fat wobbling in their navy uniforms as they attempted to run. It was a male-female duo and if Leo hadn't been so terrified he might have laughed, they appeared so comical. This was nothing like the movies. No flashing sirens, trim-waisted heroines, fit stuntmen. Nevertheless, he was terrified. He couldn't believe he was in this mess.

'Slowly,' the policewoman said. 'Put the boy down, then put your hands above your head so we can see you're not holding anything.'

Leo hesitated. If he put Albert down, he knew he would run again. And this was already quite a circus. A crowd was gathering.

'Sir,' the policewoman said. 'Put down the boy.'

'He's ill,' Leo attempted.

'Put down the child,' the policeman said.

The old man, still holding the discarded hoodie, tracksuit pants, and a balled-up pair of undies, held them out to the policeman, who grunted, screwed up his nose and took them gingerly.

Leo leant over, whispered gently to Albert, 'Please don't run, buddy. We're in a lot of trouble. A. Lot. Of. Trouble.' Then he released his hold. Albert looked at him, but as his feet touched the ground, he took off across the park, leaping over the spring and accelerating up the opposite bank. With his arms now in the air, Leo didn't know what to do. So he stood his ground, holding Malawi's leash as he watched Albert's little white bottom disappear in the distance just as another police car arrived, this time a blue light piercing the morning stillness.

Alice was going to kill him.

Making the call

She parked around the corner at the first empty space she could find, then sprinted up to the front of the police station, past a palm tree and several wanted signs. There was already a queue in front of her at the counter but one of the policemen noticed her agitation and came around the desk to speak to her.

'Can I help you, ma'am?' he said. 'Has something happened?'

'My son is here, with his tutor. They phoned me from Keurboom Park.'

'Name?'

'His or mine?'

'His.'

'Albert Louw. His tutor is Leo.' Alice wracked her brain for Leo's surname but failed to recall it.

'Have you got some identification?' the policeman asked, bringing Alice to a desk in a side room. He indicated for her to sit, which she did.

Alice fumbled in her bag, dropping Woolworths receipts, lipsticks and old tissues as she searched. She pulled out her car keys, and finally a bright cerise wallet. Scrambling to pick everything up she'd dropped, she finally retrieved her identity card from its plastic pocket inside her purse. 'Here.'

In no particular hurry, the policeman perused it. 'And a birth certificate for the boy?'

Alice breathed heavily. She hadn't thought to bring this. 'I don't have one here.'

The policeman shrugged. 'Ma'am, I'm sure you understand that we can't involve you without proof that you are Albert's mother.'

'I've got his pills, see?' she said pulling out the blister pack from its box. Albert's name and surname and the doctor's details were typed neatly on the label.

The policeman shrugged. 'Sorry, ma'am. That's not exactly an official document.' He smiled sympathetically. 'On your phone, maybe? Some people have access to their documents?'

He was right. She did.

'Oh yes. Yes.' She scrolled through her Dropbox and finally found his birth certificate. She handed it to the policeman. Carefully, the man compared her ID card with the scanned certificate.

'Follow me,' he said.

They walked out the back of the police station to a series of prefabricated offices. The policeman seemed in no particular hurry and it took every ounce of Alice's strength not to just kick him in the butt. Finally he opened a door, where a female police officer was sitting. She looked up, then stood protectively in front of Albert, who was balled up in the corner, Malawi sleeping at his feet. Leo's jersey was draped over him, but she could see his one leg sticking out. *Where were his clothes?* Sitting on the other side of the room, a sheepish and terrified look on his face, was Leo.

'Alice,' he said. 'Thank God. They tried to separate me from Albert. But I wouldn't move. I couldn't leave him alone in here with strangers.'

'You had a naked kid over your shoulder,' the policeman retorted. 'What were we supposed to think until we spoke to his mother?'

'What the heck happened? Does Albert have clothes on now? My God, Leo.'

Leo's stricken face made him look like a young boy. He seemed close to tears. 'He wouldn't let me help him dress. And he wouldn't dress himself. I'm sorry Alice, I messed up.'

Alice walked over to Albert, who studied her pensively from his curled up position. 'Baby,' she crooned. 'Time to come home.'

The policeman cleared his throat. 'Mrs Louw, it may not be so simple. Public indecency is not a small thing.'

'He's a kid not a flasher, for Christ's sake,' Leo answered unable to stop himself. 'A sick kid. How many times do I have to tell you that?'

'Watch it,' the policeman warned, shaking his finger at Leo.

Leo glared back at him. 'Anyway,' he said angrily. 'Public indecency is only relevant if you're over eighteen. What? You gave me my phone back. I googled it. What's more important is your supposed witness in the park. She's got illegal pictures of a naked boy on her phone. According to Chapter 3, Part 2, Section 20 of the Criminal Law Amendment Act 32 of 2007: A person who uses a child for purposes of creating, making or producing images of a sexual nature for personal gain is guilty of child pornography. You need to call her in and confiscate that video!'

Alice felt her temples beginning to throb. 'What are you talking about? What video is this?'

'There was a woman in the park. She filmed Albert when he was out of control and I was trying to get him back in the car. The police have her details. For all we know, she could have uploaded it.'

'Is this true?' Alice said to the policeman. 'Did you confiscate her phone?'

'She misread the situation. She thought it was an abduction.'

Alice stood up straighter. 'That is *not* what I asked. I said, did you confiscate her phone?'

'No, ma'am. She was a witness. Not under consideration.'

'She's bloody under consideration now!' Alice shouted unable to stop herself.

'Please watch your tone, Mrs Louw,' the policeman remonstrated. Though his face looked calm, Alice could see his jaw was clenching, his onyx eyes glinted.

'Well can we phone her at least? Call her in?'

The policeman hesitated, then nodded at the policewoman who'd been sitting in the room with Leo and Albert. 'Make the call,' he said. 'This mom don't like to wait.'

So bloody selfish

He marched into the house, his heart thumping. Ignoring both Lionel and Alice, he swung open Albert's door so hard it slammed against the wall.

'Once again, you little reprobate, you fucked up.'

His son was in a foetal position under the blankets, his eyes glazed with yet another overdose of Alice's Marvellous Mixtures. What had happened to this family?

'Sit up,' he said to Albert. 'I'm talking to you!'

Albert stared at him, and rather than sitting, shrank deeper under the blankets.

But Bruce was tired of this nonsense. He grabbed Albert by the arm, pulling his son from under the covers, and lifting him right out of the bed. 'Stand up or sit on the bed, I don't give a shit,' Bruce said.

Albert sat. He crossed his arms over his body defensively. Tears had already begun to form, which only made Bruce angrier. 'What are you doing, kid? Crying? What the hell are you upset about now? Think about what you're doing to your mother and stop being so bloody selfish!'

Albert said nothing. He didn't even look up at his father. Bruce wanted to give him a good thrashing but if he did that, Alice would never forgive him. He could already hear her walking down the passage behind him and whatever he had to say, he had to say it fast.

'I don't like this game you're playing, young man. You are going to pull yourself towards yourself and stop messing with your mother's head. You almost got Lionel arrested today. Doesn't that make you feel *anything*?'

And for the first time, he heard Albert mutter.

'What did you say?' he asked.

'I said,' Albert repeated, glaring at him with a piercing, deadly stare. 'Like you give an actual fuck. And his name is LEO.'

Albert's hatred was so intense, that had Bruce had time to analyse what he was doing, he might have, just possibly, wondered where that had come from. But instead, his hand was already across his son's face, the slap so loud, it resounded like a gunshot. And then his son was at him like a wild cat, his nails digging into Bruce's skin toughened from years in the sun. From tennis and running and surfing and all the time he'd spent away from his kids who were, to his mind, the biggest mistake he'd ever made. Albert tore at him. His arms, his face, his neck. Bruce was so surprised that he didn't have time initially to defend himself. Distantly, he could hear the noise of Alice shrieking. Albert was pulling on his hair. Kicking, yanking. He felt a banging in his ribs. A foot? A knee? He tried to manoeuvre away but his son was more agile, bigger than he thought.

'Stop it!' Alice screamed. 'Albert!'

Bruce was righting himself now. And when he'd regained his balance, he took a hold of his son, detaching him and throwing the flailing boy onto the bed. He vaguely heard a crack as Albert's head bumped against the bed post and then his son was crying, rubbing his scalp.

'You little bastard,' Bruce said, glowering at Albert, then he pushed past Alice and the tutor. 'I'm going out,' he said to Albert, still sobbing on the bed. 'Make very sure you're ready to apologise by the time I come back. And don't you ever, ever, do that again or I will put you on the street and never look back.'

Loving everybody

He watched Alice run after Bruce.

'You can't say things like that,' she said, holding onto his arm. 'You can't just leave after saying that. What are you thinking?'

'I *am* leaving,' he said. 'I need to calm down or I can't guarantee what I'll do or say.' Bruce shook Alice off, like an unwanted dog. When his eyes met Leo's, he grimaced. And Leo got the message perfectly.

'Why don't *I* just leave instead?' he said.

But Bruce was already out the kitchen door to the garage. His car roared and then he was gone. Alice stood by the entry, watching the garage door shut with a thud.

'I can't take much more of this,' she said. 'This constant fighting. I'm sorry you had to see that, Leo. Welcome to my life.'

Not knowing what to say, Leo said nothing at all. Then, 'Let me sit with Albert, give you a chance to collect yourself. He needs to know you're okay.'

'But I'm not okay. I'm not okay.' She wiped away a tear, waving a hand in front of her face. 'I didn't sign up for this. And I cannot for the life of me understand why you're still here when you don't even have to be.'

Leo smiled. Shrugged. 'Shakes things up a bit.'

'Or maybe,' Alice said bluntly. 'Maybe you're just a masochist.'

***

In Albert's bedroom, the boy was sitting on the edge of the bed cradling his head.

'Are you hurt?' Leo asked gently, but still smarting from Alice's comment. Perhaps he shouldn't come back. But he found the idea of it untenable. It would be like launching a paper jet and not watching it land.

'I hate him. I HATE him.' Albert massaged his crown.

'Does this happen a lot? That your father doesn't understand?' *Of course that was not what he really meant. Bruce's physical assault, well ...*

'My father is an absolute asshole.'

Leo sensed a presence behind him and without turning, he knew it was Enjoy. He didn't spend much time with Albert's sister, but it seemed to him that even she must be battling with the see-sawing of emotions in the home catalysed by Albert's moods. This was despite the fact that though not the 'birth child' in the family, she was without doubt their father's favourite. Bruce's voice softened when he spoke to her and he was always bragging about her sporting abilities and lean, taut, runner's build.

'Are you okay, Albert?' Enjoy asked.

'What do you think?'

Enjoy tried to cuddle up to her brother but he pushed her away. Leo was surprised to see her flinch slightly, as though she expected more violence, but then Albert pulled her towards him.

'It's not your fault, Joy,' he said.

'He doesn't mean to be like this,' Enjoy said wisely. 'He really loves us!'

'He really loves *you*.'

Enjoy's face crumpled. 'Daddy loves everybody!'

'Whatever.'

'You know what?' Leo said. 'None of us has eaten. Why don't we get pizza?' He knew for a fact that both kids could live off the stuff. Even for breakfast. And especially for supper.

'I've a better idea,' said Alice behind him. 'Let's pack our bags and go on an adventure.'

'An adventure? Now?' Leo said, looking bemused. It was already dusk, fat clouds parking over the sky.

'It's Friday tomorrow. Let's take a duvet day. Bunk school and go to the cottage. We can wake up in the countryside. Enjoy could sleep with me, and you and Albert can share. If you don't mind. Or there's a sleeper couch in the lounge.'

'What about Dad?' Enjoy said.

A cloud crossed Alice's face. 'Dad can catch up with us tomorrow. If he wants to.'

Leo thought for a moment about the lectures he was supposed to be attending, the paper he needed to write. 'Well,' he said. 'If anyone's hungry I guess we could get some pizza or a burger on the way?'

Disappointment

Bruce drove along the peninsula, his foot on the accelerator. He almost reached Cape Point by the time he'd forced himself to slow down. His chest was tight; like he was breathing through a thick, cold fog. His head pounded. Usually driving calmed him but it didn't seem to be doing much now. His temper was still as fired up as when he'd left the house. It wasn't easy controlling himself. As a child, he'd had a vicious fury that once unleashed was unmanageable. He'd tried to stab Gabriel with a pair of scissors once. His father, as mild-mannered as ever, had removed the weapon and told him that a person who couldn't manage his own emotions would always be at a disadvantage. So he should learn to control himself. Count to ten. Breathe. Leave. Talk to a friend. Use a punching bag. Whatever worked that did not involve taking it out on somebody else.

And over the years, he'd got better at it. Biting the inside of his cheek. Digging his nails into his hand. Walking away. Except of course, that time at rugby when he'd smacked a cheater in the face. Thank God, the kid had had a mouth guard, or he would have lost a few teeth. Not that the fucker didn't deserve it. The disciplinary afterwards had not been fun. He could have lost his university scholarship. Luckily it didn't get that far.

But tonight, he was unhinged as at that rugby match. Nothing seemed to do the trick. Last night had been the first night in their whole marriage that he and Alice had not slept in the same bed when they were both at home. This morning he'd woken to find his wife gone, Albert still asleep. Enjoy had also already left for school. And she hadn't even woken him up as he slept on in her bedroom's second single bed. How he hadn't heard her, he had no fucking clue.

Sarah arrived as he was pouring himself a cup of coffee, and though he had nothing against Sarah per se, he found himself unable to make even idle conversation with her. He had no energy for it.

She smiled at him but, clearly uncomfortable, disappeared down the passage to tidy the hurricane Enjoy and Alice had left behind them. He'd seen it. And it made him very uneasy. Alice was normally pedantic about tidying and this was just another sign of the rot festering in his own house. Soon the foundations would crumble completely.

And it was all Albert's bloody fault.

The day of Albert's first suicide attempt Bruce hadn't had meetings. Whatever he'd said to Alice. How do you feel sorry for a kid who's stupid enough to do something so selfish? So very destructive? He'd taken a few hours to contain his wrath and indignation, knowing full well these were not the emotions his wife was expecting from him. And for every moment he wanted to give Albert a clout, to wake him up to how lucky he was, he pictured Alice's face, her disappointment, in order to rein himself in. Mostly it worked. Many times it didn't.

It was just that she was disappointed so very, very often.

Like tonight.

The gate to the nature reserve was closed, not that he'd expected anything different. He was going to have to turn around. Go back home and face the proverbial fucking music.

But before that he was as hungry as a fox. And there was no way in hell he was eating any shit that Alice might throw at him tonight. (Either literally or figuratively.) He felt like a decent meal. A drink. So he turned his car around and headed north. He'd go over the mountains on the Glencairn Expressway, to the Noordhoek Farm Village. A nice, scenic drive, even in the dark and the rain. He'd grab a beer and Eisbein. Watch a bit of sport on the big screen. And head back to the loony bin when all the inmates were asleep. He'd bag the couch. It was comfortable enough.

It was a good plan. A relaxed plan. For the first time in hours, Bruce found that he was smiling. He put Daughtry up loud and his foot down hard.

A good thing

The cottage, as Alice called it, was a funny little building set in such a way that he didn't see it until they were parked right outside. As they drove down the gravel road to reach it, the rain had left the way muddy and Leo was conscious of the wheels of the car churning. Alice hadn't said much since they'd left but every so often she slid her fingers delicately over her neck, pulling at the gold chain that hung at the dimple where her neck met her upper chest. He knew from a course in body language doing his undergraduate degree that this hollow was called the suprasternal notch. He'd also learnt that in times of increased stress, certain people touched or massaged this area as a way to self-pacify.

'Like a dummy?' His friend Jen had asked him when he'd explained it.

'Exactly like a dummy.'

'But why?'

It was all about the nerve endings. The touch to this area reduced blood pressure, lowered the heart rate and acted as a calming mechanism. Yet the more Alice tugged at the chain, the more he thought how ineffective it was. It looked more likely that she was going to break it. He wondered if he should have offered to drive, but he wasn't going to be one of these macho types who thought that the men belonged in the driving seat. She already had a husband like that. And look how that had gone.

Alice turned off the engine. 'Well,' she said. 'We're here.'

The dusk was already settling like a satiated dog, the sun tiredly tipping the horizon. In the back seat, Albert danced a torch onto the bushes.

'No baboons,' he said thoughtfully.

'Well thank God.' Alice unclipped her safety belt. 'I have a belting headache. I hope there's some Nurofen in the bathroom.'

'I have something, I think,' Leo said. 'Panado?'

97

Enjoy slid out of her seat, slamming the door a little too hard behind her. Alice jumped. 'Jeepers, Joy, that sounded like a gunshot.'

'Sorry.'

'Kids, help carry the bags. Don't leave Leo to do everything. He's not your porter.'

Leo picked up the suitcases. 'Alice, it's fine.'

She grimaced. 'I hope we remembered the whisky.'

They'd packed supplies from the house. Whatever was in the fridge or cupboards, which luckily, were well stocked. Some eggs. Bread. Bovril. Milk. A block of mature cheddar. Tomato sauce. (Enjoy ate everything with ketchup). Some steaks. Potatoes. A pre-made salad. Rolls. Booze. Mixer drink. Bog roll. Packets of chips. A box of chocolates that had clearly been a gift for Bruce from a client.

No matter.

Alice dropped the keys to the house. Not once but twice. By the time she slotted them in the door they were mucky and brown.

Leo had resisted the urge to take them from her. Waiting patiently, he looked at Albert, whose little face was drooping with fatigue. The manic moods, he'd learnt, tired Albert out and though he had slept a little in the car, it clearly hadn't been enough. Enjoy held a unicorn against her tummy. It was bright purple with a rainbow tail. Well loved.

The door swung open suddenly, banging against the wall with a loud thump.

'Oops,' Alice said. She walked inside the lounge. It had a sleeper couch along the one wall and a fireplace on the opposite one. Above the fireplace and alongside it, the entire wall was made up of horizontal shelves, divided into triangles, with points facing alternately up and down. Inside each triangular prism, was a pile of wood. It gave the room a rustic, attractive feel. Alice breathed in deeply. Smiled. 'Listen, Leo, the reception here is crap. If you need to make any calls, you have to walk to the end of the path over there.' She gestured towards the side of the house. 'There's a pond there and you'll get a signal if you stand on the bench.'

'Ah,' Leo said. 'Very specific, thanks. But I don't need to call anybody.'

'Okay then,' Alice said, placing her grocery bags on the kitchen counter. 'You kids exhausted?' she said.

Both Enjoy and Albert nodded.

'Come on then. Leo, will you be an angel and pour us a drink? After today I could use one.'

Alice retreated into one of the bedrooms but exited almost immediately. 'Hey Leo?'

'Yes?'

'Are you happy to sleep on the couch in here? I was going to put Enjoy with me, but she insists on sleeping in *her* bed. I'm just too tired to argue the toss tonight.'

'Of course.'

'Great. Thanks.'

'Night Leo!' Albert and Enjoy called.

'Sleep well guys. See you in the morning.'

Leo stood up and wandered around the main area of the cottage. There were little touches that were so *Alice* that he smiled. Hanging in the centre of the lounge was a chandelier of origami birds, each with quirky little expressions drawn on their faces. In the kitchen, were storage tins of tea, coffee, flour and other things but on the side of each one, the name of the contents was hand-painted in various languages. The tiles on the kitchen floor started as red on one side, but as each row progressed, there were other colours. Lime green. Turquoise. Orange. Black. He would have never thought of it and it looked amazing. The stove was a retro freestanding cooker – also crimson – with an oven below and a bright blue kettle on one of the plates. The fridge a SMEG (also red), with a whole lot of photos in mini frames plastered all over it, hulked in one corner.

He studied the pictures. Albert and Enjoy as babies. Toddlers. A wedding picture of someone Leo didn't know. Malawi as a puppy with a bright yellow ribbon round her neck. A few landscapes. And then Alice and Bruce. Alice and Bruce. Alice and Bruce.

Leo turned away. Kindling and wood were already laid out in the fireplace, a box of matches on the mantelpiece. *Why not?* he thought, bending down to light the fire. It took surprisingly quickly, sending a soothing heat into his face. The crackling was a wonderful sound to him. Like a promise.

***

By the time Alice emerged, she had the harried look about her that he recognised as both despair and exhaustion.

'Hey,' he said. 'Come sit. I've got you a drink. And some Panado.'

'You're a lifesaver, and look at that amazing fire!' Alice said, sitting down heavily next to him and throwing back the pills without any liquid at all. 'Well,' she continued, 'wasn't that a day for cheap thrills?'

'I think you're superwoman,' Leo said honestly.

Alice laughed bitterly. 'Yip. I rescued my son, my dog and you from jail. My husband smacks my son's head against a wall. And we escape into the wilderness with only enough supplies to last us for a few nights.'

'This isn't exactly the wilderness. This place is fantastic.'

Alice smiled. 'It is, isn't it? It's been my project for years. Each time we come down, I do something. She pointed at the bird chandelier. 'From 2010. I was bored with the endless World Cup nonsense.' A painting of a comical zebra unwinding his stripes. 'From 2012. Albert had the flu. He slept a lot but I couldn't leave him; if he gets sick it turns far too easily to pneumonia. Bruce and Joy were hiking a lot.' A ceramic jug with a huge pair of luscious red lips. 'From 2014. I came here with Albert and my friend Gill and her sons. We all painted something. It was fun.'

'This house feels like you.'

Alice laughed. 'I hope that's a good thing. The way Bruce has glared at me the last few weeks has made me think that Alice is not the flavour of the month.'

Leo looked at her, and unable to stop himself, he trailed his finger from her cheek down to her chin. 'It's a good thing to me.'

Alice stared back. Her eyes were wide and with their faces so close together, he noticed the length of her eyelashes. His heart gushed like a river after a storm. Their bodies were almost touching on the couch and yet, she seemed too very far away. The breath roared in his ears as he inclined his face.

'Leo,' she said, hesitantly.

She looked so beautiful in the firelight. Her eyes sparkled in the glow. Her skirt, already above the knee, rode up on the one side to her thigh. Alice was petite and perfectly proportioned but it was more than this. He felt like he wanted to protect her from the onslaught that was her life. But he didn't want to be just another person pressurising her. He smiled, sat back in the couch. Alice cocked her head, a crease wrinkling her forehead, before she sat back too. The silence between them felt like a thread rather than a weight. Alice lifted her whisky glass, clinked it against Leo's.

'Thank you,' she said softly.

'To better times,' he replied.

***

The fire burned low as they chatted. Once, Enjoy pattered in. She was thirsty and her blanket had fallen off her, so she was also cold. Alice tended to her daughter, fetching a glass of water and tucking Joy's blankets around her tightly. Leo could hear their murmurs, the soft lilt of Alice's voice. They'd eaten hours before and he was hungry, so he went to the kitchen, looking for something to eat from what he'd unpacked. He remembered a box of crunchies he'd put in the empty cupboard and extracted one, biting into it hungrily. He turned on the stove, filling the kettle with water to boil. He could do with a coffee, and he'd seen a plunger earlier as he'd emptied the bags. When Alice walked in, he felt her rather than saw her.

'Coffee?'

'Tea?' she said hopefully.

'Sure.'

He poured the boiling water keenly aware of her closeness.

'I should tell you,' Alice said. 'That the wood you see stacked inside is only for decoration. Firewood is outside under a shelter, when you turn left out of the lounge.'

'You want me to get some?'

'Oh no. Don't worry. I'll get it. Just thought I'd tell you while I was thinking about it.'

Alice put on her jacket. He didn't like the idea of her out there in the cold and dark, and without thinking further about it, followed her outside.

She was trying to use her phone as a torch and lift the kindling at the same time.

'Alice,' he said.

She started but seeing him, smiled. 'I thought I said I'd do it.'

'But that's just it,' Leo said. 'I'm here and I *want* to help you. There's so much you have to deal with as it is. This is something I can do for you.'

'I'm a tough cookie, Leo.'

'Don't I know it,' he said. 'It's one of the things I love about you.' He could feel the blush rising up his cheeks and was glad for the dark. 'Please, just let me help you.'

But instead Alice dropped the wood. There was a silence. Electric. Intense. Then Alice stepped closer to him. Definite. Like a clicked switch. And when she kissed him, her lips were warm and full. At first her kiss was soft, but then the pressure increased, her tongue like a laser, searing him, the heat between them intensifying by milliseconds. He pushed closer, holding her tightly against him.

'Are you absolutely sure about this?' she asked.

He'd never been surer of anything in his life.

Brave

Alice felt Leo's arms around her, solid and strong. When he lifted her up onto the window ledge, it was as though she were weightless. She was just the right height now to reach him, to embrace him and she found herself falling into their kisses like water over a ledge. Leo smiled at her, and though the light was vapid, it was bright enough for her to see the shape of his full lips, the brightness of his teeth. She tugged at his shirt, putting her hands up along his back under the material. His skin was smooth, the blades of his shoulders angular. The muscles in his back rose to her touch, the skin rising in goosebumps.

Leo gasped. She wanted to breathe him in, the smell of his lemongrass aftershave. The licking smoke from the flames inside the hearth.

His hand traced up over her jumper to her breast, and she grasped it gently, guiding him to the skin under her top. Surprisingly, he had warm hands. They were soft, pliant, travelling so lightly over her that it felt almost like he was tickling her. For a moment, she thought about Bruce, who never bothered much with kisses, with gentle touch. Foreplay was cursory; predictable. She should have felt guilty. But instead she felt brave. Defiant.

She lowered her hands to Leo's belt buckle; their eyes locked. He was breathing heavily enough for her to hear him and it made her feel powerful. She unhooked the loop, tugged. The belt unfurled like a fern leaf as it fell to the ground.

'I'm not prepared,' he whispered. 'I don't have any protection.'

'I don't care if you don't care,' she said.

'Right now,' he replied, as she tweaked his jeans button, releasing it. 'I really don't care.'

His hand moved up her thigh. She lifted herself slightly so he could pull at her knickers, sliding them down, over her legs, her boots. They fell

102

somewhere in the dust. His hand moved so slowly along her thigh that she felt herself turning to him, like petals opening to the sun. She slid her hands down the back of his jeans, cupping his bottom to pull him closer. When they finally merged, it was more than something physical. It was an instant connection, a closed circuit. Every part of her was turned on as though he'd flipped a switch. And even when he was inside her he looked into her eyes, kissed her. There was no doubting that he was with her, with *her*.

She'd never experienced anything like it, the sensations pulsing from the core of her. His eyes flickered, and she knew he was close. Alice pulled him harder towards her and when he shuddered slowly to a stop, she held him against her. Kissed him. Possessive. Tender. Captivated.

He ran his fingers through her hair, kissed her back.

'Wow,' he said.

'Wow,' Alice agreed, smiling at him. She shivered. 'It's freezing out here,' she said. 'Let's go inside, build up the fire and do that again.'

He grinned, tracing her face with his fingers. 'Now why didn't I think of that?'

Starving

The Toad was busy and he found a table upstairs near one of the screens. He ordered his plate of food with relish, and drank his first beer in a few gulps. He flipped through Insta, looking at pics of some mates on a holiday in Greece, some new grey-water innovations. Then the random images that popped up. Hot chicks. Scenery. Cat photos, which bored him. He couldn't understand the attraction. He flipped to SuperSport. Ran his eye down the scores for the golf.

Bruce realised he was missing Alice. Not the new Alice who skulked around the house accusing him with her eyes of his poor parenting. But the fun, spontaneous Alice he used to know who once screwed him behind a waterfall on a hike in Iceland. That laugh. He hadn't heard it for months, except that night when the tutor was around and they were playing 30 Seconds. The night she shoved that vomit-concoction onto his plate and stalked out the room. Her anger had kind of turned him on. It showed him the fire was still there. Misdirected. Sure. But he could work with a spark. It was better than the absence of one.

Bruce's stomach growled. He was fucking starving. Waving down a waiter, he asked for something to line his stomach. A few slices of bread, maybe? He slathered on butter and chomped it down quickly. The light where he was sitting was dimmer than certain places in the restaurant, placing his body in shadow. It felt symbolic, somehow, that he was on the dark side of the moon, part of a life eclipse. He studied some of the other people in the restaurant. The body language between couples, children out too late and whining. Groups of friends laughing. He and Alice used to love people watching. It was revelatory. Imagining lives for people whom they'd never actually meet. He thought he could do it now, while he waited for the pork. His sauerkraut. And it was only at this point that he noticed Martini sitting on the opposite side of the restaurant. His back was to

Bruce, but he knew it was him. The neck was a dead giveaway. Martini had a neck like a Staffie. Short, thick, solid. It needed to be that way – carrying his largish head on his too-small body built into muscle through years at the gym.

***

He smiled, almost stood to say hello until he saw the statuesque black woman sitting across from his friend. He didn't recognise her but she wasn't Elaine. That was for fucking sure. Her short-cropped hair and queenly bearing was nothing like his friend's wife's. And so what if they were eating together? It didn't mean anything. Not really. Business. An evening meeting. But even after a few seconds of scrutiny he could tell the vibes. It was a hell of a lot more than that.

Each time Martini leant forward, she did the same, mirroring him like a reflection. Her wide smile looked almost coquettish, her long, thin neck exposed as she lifted her head. Once, she looked up, caught him staring. Her dark eyes met his frankly. Carrying a challenge. But he looked away, picking up his menu to study it.

Where the hell was his bloody Eisbein? Frankly, he didn't give a fuck about what Martini was up to but he had enough complications in his own life. He didn't need his friend's entanglements on top of it. And it's not like Martini had asked his opinion. Even if he felt for Elaine (hot but annoying), he still felt weird. Like he was consenting to a kind of, well, deviant, behaviour he had no control over. But did it even matter to him? No. It was, however, putting him off his food. Which still hadn't bloody arrived.

He called over a waitress. Demanded another beer. He was well over the limit now. Perhaps he could get an Uber. Or ask Martini for a lift. Ha, ha. The way those two were mooning over each other, he wondered if they'd make it out the car.

The waitress put the beer in front of him, then a metal plate on a wooden board. It was still sizzling and he licked his lips hungrily. Best meal in town. He sliced off the crackling, putting it to one side. He liked to eat that last. The mash was soft, buttery. The sauerkraut tart and delicious.

It seemed that Martini's dalliance hadn't put him off his meal after all.

With clothes on

He woke early, slipping out Alice's bed as he'd promised. The figure next to him was still curled in a little ball, like a kitten. He smiled. That, he had to admit, had been the most unexpected night of his life. Scenes of them together flicked through his brain, and he tried to banish them, already growing hard again. He was going to have to control himself.

The kids.

But God he wanted to touch her again.

He began to tiptoe out the room, when he heard her voice murmuring softly. 'Thanks, Leo.'

Leo stepped back, kissed her gently on the forehead. 'Thank YOU. That was unforgettable.'

She laughed. 'I aim to please.'

He grinned at her. 'I'm going to go to the lounge and look innocent. Can I make you some coffee?'

'You really are a man of many, many talents.'

'Is that a yes?'

She nodded. 'Yes please. I kind of wish you could get back in here with me, though.'

'Later,' he promised.

'I'll hold you to it.'

He wondered, though, if that was something he could promise. Last night had been so unplanned, so unanticipated. The clear light of day was probably going to change things. Not for him, because he already knew exactly how he felt about Alice. No, it was more that she was going to have time to reflect. And feel guilty. Responsible. Because he knew too, that's who she was. A good mother. A good wife. And last night had been an aberration.

But he really, really hoped he was wrong.

In the lounge, he mussed some pillows, a duvet. Placed them on the sleeper couch. Albert might have been mental, but he wasn't stupid. He had the eyes of a predator, the nose of a bloodhound. He would pick up the slightest indication of something different.

As he fluffed the pillows he'd never used, Leo heard the steps of someone behind him. Enjoy was already dressed in a very short pair of shorts, a running top and a pair of tackies.

'Dad always goes for a run with me, here,' she said. 'But he's not with us.' Her nose crinkled disapprovingly.

Leo smiled at her. 'I could go with you, if you like. Not sure I'm fit like your dad though.'

Enjoy studied him for a moment. 'No, I think you could probably keep up. Get your running shoes on.'

Her earnestness made him laugh. 'I tell you what, boss. I'll make some coffee for me and your mother and a hot chocolate for you and Albert and then we'll hit the dirt.'

She nodded. 'And maybe a rusk,' she suggested.

'Yeah sure. Why not?'

Sensitive to both Albert and Enjoy's antennae on alert, Leo sent Enjoy into Alice's room with the coffee. As she disappeared, her butt barely covered by her tiny running shorts, Albert emerged from the room he shared with his sister. He looked at Leo.

'Why are you up so flipping early?' He rubbed his eyes, then tried to flatten his hair.

'Enjoy and I are going for a run.'

'You are?' He looked irritated. Or upset.

'Come with us, buddy,' Leo said. 'I could use the support. Your sister looks like a Kenyan long-distancer in her outfit. I'm a little bit intimidated.'

Albert smiled. 'How do you know I can even run?'

Leo laughed. 'Mate, you sprinted across Keurboom Park with that fat cop after you and you didn't even have shoes on.'

Albert grinned. 'I did, didn't I?'

'But maybe this time, you can do it with clothes on?'

***

They ran hard. Enjoy was ahead of them, her feet splattering through the mud. Leo tried to avoid the puddles, but soon he was following in her steps just trying to keep up. He'd thought until then that he was fit, but it appeared he was not. He rolled up his sleeves trying to cool himself down. Albert matched his steps as they followed the path through the wheat field.

Malawi was running ahead of them, darting in and out of the rows, her tongue hanging out. Her tail wagged furiously. When she stopped, she sipped from the puddles, the bright pink tongue lapping spiritedly. As they ran, images of his night with Alice flashed through his brain. Her body pressed against him. The urgency of her kiss. They'd tumbled into her bed, the door locked. The second time had been slower, careful. Appreciative. But they hadn't managed to get all their clothes off that time either.

As Alice lay against him afterwards, she was quiet at first. It frightened him, like she'd been filled with regret. Enough to send him packing.

But instead she'd said to him, 'This is probably a bit late in the game, but I don't even know if you have a girlfriend.'

He turned onto his tummy, propping himself with his elbows. 'Alice, I wouldn't be here if I had a girlfriend. I'm not really that kind of guy.'

'I didn't think I was that kind of girl either, but here I am. And I have a husband.'

They were silent a moment.

'Do you want me to leave?' Leo asked.

'No, that's just it. I'm so happy here with you I could burst. What kind of a person does that make me?'

'One with excellent taste,' Leo quipped. It had lightened the moment. Because she'd laughed. And then he'd kissed her again, not wanting to ruin this time they had with ominous thoughts. There'd be ample opportunity for that.

And now as Enjoy turned the corner, the folds of the Langeberg Mountains were just bursting into light in an orange glow from the sun piercing through the clouds. Hovering at the base of the mountains were ghosts of mists, the fields nearby beaded with frost. Leo's breathing was heavy and the cold air burnt down his windpipe. Albert was already falling behind and this filled Leo with relief. He could slow down a bit himself to allow the boy to catch up. Albert's cheeks were crimson, the strain registering on his face in a large frown. He staggered a little, and the mud splashed up his pale, white shins, his knees like toffee apples on his stick-like legs. But he kept on going, like a determined toddler. It made Leo more determined too. If he allowed himself to focus on the scenery, it certainly made the run easier. In the distance, he could see the canola fields, the yellow flowers painting the fields in a palette of gold. There were circular patterns in the fields, as if someone had taken a lawnmower, lopping flower heads as they passed.

They came to a large dam, where a flock of Egyptian geese skittered over the water like pebbles.

Enjoy stopped at the edge of the dam, bent down. With cupped hands she poured a bit of water over her head, then waved at them both.

'Isn't this beautiful?' she said.

'You're killing us,' said Albert grumpily.

'I didn't force you to come.'

Rubbing his leg, Leo remembered the phone in his pocket. 'Cheese, guys,' he said, snapping a shot of them before they had a chance to protest. He stared down into the water.

'There are fish in here,' he said.

'Yip. We catch them sometimes. Some carp and bass,' Albert commented. 'Catch and release ... I hate fishing,' he added, almost as an afterthought.

'Then why do you do it?'

'Dad,' Albert says simply. 'He's an asshole. He's never wrong.'

Leo's confusion clearly registered.

'We do what he wants. Including torturing defenceless little creatures swimming past and generally minding their own business.'

'But why don't you just tell him fishing's not for you?'

'Yeah. That's a great idea. Then I'll be the *moffie* he loves to hate.'

Enjoy sniffed. 'He doesn't hate you, Bertie. You're just really different from each other.'

The platitude sounded like something she'd repeated a thousand times before.

'Yip, whatever.'

Enjoy was sitting on a rock, her legs stretched out in front of her. The sun's rays warmed her exposed skin.

'Are you tall for your age?' Leo asked.

She shrugged. 'Dad says I'm going to have to grow into my legs.'

'The gospel according to Saint Bruce,' said Albert bitterly.

'What does that even mean?' asked Enjoy.

Leo studied Albert's bright red face, the anger on Enjoy's. The girl had straightened up her back, her shoulders pushed back as though she was going to fly at Albert from where she sat. He moved closer, but Leo put his hand gently on Albert's arm.

'Come on guys, your dad's not even here to defend himself, let's hit the road and head home for breakfast.'

***

As they approached the house among the blue gums, Leo watched for Alice. He was sweating profusely from being put through his paces, his back damp and the sleeves tight over his biceps wet through. With all the exercise since the previous night, he could have ploughed through a breakfast buffet on his own. Enjoy was falling a little behind now and he was glad for it, since the first thing he noticed as they neared the cottage woodpile was a flash of bright pink below the window ledge. He leant down casually, pocketing the item and grabbed a few logs under his arm. Albert walked straight past, not offering to carry anything.

'Hey buddy, bring some wood in too, won't you?'

Albert sighed heavily but turned around and picked up a few logs.

'Happy now?' he said in the cutting tone he normally reserved for his father.

'So delighted. Thanks mate.'

Inside the house, Alice was standing in the kitchen. When he walked in, her eyes lit up and he wished he could take her in his arms and kiss her. Right there. Instead, he smiled. He came around the counter to see that she was wearing her trademark skirt and boots. She was at the stove and the smells coming from the pans were magnificent.

As he passed her, he brushed his fingers along hers, so softly that it could have just been a mistake. But they both knew that it wasn't.

'You hungry?' she asked.

'Famished. Been rather active since we got here,' he said. 'You know, the run and all.' He winked and her cheeks flushed.

Leo poured some glasses of water for him and the kids, noting that Alice was still sipping her coffee. It must have been cold by now.

'Water?' he asked.

She shook her head. 'You guys want to take a shower before we eat? I need a few more minutes anyway.'

'Sure.'

'Enjoy, Albert. Why don't you go shower in your bathroom? Leo can use mine?'

Albert sighed dramatically. 'I'm clean, Mom. I washed yesterday.'

'Yesterday *morning*!' she corrected. 'Go. I can smell you from here.'

'But Mom …'

'Go!'

Enjoy had already disappeared. The sound of water gushing and a cranking geyser made Albert turn. Leo smiled at Alice. 'You okay?'

She nodded, flipping over a sausage with a spatula. 'There's a fresh towel hanging up on the hook behind the door.'

***

The shower felt good. Really good. Scalding water came down hard along his back. The soap in the shower smelt of rosemary, and he lathered himself well. Foam trickled down his face, his chest. He felt great. Better than great. He was happy. While Alice was standing there in the kitchen just a few metres away, he was naked and thinking of her. He didn't want this time away to end because the reality of their return was going to change everything. Leo shook his head as though trying to shake the thoughts from his brain.

When he was done, he stepped out the shower onto the mat and dried himself vigorously with the towel Alice had put out for him. It was at this point he realised he'd left his fresh clothes in the tog bag in the lounge near the sleeper couch. So he wrapped the too-small towel around his waist and went to fetch some jeans and a T-shirt. As he walked barefoot and half-naked into the lounge, he could hear Alice still in the kitchen. But she must have sensed his presence, because she turned, and seeing him, dropped the spatula. She fumbled around to pick it up.

He smiled at her as she stood up again, blushing like a teenager.

'What?' he said teasingly.

'Jeepers, Leo. Put some clothes on, or–'

'Or?' he said, his hand at his waist as he pretended to loosen the towel. He walked closer to her. 'Or what?'

'The kids,' she said weakly.

'We could be quick,' he whispered.

Enjoy trailed through the lounge, pulling a duvet behind her. 'Aren't you cold, Leo?'

He turned, unfazed. 'Actually, I'm quite warm. But I've got my clothes from my bag now. Give me a few minutes and we can eat. I'm ravenous.' Leo looked directly at Alice.

'Go!' she said, waving the lifter at him, like he was one of the kids.

'I'm going. I'm going.' He put his hands above his head in mock surrender.

'Please rather hold the towel!' Alice said. 'That falls and you'll frighten my daughter.'

He laughed. 'Yes ma'am.'

A bit of air

The US Open was on one of the widescreen TVs and he followed it distractedly. He was in no rush to head home. What for? It really was preferable he got back when everybody was asleep. He studied the dessert menu. Surprisingly the Eisbein hadn't sunk him. And neither had the several beers he'd consumed. He felt like something sweet. In the end he settled on an apple crumble with ice cream that was on special (a free cup of coffee). It was the first day of the golf. Already it seemed a bit miserable to Bruce. This was the first major in twenty-three years that didn't include either Woods or Mickelson. He kind of thought that cut down on the interest levels. Not that he loved watching golf as much as, say, rugby, anyway. But it didn't matter. The sport on screen didn't have to be riveting. Just mildly entertaining. The real entertainment was across the room where Martini and the woman were gazing lustily into each other's eyes.

Bruce's phone began to ring. It was probably Alice and that was the one person in the world he did not want to speak to right now. All that recrimination. Like he was some shitty little teenager. Or Albert. But he glanced down nevertheless.

Elaine.

Fuck.

He considered ignoring the call but Martini was his mate. They had an agreement. Bros before hoes or whatever.

'Hey Elaine,' he said. 'What's up?'

'Bruce. I'm trying to reach my hubby. Is he still with you?'

'Um, yes.'

'Are you finished playing?'

'Actually. No. Thinking of playing a bit longer. Maybe a beer or two.'

'Well, can you at least ask him to call me?'

'Sure, I'll try remember. Can't guarantee it though. Memory like a sieve and he's taking a piss at the moment.'

'Charming.'

'You asked.'

'Actually, I didn't ask that.'

'You know what, Elaine? Maybe you should just go to sleep? Martini and I are planning a late one. Alice didn't mind.'

The implication did not come out as subtly as he planned it in his head.

'Nice, Bruce. I'm just worried about my hubby. Is that so bad?'

'I didn't mean it like that. I just meant, don't panic. He's fine. I'll get him home safely.'

'Right,' Elaine said, the doubt in her voice still evident.

As Bruce terminated the call, he saw that Martini and his lady were ordering another bottle of wine. For the first time probably ever, he felt a little sorry for Elaine. There was no doubt in his mind that this was not the first time that Martini had strayed but this seemed a little more … intense. The woman stood up, leaning over to kiss Martini. It went on forever. The waiter, who seemed to be carrying a bucket of ice, approached them but turned abruptly away, retreating to the bar bright-faced. Then the woman strode toward the toilets, towering in black stilettos with yellow polka dots that exactly matched the pencil skirt and jacket tightly fitting her body. She had a nice, round arse and her pins looked superb in those shoes. He actually felt a little jealous.

Bruce had had enough of the show and waved a waitress down. 'Can I eat my dessert downstairs, outside? I need a bit of air.'

The waitress nodded, looking unperturbed.

Bruce stood, collected his coat and walked downstairs. His phone vibrated in his pocket. Alice? But once again it wasn't his wife. This time it was Martini.

Mate. Cover me please. I'm at Teasers with clients. You know what the ball and chain is like. If she calls, you and I are playing squash. Some dinner. Yes?

So now Martini was lying to him too. Fuck, he'd piss himself if he knew where Bruce was sitting right now.

Amused, Bruce texted back. Am I winning?

Winning what?

The squash.

In your dreams, mate.

You owe me one.

Drinks on me.

At Teasers?

Ha!Ha!

He realised he was going to have to sit right back or Martini would see him as he and the chick left. Awkward. He chose a table in the corner. The place was already emptying out. It was later that he thought. He glanced at his watch. Almost eleven.

The waitress brought Bruce his coffee and dessert.

'You know her?' the waitress asked.

'Who?'

'The woman upstairs.'

'I don't think so, why?'

'It's just that, well, you were …'

'I was what?' Bruce retorted, irritated. 'Mind your own fucking business.'

The waitress shrugged and moved away but her face showed her hurt. Yip. He was a proven asshole. She was just making conversation. But apologise … to a waitress? He didn't think so.

He spooned his dessert listlessly into his mouth, periodically checking the restaurant exit for the happy couple. When they finally emerged Martini and the woman were hanging onto each other. They were a little drunk. A lot drunk. She giggled as she tripped over an uneven bit of pavement. Then she stopped.

'My shoe!' she moaned, letting Martini go as she removed her left heel – snapped completely in half. 'Christ. That's R3 000 a shoe, but who's counting?' Amazingly, it seemed that the only person who was watching this particular show was Bruce. He was riveted.

'Darling, we'll buy you a whole new pair. See?' Martini bent down to rub the woman's foot. He kissed her toes right there. Toe by toe. *Really?* Bruce grimaced.

Gently Martini removed her right shoe. 'I think I'd better drive.'

The woman threw him the keys. 'Sure, baby. Why not?'

When the car started, Martini revved it loudly. The bright yellow Ferrari reversed, skidded a little on the wet tar, then accelerated forward.

Bruce shivered, drunk enough to discount the visceral sensation of disquiet in his gut.

He called for his bill.

It was time to face the music at home and he wasn't looking forward to it.

ALICE

Baggage

They ate breakfast and Alice's head spun. What on earth was she doing? What had she done? The goodiest goody-two shoes in Cape Town. Jeepers. She hadn't even got a speeding ticket before and now, here she was, eating a meal with her – lover? – with her children, in the house she and her husband had fixed up for romantic getaways.

Not this type.

Obviously.

She looked at Leo. He smiled faintly at her, moving his leg so it brushed against hers. She jumped as though seared. This made him smile even more. It was a very naughty, very sexy, smile. Her stomach roiled. She wanted to vomit. Or climb into his lap and nuzzle his neck. She moved her food around her plate. Little piles of egg and bacon camping all over the porcelain. The fork in her hand shook. Not violently. But enough that she noticed even if nobody else did.

Albert, who was sitting across from her, was banging the table with his cutlery in that annoying can't-keep-still way that drove Bruce mad. It usually ended in a family argument with her mediating.

'Why can't you just be normal?' Bruce would shout, his voice almost pitchy.

'Because I'm not normal, I'm mentally unstable. But you, you are autistic when it comes to mental illness so you'll never-ever understand.'

Bruce would turn purple. And the ensuing words between them would inevitably result in a smack, threat, curses and possibly his iPad being confiscated for hours, weeks … When Albert could get the zapper to open the garage, he would run away. They'd searched for him in the dark more than once.

Rather than being irritated, though, with the noise, Leo simply touched Albert's hand. Smiled at him. 'Hey buddy, you need a drum kit.'

116

And with that, Albert simply stopped. It was like Leo was an Albert-whisperer. Something even she as his mother couldn't claim to be.

'What are we doing today?' asked Enjoy.

'Chilling,' said Albert.

'That's so BORING.'

'We could bake something? A lemon meringue pie, maybe?' Alice needed to keep her hands busy. Busy hands, quiet mind.

'We don't have lemons,' said Enjoy.

'We have the tree?'

Enjoy sighed heavily. 'I don't care. Maybe I'll just read.'

'You could walk with me to pick the lemons.'

'Naaa.' Her energy seemed to have dissipated in the short breath of their conversation.

'I'll walk with you,' said Leo. 'If you want the company.'

She tried to look nonchalant. Shrugged. 'Sure. Let me get a bag.'

Alice extracted a material bag from under the sink, then changed into a pair of tackies. No socks. It wasn't a long walk but it was going to be muddy and she didn't want to dirty her suede boots. When she turned around, she saw Leo standing outside under the blue gums. He was wearing jeans. A dark polo neck. Leather ankle boots. A red and blue scarf tied flamboyantly around his neck. She couldn't imagine Bruce in the outfit. But Leo. He looked perfect in it.

'Kids, we'll just be at the lemon tree if you need us.' The children eyed her blankly. Like mournful cattle. 'Albert, have you taken your pills?'

'I may or may not have taken them.'

'Albert.'

'I took them. Or maybe I didn't.'

'It's a simple question, buster. Just answer me.'

'Mo-oooo-m.'

'Yes or no?'

'Yes.'

For the life of her, she couldn't figure out why he had to make simple questions like these difficult. It was this sort of behaviour that drove her up the bloody wall. 'Please just answer me correctly the first time.'

'Yes Mom.' He managed even to make that sound sarcastic. No wonder Bruce, who had little patience at the best of times, couldn't take it.

'We're going now. Please try to be calm, kids. We're a short walk away.'

'Just go,' said Enjoy. 'We're fine.'

She nodded at her daughter, then thinking better of it, strode over to her and embraced her, kissing the top of her braided head. 'Love you.'

Then she whispered against her daughter's scalp, 'Come call me if he begins to lose it.'

She hugged Enjoy hard, before releasing her.

'It's the lemon tree, Mom. Not Siberia,' said Albert, thumping his finger against his head in a way that said *how idiotic*.

'Love you too,' Alice said, blowing her son a kiss.

He scowled moodily.

The air outside was still cold enough for them to see the clouds of breath from their mouths. They walked silently. Crunching beyond the grove of blue gums, to a fence. Alone again, there was an awkwardness between them that hadn't existed before. She could feel Leo trying to catch her eye, but she was suddenly shy. The turmoil she'd felt before they'd come together was mounting. Layer by layer. She was the responsible one. The wiser. This was a mistake. A wonderful mistake. She wanted to go back. And forward. She wanted to hold him. Or let him go. The sense of beautiful change, like a butterfly emerging from a chrysalis, or a tectonic plate widening with unstoppable, brutal force, was overwhelming.

She stopped. Her hand to her heart.

Leo stopped too, crocheting his fingers between hers.

'No,' she said, stepping back.

He let go. His young face transparent. Crumbling. Unmasked.

'Listen, Leo.'

'I don't like the sound of that.'

'It's just that, if I were your mother–'

'My mother?' Leo managed to look amused and horrified at the same moment. 'You are *not* my mother.'

'Of course not. But if I were, I would want you to be with someone who could improve your life, not complicate it. Weigh it down. I would want you to be free, not carrying another person's baggage.'

'Baggage?'

'A crappy marriage, a son who's bonkers – clinically. An adopted daughter, who no doubt will develop identity issues the moment she starts to think about it. If I were your mother, I would be beyond horrified at your choices and I would think that this woman – me – was a miserable, selfish bitch, taking advantage of her son's lovely, perfect heart–'

'An even more perfect body,' interjected Leo. 'And boy did you take advantage. More than once.'

'Leo, I'm trying to be serious.'

'You deny my perfect body and risk hurting my tender, young feelings.'

Alice stepped back a little trying to gauge him, then sighed. 'It *is* pretty perfect,' she admitted. 'But that's not the point. I'm not really a catch. I'm more like something you'd win on the tombola, when all the good prizes have already gone.'

'What the hell is a tombola?'

'For crying in a bucket, Leo, you're missing the point.'

'Now that expression does make you seem ancient. Like the village hag. You should lose it.'

'The village hag?' Now Alice was affronted.

'Yes. Maybe you should say something like, damn it, Leo, you're missing the point. Or darn it, if you must. It's a bit demure, but it works.'

'You're not listening to me, Leo,' Alice said, her voice rising.

'You're very perceptive for such a defective individual. And smoking hot. Even if you're about to push up the daisies, you're so old.'

'Leo!'

'I love it when you're angry. Is this our first fight? I can't wait for the make-up sex.'

Alice began to laugh. 'You're incorrigible.'

'I am.'

'You're making a big mistake with me.'

'I think I'm a big boy, old and stupid enough to choose. And I choose you. And all the baggage you bring with you, as you so beautifully put it.'

Alice looked at him, recognising the freefall of new, uncertain love, even as it began. A whisper. A shoot. It was joyous. Terrifying. 'And what about Bruce?'

'One step at a time, Allie. For now, let's just go and pick the lemons. You climb up so I can look up your skirt.'

'Oh my God.'

'Well,' he shrugged. 'If you say so.' Then he kissed her deeply and hard. 'Let's take the kids for lunch somewhere. A little outing later. It'll be fun.'

'If you say so,' she repeated.

'I do. Now stop worrying so much. I've got you.'

'You know what?' Alice said, smiling shyly, as she handed Leo the bag to catch the lemons. 'I totally believe you.'

Driving on

Fuck it. He was drunk. He realised it the moment he stood up. After coffee, he had a shot of brandy. Dutch courage to face the missus. And now his car was here and he was going to have to get home. But he was a good driver, even drunk. Better than some drivers sober. He'd be fine. Slow and steady. He paid his bill, gave the waitress an average tip. Not remarkable or unremarkable. But she was a prying little cow and she didn't deserve more.

At his car, he swung open the door. Climbed in. Checked his phone. This was not like Alice. No little message. No 'where are you?' No – 'you were an arse tonight. Come home we need to talk about it.' Actually, it was a relief. She was the peacekeeper but sometimes he didn't want any peace. Especially if it came at the cost of his own dignity.

He drove easily through Noordhoek. On the side of the road he saw a few people with torches. Probably helping the toads across the road. There'd been enough rain to bring them out. Exploring.

He turned onto Ou Kaapse Weg. There were still a few cars but not many. He was suddenly exhausted, the Eisbein settling in him like a dead weight. Bruce yawned heavily. Rubbed his eyes with the back of his hand. The road meandered and the mountains looked dark and foreboding, shadows in the grey sky.

Finally as he passed the Silvermine Nature Reserve, pinpricks of light flickered from the city below and beyond. Focus. He squinted, a weighty feeling of lethargy coming over him.

Finally he was down the mountain, turning right past Westlake. The motorway wasn't far now and when he took the onramp, he knew it would be about a quarter of an hour before he was finally in his own home, if not his own bed. At this stage, *that* was a bit doubtful.

He put his foot down, careful though to keep to the speed limit. Unlike some people, he was more compliant under the influence than he was without a drop of alcohol in him. Then he rarely indicated, swerved between lanes and crossed over single white lines. Now he did none of those things. He was vigilant, wary of any transgression.

But the flashing blue lights on the M3 ahead of him nevertheless sent a burst of alarm down his nerves. One sniff of his jet-fuel breath and he was in the chookie for sure. He knew there was no reason for him to be stopped – not from his driving in any event – but how could he avoid it? If he turned off at Kendal Road, he could see there were cops positioned there too. Lining up to breathalyse and incarcerate him. Bloody stupid. Why didn't he take a fucking Uber?

He decided the best thing in the end was to keep going. But going slowly. Not too slowly though. Nothing to make him stand out. Maybe they'd just let him pass.

It was at this point that he noticed the sirens coming up fast behind him. An ambulance. Then a second one. This wasn't a road block.

Thank God.

The thought made him feel a little selfish. Someone was clearly hurt. And it wasn't him.

He was just really, really drunk.

But when he saw the wreckage that was once a bright yellow Ferrari he knew he had choices to make. Terrible choices. Stop or move on. Help or leave. He hesitated. Slowed the car like a rubbernecker. The policemen congregated like bees over a syrup slick, their reflective jackets visible in his headlights. The ambulances were there, parked, the bands of light colouring the wet black road. On and off. On and off. Bruce turned on his indicator. Pulled out into the fast line.

He drove on.

He drove on.

But when he turned off the motorway, he pulled into a side road, opened the door of his car wide, the cold winter air hitting him in the face.

Then he vomited the dinner he had enjoyed all over the grass verge outside someone's nice, Claremont house.

His heart sore and pounding, he scrolled through his contacts to find Martini's number. He waited tensely for the connection. The sound of his friend's voice.

BEEP.

'Afraid you've missed me. You know what to do.'

Talking nicely

There was an almost Tourette's-like quality to some of Albert's quirks. He would often get caught on a sentence, his thoughts snagging on the wire of certain words. Jokes. Or things he'd read.

'Osmium,' he told Leo, 'is the densest element.'

And it wouldn't be five minutes before he'd repeat it.

'Osmium–'

'You told us, mate.'

'Osmium–'

'Albert, we heard you, love,' Alice said softly.

There were so many things strange about Albert. His hunched walk. His intellectual arrogance. His crab-like handwriting that didn't match his meticulous, fact-filled mind. He seemed unable to read body language, and for once, Leo was relieved. Anybody other than Albert would be able to sense the crazy feelings sparking between him and Alice. He'd already noticed Enjoy's forehead crinkling, a look of concern registering in her puckered mouth.

'What's up, Joy?' he asked her. 'You seem worried.'

'Where's Dad?' she said. 'Why isn't he here?'

'He knows where we are,' Alice lied. As far as Leo knew, she hadn't even left a note. Bruce hadn't been in touch. No calls. No WhatsApps. It was as though, Alice had told him, he was *glad* that they were gone. And maybe he was. 'Anyway,' Alice continued. 'Daddy has to work today. He had a lot of meetings. Maybe he'll come through tonight.'

Leo hoped sincerely that wasn't true. He had other plans for tonight. And they did not involve Alice's … husband. It was hard enough sitting opposite Alice, with just their feet touching. Lightly, but just solidly enough to know they were there, together. Leo shuffled. They had driven to a restaurant perched on a promontory overlooking the sea. A drive of

123

more than an hour, while Enjoy and Albert niggled at each other in the back, their voices strident and penetrating.

'Albert's touching me!'

'Enjoy's on my side!'

'Albert pinched me!'

'I'm hungry!'

'This is so boring.'

But now the children were devouring their stone-baked pizzas. Albert folded each piece in half, shoving almost an entire slice into his mouth at a time. His face was covered in tomato sauce, the olives plopping out the sides onto the table. There was a sense of competition in the way he ate, suggesting that if he didn't swallow quickly someone else would take the food from him. How many times had he heard Alice asking if Albert thought he was a caveman, or a chimp, a pig? It didn't affect his eating style and he surmised that as much as it frustrated her, Alice had learnt not to criticise her son at every moment. He had a fragile crust like a crème brûlée: one fork would shatter it.

Leo glanced at Alice. She smiled at him, and the annoyance of the unruly children dissolved. A seagull perched on the top of the open window. The once-grey light had turned an intense turquoise, making its fluffy white feathers whiter.

'Let's walk on the beach after lunch,' he suggested.

Enjoy yawned indifferently.

'All of us?' asked Albert.

'Of course. You could run it, Enjoy, if walking is too unchallenging for you.'

She squinted at him, her gaze penetrating. Only ten and it was clear her life experience had given her perceptiveness beyond her years. Though he hadn't spent much time with her before, this weekend away was peeling away her layers. But, he realised, it was peeling away his too, and he felt suddenly vulnerable. Unmoored. The package that came with Alice was what she had warned him about. A sense of horrible premonition came over him, an uncontainable shiver over his heart. He thought he knew what he was doing. He *did* know what he was doing. This wasn't a journey begun without open eyes. But he knew, too, even from this simple lunch, that it wasn't going to be a journey without some tremendous storms. He wondered if he was capable of negotiating them.

'Leo?' Alice asked softly. 'Are you okay?'

'Of course,' he said. 'Just a little tired. I didn't sleep too well last night.' He smiled at her but not in a suggestive way. He just wanted to connect with her, to be reassured.

Despite this, Alice looked down, the blush creeping over her face – a diffusion of colour like a science experiment. It travelled down to her neck, her chest, where her cleavage was just visible. He wanted to hold her. To take her in his arms and rest his chin on her head. To smell her apple shampoo and feel those breasts pushed against his body. Alice looked up again, blinking, then, very purposefully, she moved her leg so that it no longer just brushed against his. The pressure spoke to him. She understood. And this time when he looked at her she met his gaze frankly. It wasn't about last night, or tonight. It was about so much more than time, or presence, or challenge.

Albert was shifting in his seat again. He picked up a salt cellar, managing to deposit half the contents of the container on the tablecloth.

'Albert!' Alice said.

'The lid was loose. I'm telling you, Mom.'

She cupped her hand, caught the crystals, and placed them neatly on her side plate. 'No harm done.' She smiled at her son, patting his hand with hers reassuringly.

'Anyone for dessert?' she asked.

Leo shook his head. 'I'd love a cappuccino though.'

'I want an ice cream and a Coke,' Albert said.

'Please,' Alice corrected.

'Please.'

'You can have one or the other. You don't need the extra sugar.'

'Are you saying I'm fat again?'

'Again?' Alice said flustered. 'I didn't even mention that word once.'

'I want both then. Why can't I have both?'

'Because the sugar is not good for your mood. You know that.'

'You're not good for my mood, Mom. I want a Coke and ice cream.'

Leo cocked his head. 'Bert, buddy. Why not just settle down?'

'Why? You're speaking for her now?'

'Nope. For me. You're a great guy and guys like that talk nicely to their mothers.'

Albert grimaced, then seemed to accept the challenge. He nodded, slowly. Sat back into his chair. His pupils were already dark and wide. There was a troubled silence but as the waiter took the order for two chocolate ice creams and two cappuccinos, the atmosphere seemed to ease. Leo breathed in, glad that more arguments had been avoided – for now.

He stood up. 'Do you know where the bathrooms are?'

'They're a bit of a way. Unisex,' Alice replied. She glanced at her son, who was still sitting calmly enough – for him. This time he was fiddling with his fork, banging it against the table edge. 'I'll show you if you like. You guys stay here. Don't go anywhere.'

'Where would we go?' Enjoy wondered.

But Alice had already pushed back her chair. She edged around the table, ascending a spiral staircase to the left of the kitchen. It was dark wood, with a brushed metal balustrade. Their footsteps creaked on every stair. He followed her down a red-brick passage, with black and white prints. He was close behind her, close enough to smell her perfume. She turned to look at him, her eyes locking with his. He reached for her. Tentatively. But she was already against him, their lips full and hungry. It was a long, beautiful kiss. Flaming and hot. Wordless but full of promises. They breathed in each other's air, tasted each other. Her arms clasped him closer, his fingers raked through her hair. She gasped, as he moved her towards the nearby door. He looked at her questioningly and she nodded, almost imperceptibly. It was a flow of motion. A glide. Their bodies almost toppling into the stall. Her fingers worked his buttons, fumbling so badly that she began to laugh softly.

'Help me,' she said. And he took her hands in his, kissed her fingers. One by one. Then let her hands go. He was so hard now, the release of the buttons was a relief. As he pushed down her knickers, he only faintly heard the sound. An opening door. Footsteps.

But then Alice touched her finger to her lips. Shhh.

Someone cleared his throat, loudly. Theatrically.

Perhaps the loud knock on the door of the stall that followed was unsurprising.

'Sir? Ma'am?'

Alice began to giggle really softly, her characteristic red sheen rising across her face like a sunrise. She cleared her throat. 'Um, yes?'

'Ma'am. Do you have a son?'

Her face paled instantly. 'Yes. Yes I do.'

'You'd better come right away.'

'Is he okay? What's happened?'

'Ma'am. I think you'd better come. And perhaps your – um – companion too.'

His heart sank, but Leo simply touched her chin. Lifted it. Wiped her already tearful eyes with his lips. He retrieved her knickers and handed them to her.

Then he began to rebutton his jeans.

Instant voicemail

He drove home. What else could he do in this state? Maybe Martini wasn't in the crumpled Ferrari. After all, he and the woman could have separated and Martini could have taken his own car home. Somehow, however, Bruce really doubted it. There wasn't enough time. And where those two were going was nowhere separate. For all he knew, she was giving him a blowjob on the motorway when the accident happened. That wouldn't have surprised him in the least.

Fuck.

He hadn't a cooking clue what to do now. As he pulled into the garage he considered his options. He tried calling again: the same infuriating response. Bruce's head was spinning. The last brandy had been a mistake. He wasn't thinking easily through the fuzz of the booze. Alice would know what to do but he and Alice weren't talking. It was then, too, that he noticed her car was missing.

Where the hell was his wife?

His blood, once boiling, now turned to ice. Where the fuck was Alice?

Bruce walked into the house; amazingly and instantly clear-headed. Some of the kitchen cupboards were still flung open. He marched down the passage. No kid in either bed. No Alice in theirs.

Had she left him? Tonight of all nights? And why? Yes, they'd had a tiff, but really. That's all it was. A little argument. In their bedroom, Alice's wardrobe was still flung open. Her favourite jacket, which usually hung on a hook on the back of the door, was gone. As was her pink scarf. Her tackies that she normally used for hiking.

He checked his watch. It was after one. He'd left the house at five – maybe – but that gave them time to leave in all sorts of directions but not so far, unless they'd got on a plane, which he sincerely doubted. His wife wasn't that spontaneous. In fact, she was as routine as toast for breakfast.

127

And Alice didn't like to drive in the dark. Her depth perception was distorted. One thing he knew for sure. The kids were safe. Maybe not with him but safe. And he was fucking exhausted. Maybe he should just deal with all this shit in the morning.

Or he could call his wife.

He picked up his mobile.

Instant voicemail. So … no reception?

He left a message anyway. 'What the hell, Alice? Where are you with my kids? And no note? No WhatsApp? Get in touch, please.' He hesitated, tried to calm his voice. 'I need to know you're all okay.' When he'd disconnected he thought in retrospect that maybe he should have apologised. She might have been more likely to call back.

He started to strip off his clothes. A quick shower would calm him down. What a *kak* night. Thank God for long showers. He was a fucking genius getting them off the grid.

Bruce was only aware of the ringing at the front gate when he stepped out of the water. What now? He grabbed his dressing gown and tied the belt around his waist. Marched to the front door. He peered out the kitchen window but couldn't see much. It was dark. No moon. But a figure stood at the gate. A man? A woman? Who the hell knew?

He pushed a button on the intercom. Spoke into it.

'Hello?'

'Brucie, let me in.'

Now that was a voice he wanted to hear. 'Martini? Shit, dude, what are you doing here?'

'Just let me in.'

But Bruce had already pushed the gate opener. 'Bring your car inside,' he said.

'What car, boytjie? I bloody walked here.'

A panoramic view

She didn't even wait to extract herself discreetly. What kind of a mother was she? Shagging some young thing – or attempting to – and leaving her nutcase of a son in public, in a restaurant, waiting to explode?

'Allie?' Leo said.

She turned. She wanted him, but now she kind of hated him too. He was a distraction she couldn't really afford. Alice tried to smile but she knew her response didn't reach her eyes.

'It'll be okay,' he said.

She nodded. Turned. And began to run for the circular staircase. When she got downstairs, she could hear the commotion before she could see it. The high-pitched shrieking sounded like Enjoy, the lower rumble, Albert.

He was pulling her along the ground like a caveman, his fingers gripped between her braids. Instead of lying limp, which might have hurt less, Enjoy was flailing like a drowning cat, her claws out, ripping at Albert's ankle each time his leg came close when he walked. A waiter, trying to pull on Albert, knocked over a chair, which dominoed into one wine glass, then another. The restaurant patrons, sitting in their chairs like an audience, stared on with open-mouthed horror.

Alice walked over to Albert, and spoke to him loudly. 'Albert, let your sister go.'

But Albert was deaf to her instructions, deaf to everything. Alice moved forward, tugging hard at her son's arm, but though he was still lanky, he was already strong, almost stronger than her, and manic. He was invincible. Leo grabbed Albert's hand.

'Hey buddy, you're hurting Enjoy.'

'Good! I'm glad. She's a fucking shit. She must go hang herself!'

'What happened, guys?

'I hate her. She's a bitch! She should die.'

Alice tried to keep her voice calm. 'Albert, let Enjoy go.'

The shrieking only got worse and Leo was forced to push past Alice and manhandle Albert's arms down over his chest so that Leo could hold them there in place. With the force of the movement, Albert was temporarily winded, and loosened his grip. Enjoy fell to the floor, but instead of just collapsing there, crawled away to cower under a dining table. Albert was now kicking with both legs and Leo struggled to the glass door, which had a panoramic view of the garden. It was swiftly opened by the waiters, as guests nearby stared unashamedly.

Almost tripping, Leo faltered down the steps. With Albert bucking, Alice thought Leo couldn't have been able to see very much so he needed to use his feet to feel his way. Alice could see how he was losing his balance. She moved quickly behind him, gripping his shoulder as he shuddered to the last step. Righting himself, he carried Albert to the corner of the garden, under the shade of a large cycad. He was whispering in Albert's ear, but Alice couldn't hear the words. Gently, ever so gently, he began to let the boy go.

'Watch out!' Alice screamed as Albert bolted, grabbing one of the plastic outdoor chairs. He began to swing at the nearby plants, breaking off fronds in a green shower. This time, Alice yanked the chair away, almost falling flat on her behind. Leo picked up Albert, and flung him over his shoulder. Even Leo, who never seemed angry, looked irate. Alice scrabbled through her bag to get the car keys. She saw Enjoy, no longer cowering, but standing on the steps, her eyes as wide as planets.

'Darling, unlock the car for Leo, I need to pay the bill.' Alice was amazed that her voice seemed both calm and authoritative.

Enjoy nodded, sliding down the steps in an embarrassed glide.

'Leo?' Alice said.

'Got him; I'll be fine.' He offered a weak smile, unable to shrug in a balanced way, the weight of the boy clearly uncomfortable.

Alice thrust her own shoulders back. Remounted the steps. Then she smiled in what she thought was an entirely winning manner at the bug-eyed manager.

'Right,' she said brightly. 'How much do I owe for the damage? And the food, of course, definitely all that food.'

Not here

'Jesus, mate, what happened to you?'

Martini touched the blood still leaking down his temple. 'What a night. I got so drunk I fell off a barstool. Landed on my head. Hit something on the way down. Don't know what.'

'Where was this?'

'Oh after Teasers, we hit a few bars on Long Street.'

'We?'

'Just some okes from the tennis club. You don't know them.'

Bruce looked at his friend. He wanted to tell him that his story wasn't washing with him. But how to address the issue without embarrassing Martini?

'But how did you get here?' Bruce asked instead.

'Well, I wanted to take an Uber, but my phone was dead, so I took some random taxi. Except that on the way back home, I needed to vomit and he chucked me out the car. Told me to walk it off. Got to hand it to him; I've certainly sobered up.

'And your car?'

'I left it at the office. Thank God. No ways I could have driven. Anyway, your house was closer than mine. Maybe I can crash for the night? Send Elaine a message. She already thinks I've been with you.'

Bruce studied Martini. He was bleeding from his arm as well, and he'd have a proper shiner tomorrow. His eye was already swelling closed. The bar stool story was good but not good enough. He wondered about the woman in the car. The crushed Ferrari on the side of the road. Was that her car? Was she even alive?

'I promise I'll be quiet,' Martini added. 'Quiet as a little mouse … Won't wake the family.'

'They're not here,' Bruce said shortly.

'Really? Why not?'

Bruce didn't want to talk about it. 'I think we need to get you cleaned up. Put some ice on that eye. Do you want to phone Elaine?'

'Christ no. Can I send her a WhatsApp from your phone? I don't need a fucking lecture.'

Bruce opened his mouth.

'Not a word, Bruce. My marriage, my problem.'

Bruce shrugged. 'Sure, mate. Grab yourself a shower. I'll get you some clothes. My phone is on the kitchen counter. Have at it.'

This was turning into quite some night. His wife had left him and his friend was now making him an accomplice to something he knew in his heart of hearts was not kosher.

There was a limit to loyalty – or was there?

They'd been friends so long he could hardly recall when Martini hadn't been in his life. And as for Alice, it hurt too much to consider that she might have given up on him. He wasn't perfect but he was a good provider. Spontaneous. Generous. Most of the time he was a good dad. Not great – there was certainly room for improvement – but good enough. He resolved that in the morning he would track Alice down. Possibly even apologise. He could do that, couldn't he?

He knocked on the bathroom door. The water was turned off already. His friend had clearly perfected the thirty-second shower.

'Tracksuit and T-shirt outside the door for you, Martini.'

He could hear Martini grunt.

'You okay in there, dude?'

No answer. *Christ, now what?* He swung open the door. Martini was sitting on the edge of the bath, his head in his hands. Even without seeing his face, Bruce could tell he'd been crying.

'Martini?' he said cautiously.

Martini jumped. 'For fuck's sake, Bruce, don't you knock?'

'I did knock. You didn't answer. Do you think you need to get to a hospital? You might have concussion.'

'No!' Martini stood up, the towel around his waist, not hiding the truth. Martini was getting a belly. Some middle-age spread. And in the harsh bathroom light, he looked ten years older. 'I said I'm fine and I am. I've just had too much to drink. I need to sleep this off. A few Nurofen and I'll be right as rain.'

Bruce shrugged. How stupid did his friend think he was? Stupid enough to believe his story, obviously. He walked to the medicine cabinet, pulled out a bottle of pills. 'Go wild,' he said. 'Nothing else you want to share with me?'

'Just your phone, mate. I need to WhatsApp Elaine.'

'Yes. You told me.' Bruce stepped back. His legs were beginning to tingle with exhaustion. 'It's charging in the kitchen, next to the kettle, remember? No pin code. There's an extra charger for your phone too, if you want.' Bruce stretched, wondering if his friend had even heard him. 'Martini?'

'Hmm?'

'I'm going to shower and hit the sack. Help yourself to food or coffee. Packet of peas in the freezer for your eye.'

But Martini didn't say anything. The grey tinge of his skin, a sharp contrast to the purply-blue of the soft tissues around his left eye, was the last thing Bruce noticed before he closed the door.

Some woman

In the cottage, Albert was spiralled up in his blankets, like a hamster. Though it had been difficult to get him to take the risperidone, when they'd finally managed, it knocked him out almost immediately. Leo didn't want to say it, or think it, but thank God. Despite this, he recalled the way Alice had walked back into the restaurant, her back straight, her head held high.

That was some woman. She had serious, well, balls.

Alice sat down next to him. She'd made them both tea and Enjoy was lying on Alice's bed reading a David Walliams book. Something about a dentist. And a headmaster in all colours of grey. Charcoal grey. Grey grey. Dove grey. A bit like Leo's mood. But he'd lit a fire and the licking flames were nice to watch. Distracting.

'Well,' she said.

'You okay?'

'Hey, why shouldn't I be? This is my life.' She bit on her lip and refused to meet his eyes.

Leo reached for her hand, holding it gently between his. 'Alice.' When she still didn't look at him, he squeezed again. 'Alice?'

'God, this is such a mess. Surely that was enough to send you packing? Sometimes even I want to hightail it out of here and never look back.'

'You were amazing. Beyond amazing.'

Alice laughed. 'I seem to recall you were the poor sucker carrying out the delinquent.'

'Yes, but did you notice my sexy biceps and tight butt as I was doing it?'

She laughed. 'I couldn't help but notice those.' She punched him lightly on the arm with her other hand. 'Off the topic, buster.'

'Well, on the topic, then, I'm on your team. Team Alice all the way.'

'All the way?' she said raising her eyebrows.

'Oh yes,' he said, winking.

Leo was overwhelmed by a surge of emotion. With Hailey, his previous girlfriend, he'd often woken up to find her reaching for him. And though he'd had a physical response – she was a beautiful girl after all – he hadn't felt like this.

Hailey was sure of herself. So sure, she would climb onto him, and ride him with no words, not even a greeting. Satisfaction was about her first, always. And, considering it objectively, the connection between them had been entirely physical. A good connection, sure, but out of the bedroom, there was something not quite sincere about her. She never seemed to tell him the truth; those breasts, for instance, were not the ones she was born with. He'd felt enough tits in his life to know that, yet she wouldn't admit it. Not that he'd asked outright, but she'd had so many opportunities to tell him. It didn't really matter – they looked, she looked – great. But it was more about her inability to expose herself emotionally.

Physically, she had no trouble with that, strutting around the apartment completely naked, unselfconscious. Self-assured. Ironically, she did it so much, he got used to her. With nothing much left to the imagination, he wasn't constantly horny. He became … bored. She was almost too available, too independent. Hailey didn't need him.

Not like Alice did.

Alice cocked her head. 'Still here, Leo?'

He smiled. 'Definitely.'

She extracted her hand from between his, let it trace up along his polo neck, along the hard curve of his chest. His nipples tightened and she wasn't even touching his skin. As her hand gently followed his contours, he wanted to kiss her, but her expression made him still. She was learning his body like Braille, committing him to memory. But as she outlined his silhouette with her hand, when she reached near his shoulder, he winced involuntarily.

'Leo?'

'Umhmm.'

'That's sore?'

'It's fine. Just a bump.'

'Is that from Albert?'

'Really, Allie, no biggie.'

She sat back. 'Take off your shirt.'

'You're very bossy,' he said. 'I'm totally fine.'

'Please, Leo. Let me see.'

He shrugged. 'I know what you're doing,' he said, as he pulled the shirt over his head. 'You're just trying to get me naked.'

She smiled, but her expression was serious. Not only had Albert managed to scratch through Leo's shirt, but along his back, also, bruises were beginning to rise from Albert's shoes where the boy had kicked him.

'The little bastard,' Alice said, her voice catching. 'I'm so sorry.'

She stood up and walked to the kitchen. He could hear cupboard doors opening. Then she came back with a medical kit.

'Allie, please don't worry. I'd much rather you went back to feeling me up.'

This time she laughed. 'First I repair the damage, then I kiss you better.'

'Deal.'

'Turn around. I'll put some arnica onto these bruises.'

She sat down next to him. He turned, feeling her soft, gentle hands on his skin. The gel was icy, making him flinch. 'Ouch, that's cold.'

'Don't be a baby.'

'Yes ma'am.' Her breath on his skin was making him crazy, but at the same time, he liked the feel of her soft hands. She was gentle, her fingers lingering under his shoulder blade, where the hard tips of Albert's shoes had dug in. Amazing how much it hurt.

'I'm really sorry, Leo,' Alice said. 'This is really quite inflamed.'

'Oh please,' he said. 'It's nothing. When do we get to the kiss me better part?'

He couldn't see her face, but somehow knew she was smiling. 'Hold your horses.'

'I'm not sure that patience is one of my virtues.'

'You have virtues?'

And he was just about to turn around, to take this unbelievable woman into his arms, when he heard the front door open.

Then a voice filled the room with fury and surprise. 'What the fuck is going on here?'

The same message

He stepped into the cottage. A fire was burning in the grate and his wife was touching up the tutor over a cup of tea. Very romantic. But instead of looking guilty, Alice simply glared at him.

'What the heck are you doing here?'

Hot anger flamed in his gut. 'Last time I checked, this was my place too.'

Instead of answering him, Alice leant forward and picked up a plaster. She tore it out of its wrapping, which floated like a feather to the floor.

'Turn a little, please, Leo,' she said.

Alice wiped some antiseptic cream – he assumed – onto the skin below his pecs and stuck down first one plaster then a second.

'All done?' the tutor said casually.

Alice nodded.

'Thanks.' He slipped his shirt back over his head.

'So, mate,' Bruce said. 'Can you give me and my wife a moment?'

The bloke looked at Alice.

'What the fuck, Lionel. You don't need her permission.'

'Leo,' Alice said icily. 'At least get his name right.'

'Lionel. Leo. My message is the same.'

Leo stood up, then walked to *his,* Bruce's, fucking bedroom. 'Enjoy, I'm going for a walk. Want to come?'

Bruce couldn't hear her reply but his daughter emerged almost immediately.

'Daddy! Mom said you might come today.' She hugged him hard around his waist.

'She did?'

'Yes! She wasn't sure, though. She didn't promise.'

Bruce smiled at her. 'Mmm, so where's the terrorist?'

'His name is Albert,' Alice said, her tone clipped.

'Again,' Bruce commented. 'Same difference.'

'He's asleep. This afternoon, you know, at lunch. He broke, like, so many glasses. And he hit a tree with a chair. It was raining leaves! And he pulled my hair. See, over here,' Enjoy indicated the top of her head.

Bruce grimaced. 'What did I say, Alice? The terrorist.'

'He's asleep,' Leo commented. 'It's been a rough day.'

Bruce shot him a glare. 'Weren't you going for a walk?'

Leo smiled casually. *What a condescending prick.* 'That's right. Come on, Miss.'

Bruce watched the two leave, Enjoy skipping a little ahead. He turned to Alice. 'So, has he moved in or something? He must be milking us dry.'

'Leo came as a guest. And thank God. Albert went on a rampage. Leo had to carry him out. You should see the bruises on his back from Albert's shoes.'

'Yes, I saw you checking those. Anything else you were checking out?'

Alice's face scrunched up the way it always did when she was in a rage. 'Fuck you, Bruce,' she said. 'Why are you even here?'

'You didn't leave a note. You didn't answer my calls. I was worried.'

'How sweet,' Alice said caustically. 'Well, as you can see apart from a few cuts and scrapes, we're fine.'

'Then it's time to come home.'

'Why? It's Saturday. I'm in no hurry.'

Bruce studied his wife. She seemed … different. Surer of herself. Bold. He didn't like it.

'Alice, we need to talk properly. That kid is breaking up this family. We need to have a plan.'

'That kid is our son. And he is ill. Maybe you should think about your own behaviour. You threw our child against a wall, for goodness sake.'

'*That* was an accident.'

'You mean like the slap across his face was an accident?'

'He attacked me. I was defending myself.'

'Big man. So brave he can beat up a little boy.'

Bruce flinched. 'I did *not* beat him up.'

'You're abusive, Bruce. Even if it's not so much with your hands. Your words are bad enough. You're supposed to be his touchstone, his role model. But you say the most terrible things. And you can't take them back.'

Bruce sat down next to Alice, trying to catch her hands between his. 'That's a horrible thing to say, yourself. You make me sound like a monster.'

Alice was silent a minute. 'Honestly, Bruce, I have no idea who you are anymore. Since Albert became sick you're hardly around.'

'I'm here aren't I? I risked the fact that you would be here and drove all the way without knowing. That's got to count for something, doesn't it?'

Alice didn't answer. He couldn't read her expression and it chilled him. 'Is there something you want to tell me?'

'I'm not going back today. You go if you want. But I'm happy here with the kids.'

'Leo and the kids, you mean?'

'Oh whatever, Bruce. Stay. Don't stay. You decide.' Alice stood up and though Bruce stood up trying to catch her shoulder, she deftly avoided him to stomp to the kitchen. She flung open the freezer, extracting some meat. Then she opened the fridge, threw lettuce, tomatoes and cucumber on the counter. Out came the wooden board, a dangerous looking knife and a scary expression. He found it just a little sexy. She was like a different person. The knife slid down, chop-chop-chop! Alice leant down, pulling a glass bowl out from a lower shelf, pitched the massacred tomatoes into it.

Bruce was at a loss. He'd not been expecting an open-arms welcome. A bit of a cool-off, perhaps, and then, back to normal. That's what had had happened before on the rare occasions they had fought. But he was beginning to realise that this *was* the new normal. An angry wife. A sulking, suicidal tween. A clean-cut, too-perfect tutor and a running-obsessed ten-year-old. That, the running, at least he could handle.

He walked outside, set some wood onto the braai outside. Kindling in between and below. In the drawer in the lounge he found some firelighters and matches. When the blaze started, he watched it fixedly, resting his weight on his right hip. Uneasy. He pulled out a chair from the shed outside, unfolded it and sat himself down in front of the flames, brooding.

Martini had left the house early, by Uber, Bruce assumed. When he'd woken up, his mate was already gone, a lone coffee cup sitting inside the sink. Martini had scribbled his version of a detailed note on the notepad attached to the kitchen fridge. *Thanks mate. Out of here.* Bruce found his clothes dumped next to the washing machine. Then later, when he'd turned on the radio, he heard the news. It wasn't entirely unexpected, of course.

Lebogang Dinangwe, married actress, model and socialite, was tragically killed in a car accident last night near Constantia. Thrown from her yellow Ferrari, Dinangwe's body was discovered some distance from the car. It is believed she died on impact.

On impact with what? The barrier or the windscreen?

Needless to say, the yellow Ferrari was the giveaway. The proof.

He'd never heard of the woman before, but googling her, recognised her face immediately. Posed in front of some banner, her regal stance was the same as he recalled from the Toad. Bruce changed stations. Checked on News24. But more details on the accident did not seem to be forthcoming.

And the tension pitting his stomach made him more focused to find his wife and talk to her. Alice was always the calm presence, the oil on the water, and despite the recent tension between them, he needed to confide in someone about what he suspected.

What was he supposed to do?

Without any doubt whatsoever, he knew his friend had driven that car. Which meant that he'd staged the body.

How the fuck did he have the wherewithal to do that? The *cojones*?

But what then, really, was the point in confessing? Martini would be up for manslaughter and locked away for good. What purpose would that actually serve? Whose purpose? People in South Africa had been let off worse crimes. Justice wasn't exactly a working currency here.

From a distance he could hear the sharp pitches of his daughter's voice. They'd be coming back soon. Her and the tutor. Leo. Leo … Leo … Leo. Bruce could make nice if he wanted to.

As the two approached, he stood up.

'A brewski, mate?' he said to the young man, hoping there was actually some beer in the fridge.

Leo shrugged. 'Sure, why not?'

'Run into the kitchen, be a love, Enjoy. Fetch us two beers.'

'Can I have a drink too?'

'Yes, okay. If your mom says so.'

Enjoy ran into the house and Bruce indicated the free chair. He fetched another two from the shed.

'So,' he said.

Leo looked at him. He had this placid, almost docile expression. With a touch of fear. And Bruce immediately felt better. He was still on top, like he'd always been. It was just a matter of establishing hierarchy. And it was clear the young man was apprehensive about him. As he should be.

'You and Albert getting along?' Bruce asked.

Leo sat back in his chair. His legs were aggressively open but Bruce allowed him a little leeway.

'He's a great boy.'

Bruce wasn't so sure about that. How a child of his could turn out so weird was a point of shame to him. He'd been successful at everything in his life. A hot wife. Good money. Great house. Fabulous car. Trophy rainbow daughter (although Alice would be horrified by that description). And the one thing he needed to round it off, a perfect sporty son, was so

140

different from what Albert actually was that Bruce sometimes wondered if the kid had been swapped in the hospital. He was weedy and weak, emotional and aggressive. Unpopular and irritating. And he couldn't blame the other kids really. If Bruce couldn't stand to be near Albert these days, how was he supposed to expect others to?

Bruce realised then that they were sitting in silence. He cleared his throat. 'So you're getting along?'

Leo's eyes opened slightly, a micromovement of a smirk at the corners of his mouth. 'He's a cool little guy. Amazing brain. Can't keep up with him sometimes.'

'Really?' Bruce tried to keep the amazement out of his voice.

The tutor tipped his head, then straightened it. Looked him straight in the eye. 'Abso-damn-lutely.'

A new language

In the kitchen, Alice was preparing a *paptert*. That and avoiding her husband, who had camped outside and set up a bonfire of such astronomic proportions she could almost feel the heat from where she was standing. Overkill. Like always.

When Enjoy came inside to fetch the beers, Alice helped herself to a stiff gin and tonic, with some of the lemon they'd picked that morning. They'd never got to the meringue. More gin, perhaps, than tonic, but she needed a bit of courage. Later she would regret this, probably. She always talked a little too much, a little too honestly with a bit of booze in her. Clearly Bruce had decided to stay. Sadly. She'd thought his lukewarm reception would send him on his way, but apparently he was made of tougher stuff. When she heard footsteps coming around the corner, she expected Enjoy to arrive with another order from Bruce. But instead she saw Albert, who was rubbing red, swollen eyes and stumbling a little as though trying to find his balance.

'Darling, you're awake.'

'Has Leo left? Does he hate me now? Like Dad?'

'Dad doesn't hate you. And neither does Leo. They're both sitting outside next to your dad's enormous braai fire.'

'Oh.'

Albert scratched his neck. His stringy hair needed a wash and Alice wondered if she could suggest such a thing without triggering another reaction of astronomic proportions. She smiled at her son.

'Darling, why don't I run you a lovely hot bath, with some of my bubbles – the ones you like?'

Albert stretched. 'Okay. But I need a snack first. I'm starving.'

'Well, you burnt quite a lot of energy in that restaurant,' Alice said brightly, putting her hand across her mouth in an attempt to stop herself from giggling.

Albert cocked his head. 'Are you laughing at me?' But he didn't seem angry.

'*With* you, Bertie. It's not every day you get to leave a restaurant in a fireman's lift.'

'Oh God.' Albert scratched at his neck again, brightening to a mild puce.

'Oh goodness.'

'What?'

'Goodness. Not God.'

'Whatever, Mother. Now what's there to eat around here?'

***

With Albert safely ensconced in the bathroom, Alice breathed a little easier. In their house, their lives, the trip wires were everywhere. A 'cheeky' look. A short temper. A long day. It was like Alice was the bomb disposal expert, constantly disarming explosive situations before they detonated. But it was tiring work, exhausting, in fact. How could one ever relax? When Leo was at home with Albert and she could get on with her work, she felt free for the only time in the day. It allowed her to breathe, if only for the shortest of times. She was far from bulletproof, and she didn't have the resources to keep going. Yet, there she was. Trying her best.

Her family of origin, the one before Bruce, the one of her childhood, had been a happy one. Of course, there had been issues. Her mother's illness when she was ten – a breast cancer scare, mastectomy and recovery. A few financial difficulties, when they'd had to 'tighten their belts'. But it had never lacked spirit or love. Sometimes she felt that Bruce and Albert actually did hate each other. And she was stuck in the middle while they vied for her attention. That left Enjoy somewhere on the side. Flitting between them like an uncertain moth, not knowing where to rest her wings. Alice often felt that's why she could never be still; like the rest of the family, she was searching for something. But Alice, and Enjoy, probably, didn't know what that was.

Alice felt like she was learning a new language. A new state of being. She wasn't equipped for the kind of tension reverberating through their house, Albert at the epicentre, usually. But sometimes, more often these days, it was Bruce. It made him unlikeable. His inability to even try to be flexible, try to understand the mind of a child at a gallop, uncontrollable like a fleeing horse. Which is what made Leo so attractive.

He seemed mostly unfazed by Albert's moods, nurturing. And of course, he was so hot that it was difficult not to stare at him. Discovering his body was like unwrapping a beautiful gift; and ironically, despite a lifetime of living by the rules, of putting everybody else first, she felt that she deserved him. The guilt would come, no doubt, she knew herself well enough to recognise that, but whether or not she was going to succumb to it was another matter. Frankly, she wished Bruce would just go home so she could continue what she and Leo had started.

In the bathroom, she could hear the taps turning on again. With Albert, she realised, it was often a good choice to make him think something was his idea, or at least encourage rather than order him. He didn't take to authoritarianism, the type of parenting Bruce preferred. No wonder they clashed so much.

Alice ground pepper over the top of the tart. The oven was already on, and she slid the large Pyrex dish into the middle shelf. Twenty minutes and it would be ready. But that also meant she'd have to emerge from the kitchen.

Truthfully, she was a little afraid.

How would she be able to hide her feelings for Leo from Bruce? Surely they must be written all over her face, unscrubbable, like permanent marker? But perhaps not. He was so lost in his own ego these days it was difficult to ascertain if he noticed anyone but himself.

She picked up a wooden bowl from the cupboard below the counter. Poured a packet of salt and vinegar chips inside. With one hand, she clutched the bowl against her stomach like a shield, with the other, she held the gin and tonic (refilled) like a weapon.

Outside, the men were sitting peaceably enough. Between them, Enjoy was burning a long stick, the flames flickering as she poked it into the coals. Alice worried about Enjoy's braids. She'd heard some horror story of a girl blowing out her birthday candles and catching fire. But Alice bit down on her lip, and refrained from saying anything. She had to stop being such a mother hen. She knew that about herself. Enjoy was ten. Perfectly able to roast a marshmallow or play with a stick.

As Alice emerged, she saw Leo look up. His eyes burnt into her. Hotly. Inside her, she felt like she was turning to liquid.

She set down the bowl and glass on the garden wall. There was no chair set out for her, and instead of waiting for one of the men to fetch one, she walked to the shed herself, trying to blot out the colour rising in her face by thinking of things other than Leo's hands on her and the hard muscle of his abdomen. She was failing and not for the first time in her life she wished she were better at subterfuge. Once she'd thought her inability to lie was a quality to be admired. Now she just wished she'd practised more.

'Okay in there?'

Leo's voice behind her made her jump.

She tried to level herself, but she felt like she was still levitating.

'I can't stop thinking about you,' he whispered at her neck. 'I just want to–'

'Mom?' Albert.

Leo turned with an easy assurance that Alice both admired and feared. 'Hey bud. Need a chair? We're doing a braai.'

Albert studied them for a moment, biting on his lower lip. 'I'm sorry, Leo. You know. About earlier. Are you cross with me?'

'Bertie, you're my friend, aren't you?'

The boy nodded uncertainly.

'So as your friend I'm going to tell you the truth.'

Now Albert gulped, his eyes widening. It was clear he didn't want to hear this truth and Alice felt herself holding her breath.

'So, I was really upset with you this afternoon. Annoyed. Irate. All that's totally true. You're not stupid and you knew it. But you and I, we're better than that. And I'm not angry anymore.'

Albert smiled. Then shyly he moved forward and hugged Leo, darting out the shed before Leo could hand him a chair.

Alice looked at Leo. 'I could seriously kiss you right now,' she said softly. 'Like, seriously …'

He cupped her chin, smiled his perfect smile. 'I'm going to hold you to that. Rain check?'

She smiled, picked up a fold-up chair. 'Game face, Mr Amirante.'

He extracted another chair for Albert, stared at her long enough to make her squirm. 'You're even sexy when you call me that,' he said.

The real game

If he'd pictured himself three months ago, this is not at all what he would have imagined. Sitting like a little family around a fire chatting to the man of the house while trying not to give the *real* game away.

Bruce was a good-looking man. And charming. He could see what would have attracted Alice. He should have felt overwhelmed with guilt. So why wasn't he?

Bruce waved the braai tongs as he spoke.

'You like camping? You look like an outdoors oke?'

'Sure. I only have the basic kit though. I'm not exactly equipped for glamping.'

'Oh I know all about that. Remember, love? When we were in Florence and had to camp in that horrible site so far out of town it took almost an hour to get in? And we had nothing but the mattresses and our sleeping bags? Recycled bread to last the whole day?'

Alice smiled. 'And then we stopped at that petrol station and this guy tried to climb in the back to steal my handbag but the door was locked. The look on his face as you chased after him!'

Not to be outdone, Leo spoke: 'I was travelling in Malawi and my car broke down. I had to camp on the side of the road. By myself. In the middle of the night, I heard this weird sniffing and crunching around where the zip of the tent was. I freaked out. Thought I was about to be murdered.'

'What was it?' Albert asked wide-eyed.

'A cow! Eating my tent from the outside.'

They all laughed.

'And then I couldn't chase the damn thing away. In the end, I had to pack up the entire tent and sleep on the back seat of the car. It was so uncomfortable. And noisy. That damn cow farted so loudly it sounded like a gunshot.'

The kids giggled especially loudly. They were an appreciative audience.

'You do a lot of travelling?' Bruce asked.

'Oh a fair amount. I've spent a lot of time in Italy. You know, with extended family.'

'You speak Italian?'

'Sure.'

'Wow!' said Enjoy. 'Say something.'

'Like what?'

'Oh anything.'

'Well, I'd better choose something romantic then. Italians are known for that, right?' He looked at Enjoy but he could feel Alice's eyes on him.

'I thought they were known for pizza,' Enjoy said matter-of-factly.

'And ice cream,' added Albert.

'And fashion,' said Enjoy.

'Well, those, first, and then romance. Here's one: Ho scritto una storia d'amore senza inizio e senza fine ... per scriverla con te.'

'What's it mean?'

'I have written a love story without a beginning or ending ... so that we may write it together.'

Both Albert and Enjoy pretended to retch. 'That's pretty bad, Leo.'

'I know, right?' Leo said, smiling but he looked over at Alice, who bit her lip and looked away.

'You got a girlfriend?' Bruce asked.

'No,' said Leo. 'Not right now.'

'Then maybe you should work on your pick-up lines,' Albert said seriously.

Leo laughed. 'Thanks for the advice, buddy.'

'Well, I don't know,' said Bruce. 'What did you think, Alice?'

Inwardly Leo baulked. But Alice just smiled. 'I think a pick-up line depends entirely on the person delivering it.'

'See?' Bruce said. 'Your mother, the diplomat.'

With the braai tongs in his hand, Bruce chatted amiably but not about himself. Instead Leo found himself being quietly interrogated. His life. His parents. His friends.

It was strangely flattering.

By the time that the marshmallows were roasted, the s'mores made from them devoured, Leo felt heavy. Exhausted. A combination, perhaps of subterfuge and child removal. His shoulder blade ached. But one thought still gnawed at him, keeping him at the fire. He didn't want Alice with *him*. Or near *him*. Or touching *him*.

It was these thoughts that made him realise entirely what he was up against. An institution versus a flickering of – what – lust? Love? He wished, not for the first time that evening, that Bruce had just stayed in Cape Town. And it wasn't like he could simply get rid of him. Leo wished he had his own car here. Maybe then, he could have left, not having to live through the family's nightly rituals of brushing teeth and goodnight kisses. And padding off to everybody's respective beds. Not having to lie awake and picture what was happening behind closed doors.

It made him feel physically sick.

Alice, who was opposite him, across the fire, was sitting with her arms wrapped around her knees. Throughout the evening, their eyes had met, and each time he'd forced himself to look away. But not before the slight twitch of a smile at the corners of his lips. She was worth all the *angst*, he knew that, but she wasn't sure she'd think the same. After all, she had everything to lose, while he, he had everything to gain.

'I'm getting cold,' Alice said suddenly. 'Let's go sit inside.'

They hadn't bothered yet to light the fire inside, but Leo was happy for the chore of moving coals on a shovel from outside into the hearth. He and Bruce stacked some smaller logs over the coals and kindling, watching the fire spring back to life.

Sipping a cup of coffee, he felt the tiredness seeping into his feet, his limbs. But he wasn't going to be outdone. The kids were still awake and Alice seemed reluctant to let them turn in. To let them sleep was to admit the night was over.

Albert snuggled up against Alice, leaving no room for Bruce on the couch. Enjoy was yawning heavily, her head on Bruce's shoulder. Alice sipped a potstill brandy that her husband had poured for her, quietly staring into the flames through the amber liquid. It was very clear they were going to have to separate to their respective bedrooms and Leo realised he was just going to have to man up.

'Do you mind if I use the shower, kids?' he asked. 'Think it might be time to crash.'

'Let me get you a dry towel,' Alice said, gently moving Albert so she could stand. 'Bruce, maybe you can put Enjoy into bed. She's knackered. Albert, honey, we need to give you your meds. Just wait here and I'll be back.'

As Leo followed Alice down the passage to the linen cupboard, his feet felt like lead. He wanted to say something, but he didn't know what. It was too early; everything between them too new.

Alice touched his arm, meeting his eyes. 'Only sleep, Leo. Nothing else is going to happen.'

He tried to smile. 'This is a new one for me, Allie.'

'Tell me about it. It's going to be okay.'

'Mom!' shouted Enjoy. 'Come kiss me goodnight.'

'Me too,' whispered Leo, making her laugh.

'Goodnight Leo,' she said, handing him the towel. As their hands touched, they stood together, a surging energy passing between them.

'Goodnight, beautiful Alice.'

Frigid

He kicked off his shoes. God. What a fucker of a day. He wondered about Martini. The bugger wouldn't be able to contact him here. And maybe that was for the best. Bruce was still trying to work out what the hell to do about what he knew about the accident. He didn't know that Lebogang woman, but she deserved some sort of truth, like anyone else. And he had to admit it. That Martini had left a dead or dying woman on the side of the road to save his own hide was rather disturbing. Bruce wasn't perfect, but he couldn't have imagined doing *that.*

He could hear Alice talking to the kids next door. When was she coming to bed? They'd done a good job of politeness, even affection, in public. But he knew that look. He was in the dog box. No getting around that. He sighed. Stripped down to shower. It would do him good to wash off the day. But when he turned on the tap, he could see he was competing with Leo for hot water. His temper flared. He'd brought that dipshit into their lives; it was time to get him out. But then he thought about Albert. More time with the twerp. Well, so be it. He'd have to show him who the alpha male in the house really was.

Bruce stepped out the shower. Dried himself off. It was cold in the bedroom and he pulled on his pyjamas. In the summer, he liked to sleep naked but he wasn't going to freeze his arse off tonight. He looked up as Alice opened the bedroom door. Her expression was neutral.

'I'm going to bath,' she said.

'Good luck with that. The tutor's taken just about all the hot water.'

'Leo,' she said.

'Really, Alice? You're going with that again? I know his bloody name. I just don't care about it.'

'I'm not fighting tonight, Bruce. I'm going to bath and then I'm going to sleep.'

'Oh, I thought we could maybe … catch up? A little one on one?'

'No thanks.'

'No?'

'You heard me. I didn't ask you here and frankly, I would have preferred a bit of time apart. You don't get to do what you did to Albert and then pretend like everything is the same.'

Bruce felt himself go cold. 'I'm trying to make it up to you, Alice. I don't like how things are going between us.'

'Well, maybe it's time to put other people before yourself for a change. People like your son.'

Bruce sighed heavily. What a bitch she was being right now. It was all just too much effort. 'You're right. Let's just go to sleep.'

He rolled over, turning his back to her. He could feel her frigid vibes and was glad for the pyjamas. The bloody bed was freezing over.

The book

A week had passed since the cottage escape.

'I'm going to drop Enjoy at Charlotte's,' Alice said. 'For her sleepover.'

Bruce looked up from his computer. 'Okay.'

'Albert is sleeping. He'll be okay for a few hours as long as you're here ... Bruce?'

'Christ, Alice. I can look after my own kid.'

'Sorry. I just thought you hadn't heard me. I thought I'd take some time to go shopping. I need some new trainers. Cavendish closes late tonight.'

Bruce nodded. 'Okay. Cheers, babe.'

'Bye Daddy!' Enjoy said, running back to hug him.

He smiled. 'Tomorrow, we're running a ten. Think you can handle it?'

'You bet.'

'Hey Alice, what are we doing for dinner tonight?' Bruce asked. 'When you get back?'

'Pizza?' Alice said. 'If you can order?'

Alice clipped her safety belt, reversed the car. Her heart was battering her rib cage. So much for subterfuge. She was simply awful at it.

As she drove, Enjoy babbled next to her. Alice's mind was spinning.

'You're not listening, Mommy,' her daughter said crossly.

'What?'

'Can you look at new tackies for me too?'

'I think it's better if we go together. You'll need to try them on.'

'Well, we need to do it soon. I have holes near the toes.'

She was glad when her daughter was safely with Charlotte. Tonight Alice was feeling reckless. She drove faster than she normally would, remembering her younger self, hitting the highway for a girls' weekend. Liberated. Light. Carefree.

She parked her Audi outside on the street, checking the address on her phone. Hesitating, she was overcome by shyness. But also resolve. She stepped out the car, slammed the door behind her. The main gate to the complex was wide open and she walked through it, looking for a sign to indicate which direction she should go. There was a staircase, the paint peeling slightly. Number 12 was on the top floor. When she stood outside the door she didn't even let herself hesitate. Alice lifted her hand and knocked. Music blared from inside. A band she didn't know.

'Just a minute.'

And then the door swung open and he was there. Barefoot. In shorts and a bright orange T-shirt. His hair wet and tousled. That beautiful open face. A surprised look.

'Allie!'

She stood there uncertain. Since their weekend away and Bruce's arrival, she hadn't stopped thinking about him. He'd been at the house but in no way that indicated what had transpired between them. He was back to being Albert's tutor. Albert's. And that made her feel sick. 'Hey,' she said. 'Good time?'

He hesitated before he smiled. Alice felt her heart diving into her feet. 'Come in. Where are the kids?' He peered past her down the corridor.

'What kids?' she answered and shrugged, trying not to let her hesitation show. She opened up her palms. Empty-handed.

Leo stepped inside, and she followed. He didn't touch her at all and already her shield was crumbling. She was such an idiot. But it was then she noticed the voices. Inside the flat. Voices. So very many of them. Oh God.

In the kitchen, a whole lot of twenty-somethings milled together. One girl, the first to catch her eye, was sitting on the counter, her long, tanned legs hanging down like pendulums.

'Guys, this is Allie. A friend of mine.'

'Hey,' the long-legged girl said. 'I'm Jen.'

There were other names, introductions. Alice felt like throwing up. What had she been thinking?

'Drink, Allie?' one of the guys said. Chris, she thought. Was that his name?

'Thanks but no. I've just come to collect a book. Remember, Leo?' Leo looked at her a bit blankly. Usually he was quicker to catch on. 'That book you borrowed?'

Then Leo smiled. 'Oh, yeah right. I've had it for so long I can't even remember what the cover looks like. Come help me. Please?'

They left the kitchen. She could feel the curious eyes stabbing her in the back and she couldn't blame them. It was pretty obvious she didn't belong here. And who were all those people to him? Coltish Jen, for example.

Leo opened the door to his bedroom. It wasn't neat as such, but it looked clean and comfortable. A guy's room. Inside, the beige curtains were still wide open and the dark settling like a blanket over the mountain. The bedside light was on, a laptop open next to the bed, whirring.

Alice shut the door behind her. 'Look,' she said. 'Clearly I should have called.'

Leo smiled. 'You look very pretty.'

'I'm so embarrassed,' she said, undeterred. 'This isn't at all how I pictured this. Just give me a book, any book, and I'll get out of this place. You carry on like I was never here.'

He studied her a moment. 'Yes, I could do that.' But he didn't move.

'Leo, seriously. I'm dying here.'

But Leo stepped a little closer to her. 'You pictured this? What did you picture?'

'Stop it,' she said. 'I'm an idiot.'

But Leo moved even closer, his dark blue eyes deep enough to swim in. He put his arms around her, his hands on her butt, pushing her against him, his hardness undeniable.

'The people,' she said. 'In your kitchen.'

'What people?' he said, guiding her to the door.

A click of the lock.

Then he kissed her so hard that she felt herself slipping.

'Did you picture this?' he said, as he pulled off her skirt, her knickers; his mouth so hot on her that she gasped out loud. His tongue probing, his warm breath on her body. He took off his shirt, his shorts. Undressed them both completely. Guided her down onto the bed. And then he was inside her, on top of her, through her. She'd never felt like this before. Never. The intensity of the sensations, the emotions so overwhelming that she couldn't keep them in. She called out. And Leo just laughed, a laugh of pure joy. And she laughed too. He kissed her, and kissed her. Tongues, and skin, and her body screaming with want for him. She felt like he knew her. Like she knew him. Absolutely. Completely. Her heart was full of him. Her body alive in every cell, every pore.

She didn't want it to end.

She didn't think she could take any more.

And then, miraculously, they didn't have to, as this rollercoaster of sensations and emotions ground to an incredible, unforgettable stop.

Leo rolled off her, grabbed her hand and held it tightly against him. Then he looked at her, and smiled.

'Good book,' he said. 'I'd highly recommend it … I liked the pictures the most.'

And overwhelmed by what she was feeling, Alice began to speak. 'Leo, I–'

Leo put his finger over her lips, shook his head gently. Then he kissed her.

She didn't understand. Did he know what she was going to say? Then why couldn't she say it? Did he feel differently? But she kissed him back, luxuriating in his smooth, beautiful skin against hers. He smiled at her and the emotion in his eyes hadn't changed. He had his reasons. She was going to have to trust him. She *did* trust him.

'So …' Leo said.

She smiled back. 'So.'

'How long do I have you for?'

'I'm supposed to be shopping at Cavendish.'

'Right, and what are you getting there?'

'Trainers. For gym.'

'Okay, and what time does Cavendish close?'

'Seven.' Alice looked at Leo's expression. He was mulling something; that was clear.

'So is there anybody you could "bump into"?' he said. 'Have a drink? Dinner? Someone you trust?'

'Leo Amirante. Are you asking me to find an alibi?'

'I might be. You think I'm just going to let you leave me after this?'

'This?' she raised her eyebrows.

'This,' he confirmed, his hand skating her body, sending flames down her spine.

Suddenly she felt reckless. 'I could ask Gillian. She'll ask questions, though.'

Leo nodded. 'I don't care. I want to pretend tonight that you're just mine. I want to hold your hand and eat pizza and fuck you senseless.'

Alice grinned. 'Pass me my phone. I'm on it.'

***

They emerged from the bedroom several hours later. Alice had felt safe in there, but now it was like breaking free from a cocoon. A hostile world awaited them. Leo threaded his fingers between hers, leading the way. Shame-faced, she followed him into the kitchen, where his friends were louder and drunker than they had been when she arrived.

155

Leo's hand squeezed hers and she wondered if he was nervous too. He'd never seemed particularly perturbed by what other people felt but maybe this was an exception.

'Hey,' one of the guys said with a lascivious grin. 'That must be one helluva book. No wonder Leo hasn't given it back.'

'Great climax?' offered Jen and everyone guffawed.

But Leo just smiled and put his arm around Alice, pulling her close. 'Be nice, people. Remember you're in *my* kitchen, drinking *my* booze.'

'And quite the host you've been too, so attentive,' said Chris. 'Allie, glass of wine? Water – for the dehydration?'

'Actually,' she said. 'I'm more of a whisky drinker. If that's okay with Leo.'

Leo nodded, pointing to the corner cupboard.

'My kind of girl,' said Chris, opening it up and pulling out a bottle of Bell's.

'That's where you're wrong, Chris,' said Leo, kissing her there in front of everybody. 'She's *my* kind of girl.'

Trouble in paradise

Mooching in front of the computer, Bruce contemplated the screen. It wasn't like Alice to go shopping on a Friday evening. Actually, it was damn weird. Obviously, she was avoiding him. He wasn't stupid. He was glad though, that Albert was still asleep. Those pills knocked him for six. The house felt a bit like a mausoleum. A remnant of its former, happier self.

He stood up, grabbed a CBC Amber Weiss from the fridge and twisted off the cap. And feeling peckish, took a tube of Pringles out the pantry. He wouldn't eat them all. Or maybe he would. Right now he was feeling damn sorry for himself. Maybe he could eat himself into happiness. He couldn't go and exercise now. Alice would have his balls if he left the kid alone.

He turned on the DStv hoping to see a replay, and he'd only just sat down when the doorbell rang. Bruce had half a mind to ignore it. In this mood, company would just give him a fucking headache. But he stood up. If it was one of those beggars and they worked out no one was home, he could be in for more drama than he was prepared or equipped to handle.

Looking out, he recognised Martini's car. He sighed. Fucking fabulous. He hadn't seen his friend since he'd crashed over (and crashed), and he wasn't sure he actually wanted to. How could he look him in the eye and pretend it was all fine? There was a lot about himself that he wasn't happy with right now, but he did still have a conscience.

He pushed the buzzer, and Martini drove in under the carport. Whoop! Whoop! The alarm on the vehicle activated.

Martini looked pale. But seeing the beer in Bruce's hand he smiled. 'I'll have one of those.'

'Oh you will, will you?' Bruce commented. 'I think you may have just abused my hospitality a little too much already.'

157

'Oh that,' Martini said. 'Sorry, mate. If it's any consolation, you probably saved my marriage.'

'And you care about that?'

'What the bloody hell do you mean? Don't be a dick, Bruce, just because I didn't kiss you goodbye. I can give you a smooch hello instead, if you like.'

Bruce couldn't help it.

He laughed.

'Alright then,' he said, handing the bottle to his friend. 'I'll pop another. But you're buying the pizza.'

Inside, Bruce had swung the back doors wide open. Despite being the middle of winter, it was surprisingly hot. He was wearing a T-shirt and jeans, and hadn't felt a need for a jersey all day. It was going to be a hot weekend. A heatwave in July. No wonder the dams were so bloody empty.

'Where's Alice?' Martini asked.

'Out.'

Martini frowned a little. 'What's going on, Bruce? Every time I come around your wife is missing. Bit of trouble in paradise?'

'Of course not,' Bruce answered. 'She's buying shoes. Albert's asleep and she doesn't have to worry.'

'Mmmhmm.'

'What?'

'Brucie. You get this little twitch between your eyes when you're lying. You know that, right?'

'So what? We had a little tiff. Nothing insurmountable. That's marriage, isn't it?'

Martini clinked his bottle against Bruce's. 'I can certainly drink to that.'

Just then, Albert emerged. He grimaced as he took the men in. 'Where's Mom?'

'Don't be rude, Albert. Greet Martini.'

Albert looked at Martini and grunted.

'For God's sake, Mister. Shake hands. And look at him. Firm shake, boy.'

Albert moved slowly towards Martini, so slowly that it seemed to Bruce that he was purposely taunting his father. A snail's pace of forward movement.

'For fuck's sake, Albert. Move it. Shake the man's hand.'

Martini glanced at Bruce, a questioning look on his face. 'Chill out, he's just woken up, from the look of him.' He touched Albert on the shoulder. 'Hey boytjie. How are you?'

'Shake, damn it.'

Both Martini and Albert shook, then Albert darted out the room at an inversely proportional speed.

'What's with you, mate? He's a kid. A troubled kid.'

'What the hell would you know about it? It's not like *you* have any.'

Martini winced. 'I came over to make nice. Six years of IVF and that's what you have to say? Fuck you, Louw. I've been a kid, even if I can't have one.'

Bruce felt his face redden. 'Jeez, I'm sorry. It's just been a bit stressful around here.'

Martini gave him a hard look. 'Frankly, Bruce, you're being a real arsehole. Not sure I want to stick around.'

'Oh come on. Let's just get pizza. Alice said she'd be home just after seven. We can even get the little runt his Hawaiian.'

Martini cocked his head. 'Try again, Bruce.'

Bruce corrected himself. 'I'm sure my beloved first-born would love a Hawaiian.'

'See?' Martini said. 'Amazing possibilities when you behave yourself. Now what does Alice like?'

'Something with blue cheese?' Bruce pulled the Butler's menu off the fridge. 'Have a look. I'd prefer something low-carb ... um ... please?'

Martini began to chortle. 'Fine.'

Bruce's phone buzzed in his pocket. He checked the screen. 'Alice,' he told Martini. 'Hey, babe,' he said, speaking into the phone.

Alice sounded upbeat. 'You're on your own tonight, Bruce,' she said. 'Is that okay? I've bumped into Gillian and she's suggested a girls' night. It's not like we had plans or anything.'

'Martini's here,' Bruce said.

'Oh, good. Enjoy yourself and don't forget that you have to order the Hawaiian without the ham. For Albert. Is he awake?'

'Yes.'

'Well tell him I love him. Don't wait up. Not sure how late Gill and I are going to be.'

Bruce ended the call. 'Fancy another beer, dude? It's boys only tonight. And the sprog doesn't eat the ham on a Hawaiian, so help me God.'

***

Later, they sat on the stoep. Albert had emerged only to eat his food, shoving it in like a messy gorilla, the sauce running down his face in rivulets. His T-shirt the flood plain. Bruce found it hard to watch but mindful of his manners, and Martini's disdain, restrained himself. Apart from handing the kid a serviette. Three times.

Martini ate very little. Despite his physical presence, he didn't seem entirely there, his distraction increasing markedly as the beer went down. Martini was generally not a belligerent drunk. He was much more likely to get soppy; sometimes he'd even cry. It had been a source of extreme mirth to all their mates for years. But tonight he was quiet rather than tearful.

'What's the plan for the weekend?' Bruce asked eventually, as their usual light banter dissipated.

'Leaving in the morning for Elgin. Elaine left at lunch. I would have gone but I had a meeting and I can't be asked to go through that afternoon traffic.'

'I get that.'

'Anyway, Elaine likes the time alone. She'll do an early-morning ride. By the time I get in we'll both be ready for brunch.'

Bruce nodded.

Then Martini's posture changed. 'We need to talk a little shop,' he said. 'Have you confirmed with Hing and Nyembe?'

'You know I did. Jesus, Martini. You know I was being cautious. A smaller order first, to check the quality. I've ordered everything else now. You know that. I told you the taps were great.'

'Of course they bloody were. I vouched for them, didn't I? Anyway, a two-step process is going to slow everything down. It already is, isn't it?'

'No, I don't think so. Expecting the delivery soon. Told me two weeks or so.'

'Okay.'

'Why?' Bruce said, suddenly concerned. 'Is there something I need to know?' (Apart from the fact, he thought, that you murdered your girlfriend drunk driving? It hung between them, unspoken, but to Bruce, almost tangible.)

'Well, not really. It's just that—'

'Just that what?'

'There may be a few delays. Some family issues. Nyembe, you know?'

'What have family issues got to do with it?'

'You may need to go down to the port and clear some of the stuff. The cargo.'

'Why the hell would I do that? It's a door-to-door delivery. I thought that's what we were paying for?'

'Most of its taken care of. Thought I should mention there might be a delay. It just seems Nyembe's lost a sister or something. Car crash.'

Bruce felt a chill running through him. *What the fuck was going on?*
'Dude. There's more to this than you're telling me.'

160

'No, I'm just saying.'

'Who's the sister?' Bruce asked, already knowing.

Martini shrugged. 'Don't know. Just cut the guy some slack, is what I mean.'

'You're sending mixed messages, Martini. One moment we're in a big fucking hurry and now I must chill? What about Hing?'

'What do you mean?'

'Can't I just deal with him?'

Martini sighed. 'He's in China, dude, that's where he lives after all. And China is one massive bloody country.'

The pissing contest

He woke, stretching across the bed. The sounds of hadedas calling outside seemed too loud. Jarring. Alice had left as late as she could get away with. Almost midnight. By that time, some of his friends had peeled away. Night clubs. Home. Ubering into town to see other mates. They'd urged him on too but he wasn't having any of that. He was very happy where he was, with Alice. But now he was awake and she was gone and despite himself he was filled with an overwhelming feeling of loss. The pillows smelt of her but it wasn't enough. He missed her physically. Like his heart had been hacked out with a screwdriver. Jagged and rough. He wanted to talk to her, to hear her voice. But it was so early and how would he get away with calling? If Bruce answered, what then?

He pulled on his T-shirt from the night before.

Coffee. That would help somewhat but as he passed through the lounge to the kitchen, he realised there were two bodies sprawled on the couches. He found himself irritated. *Why were they still here?* He wanted Alice, not this useless lot.

Chris stirred as Leo turned on the grinder. Jen seemed passed out cold.

'Christ, Amirante. Are you drilling a borehole? My brain feels like it doesn't fit in my skull.'

'I need coffee,' Leo replied.

Chris sat up. 'You need your head read, is what you need, mate.'

Leo looked at his friend. 'And why would that be?'

'Jeez. She's hot and all. But she's married, isn't she? You into cougars now?'

Leo grimaced, extracted an espresso cup from the shelf. A pure shot of caffeine might help. Better than rage.

On the couch, Chris looked pained. Clearly Leo's anger had registered. As he stood up, his blanket fell onto the floor, exposing his bare legs.

162

Among other things. 'I was going to offer you a coffee,' Leo said. 'But after that comment, you can just pull on your pants and leave. Come on. You slept like that on my couch?'

Chris looked down, his dick hanging down from under his T-shirt. 'Oh, this.' He shrugged. 'Just needed to hang loose.'

'On my couch?'

Chris shrugged. 'Oh please. You're offended now?'

Leo gulped down the hot liquid. 'Seriously. You can wear or not wear what you like. But not on my couch.'

'Sure. Whatever.' Chris pulled on his clothes. 'You *pomp* some married chick and I'm offsides?'

Jen stirred on her sofa. She groaned. 'Guys. Stop the bloody pissing contest. It's too early.'

Chris sighed. 'Well, you're a woman.'

'Thanks for noticing.'

'Then what do you think?' Chris continued.

'I liked her. She seemed cool.'

'I didn't ask what you thought of her sparkling personality. She's *married*. And *old*.'

Jen threw her duvet off her. Leo thought she looked a lot better in her T-shirt than Chris did. But she was clearly wearing knickers, the line visible. 'Hey, Chris,' she said. 'This is Serious Leo we're talking about. This is the most adventurous he's ever been and you're ruining his vibe.'

'Thanks, I think,' said Leo.

Jen shrugged. 'I saw the way you looked at her, dude.'

'And how was that?'

'You're in luuuurvve.' Jen smiled in her most annoying way and Leo's head began to pound. He looked away, saying nothing. Removed a box from the top kitchen cupboard. The foil wrapping inside rustled.

'So it's true then?' Jen persisted.

Leo opened Rascal's cage and pulled out the rat to pet her against his chest. The little animal nuzzled into his hand, where he was holding a small dog biscuit. The rat was strangely calming, therapeutic. But he still had the jitters.

'When are you both leaving?' he said. 'I have work to do.'

'On a *Saturday*?' Chris replied, pulling on a discarded pair of shorts.

'Oh come on, Leo,' Jen said. 'You've got to expect a bit of ribbing. That's what friends do, right? And you weren't exactly subtle about her last night.'

Leo clicked under his tongue, his pet rat dancing down his outstretched arm. 'Can you both just go? I don't like you making light of a situation that's really serious to me.'

Jen sighed. 'Yes, Leo, we can see that. But I guess what Chris is trying to do is protect you. Situations like these blow. However great Allie is.'

'I know what I'm doing.'

'Really?' Chris replied. 'Breaking up a family?'

'Honestly, Chris,' Leo said. 'That family is already long broken. And it's none of your freaking business anyway.'

Chris grimaced, then shrugged. 'Jen, let's go get breakfast at La Belle. Leave him to his wallowing. And home wrecking.'

Jen pulled on her jeans, kissed Leo on the cheek. 'Ignore him,' she whispered. Then, louder. 'We're leaving. Don't forget about us minions on your way to the top.'

When they had finally departed, Leo reached for his phone. He scrolled down for Alice's number and called.

She answered almost immediately. 'Hey.'

'Hey yourself, can you talk?'

There was a slight rumbling in the background. 'Give me a second. I'm going to go outside. Albert is making a horrible noise.'

Leo could hear her footsteps, a sliding door opening. His stomach roiled.

'Hi,' she said again. 'I'm so glad you phoned.' A silence floated between them like a cloud. '... Leo?'

'I love you, Allie,' Leo said, finally. It isn't what he'd expected to say, especially as he couldn't see her expression. But in her response, he could hear she was smiling.

'I love you too.'

'I guess this leaves us in a bit of a predicament,' he said.

'Yes.'

'Can you slip out today?'

'Oh God, I want to. But Albert is hyper this morning. There's no telling what he'll do. And you know Bruce. He's out on some run with Enjoy. But I don't know when he'll be back.'

'Then can I come there, to you? Help you with Albert?'

'I wish. If Bruce sees you on a Saturday two weekends in a row ...'

'I know. I know.'

'I miss you,' Alice said. 'Last night was pretty amazing.'

'Pretty?' he teased.

'Mr Amirante, are you fishing for compliments?'

'Hey, I don't get to see you all day. Especially like *that*.'

Alice laughed softly. 'The beach tomorrow morning? Muizenberg? Nine? But I'll have to bring the kids.'

'Yes.'

'Yes?'

164

'I'll be there.'

The beach

When Alice woke, Bruce was already gone. Running again. Or surfing. Whatever. And then he was checking the building site. She called to Enjoy and Albert, her heart too big for her chest.

'Let's do something fun, guys. Beach. Ice creams. Boogie boards.'

'Yay!' said Albert, air-punching.

'Can I wear my new bikini?' asked Enjoy.

'Of course. Get yourselves into your cozzies and I'll spray you both with sunscreen before we get in the car so it can dry properly.'

The kids dashed to their bedrooms. Going to the beach wasn't a common occasion, despite living so close to the sea. Bruce wasn't a huge fan of the sand, unless he was running on it. And lately, they'd worried about Albert and what he might get up to. Whom he could hurt.

Alice packed a cooler bag of soft drinks, a few packets of Fritos, some apples and drinking yoghurts. Some extra meds for Albert in the side pocket. There were two large bottles of water she also slipped into the bag. At first when Gillian had asked if she could come along, Alice had been resistant. But then the thought that Gill might be able to watch the kids while she and Leo talked alone was enough to change her mind. Besides, interaction between Albert and Joshua would be good for him. Enjoy and Gillian's son Rhys weren't exactly friends, but they got on well enough. Truthfully, Enjoy got on with everyone. Except maybe her own brother. And that wasn't really entirely her fault.

The parking at Muizenberg was almost full already by the time they arrived. Alice slung the cooler bag over her shoulder and carried the umbrella under her arm. The kids held the towels and a beach chair each – they only had two. They were near the beach huts when Gillian waved at them, having staked a spot against the wall along the path.

'Hello babe!' Gillian said.

166

Alice hugged her, her eyes scanning the beach over her friend's shoulder. But Leo was nowhere to be seen. Josh and Albert eyed each other, almost suspiciously.

'What's with them?' Alice whispered to Gill.

She shrugged. 'You know tweens. One day they're friends, the next they're not talking. Not our problem. Chuck them in the ocean; they'll be fine.'

'Enjoy, Rhys?' Alice said. 'You reckon you could build a sand castle?'

'Mom! We're a bit old for that,' Enjoy said. 'We're going to collect shells, aren't we Rhys?'

He nodded uncertainly. 'We have buckets?'

'And you two,' Gillian said to the older boys. 'Take the boogie boards. Go and swim. The mommies need some adult time.'

The boys scarpered.

'Alone at last,' Gillian said. 'Now dish!'

Alice laughed, and shook out her towel. She opened up her beach chair to sit. But then just as she was about to speak her eyes settled beyond Gill down the beach. Gillian turned, following the direction of Alice's gaze.

'That's him? That guy over there? Oh my God. If he shags as good as he looks, I'm surprised you *ever* left his bed.'

Seal of approval

As Alice turned and saw him, her face lit up with such happiness that he had to resist the urge to run to her. She was wearing a blue bikini, a sarong tied around her waist. Alice walked towards him, barefoot and limber and pulled him into a long hug.

'Fancy meeting you here,' she whispered. 'Let me introduce you to Gillian.'

Leo hadn't been happy about Gillian joining them, but he remembered that Allie had put up with his reprobate friends for a long evening. He was going to have to meet hers, reprobate or otherwise.

Gillian eyed him over her sunglasses. She stood up, approached him.

'So,' she said, rather aggressively. 'You're *The Lover*.'

He smiled disarmingly. 'I guess that makes you *The Alibi*,' he said. 'So, thank you. We made *very* good use of the time.'

She grinned. Glanced at Alice. 'I like him. Quick on the draw.'

Alice laughed. 'I like him too. A whole damn lot.'

But then Gillian pushed her face right close to his. He flinched, stepping a little back from her coffee breath. 'But listen here, matey,' she said. 'Don't think you can charm the pants off *me*. You hurt my friend and I will use tweezers to rip out your pubes, one hair at a time. Are we totally clear?'

Alice shrieked. 'Gillian – what the heck?'

But Leo just nodded seriously. 'Crystal. But it's not going to happen.' He glanced at Allie. Shrugged. 'I'm mad about her.'

Gillian's shoulders relaxed. 'Well, now. Since we've cleared that up, Alice will give you my number. If you guys need help. I'm here. I have to say this is the first time I've seen Alice happy like this in literally years. So you have my seal of approval. For whatever that's worth. Have a seat, Lover Boy.'

Alice smacked her friend lightly on the shoulder. 'Can you stop calling him that, please?'

'Why? Am I embarrassing you?'

'A bit. Besides, the kids could arrive at any second.'

Leo looked around. 'Where are they?'

Gillian gestured vaguely towards the water. 'Blue and orange boogie boards. And the rock pools. I might actually go and have a quick wander down there and check on them. I might even also dip a toe in. I could be gone with the kids for say, twenty minutes?' She picked up her towel off the back of the chair. 'Behave yourselves, children. This is a public beach.'

Gillian strode down the beach, her pony tail flopping like rope behind her.

'I'm a little scared of her,' Leo admitted to Alice, watching her leave. 'She almost has bigger biceps than I do.'

'No chance of that,' Alice said, running her hand lightly down his exposed arm, tracing the curve of his tattoo. 'But she does have a good left hook.'

Leo grabbed her fingers between his. 'You'd better keep your hands off me. I'm horny just sitting next to you.'

'I'm not sure I can.'

'Good, I was hoping you'd say that,' he said, springing up and pulling her by her hand to her feet. 'Let's go,' he said.

'Where are you taking me?'

'We're going to be teenagers and make out in my car.'

'Leo! You're joking, right?'

'Oh, I never joke about making out in cars. It's a very, very serious subject.'

The world off her shoulders

They emerged flushed and a little dishevelled. Alice combed her fingers through her hair, feeling the warm thud of where they'd joined together. Her legs were unsteady from the shaking.

Leo studied her, his eyes twinkling. 'That might have been a little more advanced than mere teenagers,' he said.

'I don't know so much. Teenagers these days seem pretty advanced,' she said. 'But not sure they could achieve all that in twenty minutes. They procrastinate too much.'

He laughed. 'Skills,' he said. 'Put to good use.'

'Exactly.'

They walked together towards the beach, and Alice held her hands interlocked in front of her in an effort not to touch him. She was lucky for the attempt because just as they stepped onto the path near the playground, she heard her name being called behind her.

She turned, her heart sinking.

'Oh Alice,' the woman said. 'I thought it was you! You here with the family?'

Of all the people to meet, it had to be Charlotte's mom, Nadia, who was unable to keep her mouth shut on even the most minor of secrets.

'What a morning!' Alice said evenly. 'First I bump into Albert's tutor, Leo. And now you. Must be the gorgeous weather. In winter! Leo, this is Nadia. Her daughter's in Enjoy's class. Charlotte?'

Leo, to his credit, kept his expression just as neutral. 'Nice to meet you.'

'Where are you sitting?' Nadia asked.

'Oh, I'm here with Gillian and her kids. Bruce is working today.'

'You're working today too then, Leo? Filling in?' Nadia asked.

'Oh no! I came for a run, and then I spotted Alice. Came over to see if my buddy was with her. But he was in the water.'

'And how's he doing?' Nadia asked leaning forward, her ears and nose almost twitching. 'Albert? Any funny turns? Incidents?'

'He's fine,' Alice said firmly. 'Isn't he, Leo?'

Leo looked over at Nadia, his nose wrinkling a little. 'Fabulous kid,' he said. 'Doing brilliantly.'

'But what about the, you know, depression? Odd behaviour. Charlotte says the kids were talking at school. Apparently he's on all these medications. And last time I saw him, well, he was looking a little, how do I put it? Chunky? Around the face?'

Alice bit down on her lip. Hard enough to bleed.

Leo glared at Nadia. 'Wow. And that's how you choose to say it? Gosh, imagine if you'd actually been *trying* to be insulting!'

'Oh I didn't mean–'

'Actually,' Leo said. 'I think you did. But what do I know? I'm just the tutor.'

There was an icy silence.

'I was going to get a coffee,' Leo said to Alice at last. 'Can I bring you and Gillian one? And maybe some ice creams for the fat kids in the sea?'

'Goodness!' said Nadia.

Alice smiled. 'Are you sure? You're not on your way home?'

'I haven't seen Albert yet. He plays a mean game of beach bats. And you know how he needs the exercise. Can't let the side down, don't you think … Nadia, wasn't it?'

And with that he strode away, leaving the women dumbstruck behind him.

***

When Alice got back to her beach chair, Gillian was lounging in her own, her face shaded by a huge sunhat with the top cut off. Her hair cascaded out over the edges, giving her a wild look.

'Oh,' she said. 'You're back from wherever you disappeared to.'

'I am.'

'My God. You're grinning like a Cheshire cat.' Gillian looked Alice up and down. 'You didn't, did you? Here?'

Alice couldn't keep her face straight. 'We totally did. The earth may still be moving.'

Gillian sighed. 'Oh my God. I'm so jealous. And where's he now? Hug and roll?'

'Shhh. Keep your voice down. Bloody Nadia is sniffing about. She and Leo just met. They may not be on the best of terms.'

Gillian crowed as Alice recounted the scene. 'Serve her right. Babe, he's a gem.'

'He is. *And* the gem is bringing us coffee.'

Just then Albert and Joshua arrived, dragging their boogie boards behind them. Their lips were quivering, almost blue. Both mothers got up, wrapping their boys in thick beach towels.

'How was it?' Alice asked. 'You were in there for ages.'

'Rad. But cold. Even with the wet suit,' Albert said. 'Unzip me, Mom.'

'Please.'

'Yes, yes.' Albert turned and Alice ripped open the Velcro, then began to tug on the zipper pull. She yanked harder but the wet neoprene was sticking fast to him.

'Need help?' said a voice.

'Leo!' Albert beamed. 'What are you doing here? Mom! Leo's here!'

'I know! We found each other on the beach while you guys were in the ocean.'

Leo approached, carrying two takeaway trays. 'Let me put these drinks down. I got you hot chocolate, just the way you like it. Hope Josh drinks it too? Allie, the coffee on the left is yours. Gillian, I didn't know if you took sugar.'

'Damn right. Thanks.'

'And here are the two extra hot chocolates for the other two kids.'

Gillian smiled. 'That's really generous of you, Leo. Can we chip in?'

'My shout.' Leo then helped Alice pull on Albert's wetsuit. 'Dude, you're getting a little tall for this. You only just fit.'

'I know,' Albert said proudly. 'I've grown like five centimetres!'

'Looking good, buddy.'

Standing in his board shorts, Albert was beaming. 'Did you know we were going to be here?'

'No,' Leo lied. 'But best surprise all day.'

Albert smiled broadly. 'Really? You mean it? Want to play a game?'

'I'd love it. But let's give you your ten o'clocks first so I can keep up with you. Alice, are they in your cooler bag?'

And Alice nodded, feeling her heart swell. She was almost sure that Bruce didn't even know that Albert took *any* medication mid-morning and certainly not the exact time he took it.

As Leo popped the pills into her son's mouth and passed Albert his hot chocolate to slug them down, she didn't feel nearly as responsible or alone. For once, the world was being moved from her shoulders.

Paling in comparison

Leo put the last of Alice and the kids' stuff into her car. Albert and Enjoy were already strapped in and Alice stood next to him at the boot.

'It's been the best morning,' she said to him.

'Especially the first bit,' he said.

She reddened, a shy smile creeping onto her face. 'Yes, those coffees were really hot and steamy.'

'Scalding,' he added, as he tucked a strand of her hair behind her ears.

'Mom!' Enjoy whined. 'My feet are itchy from the sand. When are we leaving?'

'Coming!' she called.

'But we're not even doing anything,' he said softly.

'More's the pity.' They looked at each other, unable to tear themselves away. 'I wish we could stay here all day,' Alice said.

'Me too. Real life sucks. I'm all grown up but if I don't go to this family lunch, my mother will have my hide.'

'You'd better get going then,' she said, then added in a whisper, 'because I *really, really* like your hide.'

His stomach bucked. 'Don't get me started, Allie, it's hard enough to leave as it is.' He took her hands and held them to his chest, wanting so badly to kiss her. Then he let her go, and walked to the passenger door. 'Cheers kids. See you tomorrow, Albert. Thanks for the game.'

'Bye!'

When he got into his own car, he thought about Alice straddling him in the back seat only a few hours before. He was in serious trouble, unable to focus on anything but her. As he put his keys into the ignition, his phone buzzed. He checked the screen.

Miss you already.

He smiled. Texted her back. Miss u too.

Later?

I'll call you after family onslaught.

You'd better.

As he exited the car park, he could see her Audi pulling ahead, Albert's head leaning against the glass of the passenger window. Poor kid. He'd sleep for hours now. And all Leo had to endure was his four sisters, their husbands, boyfriends and respective broods and his mother checking on whether he'd eaten or not. If he was very lucky, they might not quiz him on his relationship status and why he hadn't met anyone 'as nice as Hailey' yet.

Because he had. And Hailey paled in comparison.

He just couldn't tell them about Alice. As much as she dominated his every waking thought.

Okay?

'Where've you all been?' he asked as Alice opened her car door.

'Didn't you see the note I left on the fridge? We met Gillian and the kids at Muizenberg.'

'Oh, I did. But I thought you must have gone on somewhere else, you were gone so long.'

'We were having fun. Sorry. Lost track of time a bit.' Alice, he noticed, looked anything but sorry, but maybe he was projecting. He was a grumpy sod these days.

'And Albert?'

'Exhausted. Passed out, as you see.'

'I'll carry him to his bedroom.' Alice blinked as though surprised but held the door open so he could reach in and unclip his son. He looked so angelic asleep and Bruce felt a slight twinge of guilt at how hard he was on him. He glanced at Alice, who smiled.

'It was a good morning for him, Bruce. He and Josh swam until they were shivering. It felt like the old days.'

'I'm sorry I wasn't there,' he said, meaning it. 'It would be so much better to see him happy.'

She nodded, stepping aside as he lifted him. Bruce carried Albert down the passage. The kid was a deadweight, his feet covered in sand. So instead of putting him in the bed, he lay him on top and covered him with one of the dry beach towels. Albert snorted slightly, rolled over and lay on his side, his back to Bruce. It wasn't intentional, of course, the kid was half-comatose, but Bruce still felt slighted. And this, he knew, was ridiculous.

In the kitchen, Alice was checking her phone. She jumped when he came in, and shoved the phone in her bag.

'Secret lover?' he joked.

'Absolutely,' she said, deadpan. 'I have so much free time. And energy. Want some lunch?'

Bruce nodded and Alice pulled out some cheese and cold meats. 'We can do a hot dinner tonight,' she said. 'It's a bit late now.'

Alice was almost military in how she pulled the lunch together. Enjoy wolfed hers down in the kitchen and disappeared to her bedroom to read a book. Alice and Bruce sat on the patio but Alice didn't say much.

'You seem tired,' Bruce said, finally.

'Yes.'

'And how's Gill?'

'Fine.'

'She seeing anyone at the moment?'

'You know Gill. Always someone on the scene. I think he's a doctor or a vet? Something medical anyway. Can't keep up.'

Bruce leant forward, cupping Alice's hand with his own. 'Are we okay, Alice?'

'What do you mean?'

'It's just that lately we just keep snapping at each other. We don't laugh together. We don't spend time. It's been more than three weeks since we've had sex. I miss you.'

'You miss the sex? Or me, specifically?'

'Both. It's the same thing, isn't it?'

'Is it?' Alice looked distant. 'I don't feel much like it these days. There's too much pressure on me. But sometimes I just feel that, well, that you just go about your life the way you always did.'

'But I don't.'

'Really?'

Bruce tried to keep his irritation in check. 'I'm working my arse off, Alice. To pay for all the bills and the pills.'

'And I'm not working too?'

'I didn't say that.'

'Yes, but working and being emotionally supportive are two very different things. I feel so alone in this parenting thing. And every day you make it harder. You don't even *try* to understand Albert. What he's going through.'

'That's fucking bollocks.'

'I don't think so, actually. I'm the family glue and you just bounce around like nothing's changed.'

'I just told you I think things have changed.'

'So what? You act like you're doing me a favour when you watch the kids. It's not babysitting. It's parenting.' Alice sighed. 'You know what?

I'm tired. I don't feel like this. I'm going to lie on my bed, read a book and go to sleep.'

Bruce grabbed Alice's hand. 'Alice,' he said earnestly, 'It's you I miss. Don't go. Please. I'm asking you to stay here with me.'

But Alice extracted her fingers. 'See you later, Bruce,' she said, and walked back into the house.

Family trees

She was sitting at her desk when there was a knock and the door opened.

'Hey,' Leo said.

She turned away from her CAD drawings. 'Hey yourself. What's up?'

Leo ran his fingers through his hair. He looked nervous and Alice felt her heart constrict. This was it. He was bound to realise it eventually. She'd hoped for longer, but maybe she'd just been lucky to have him for the short time she had. She was, after all, the one who'd warned him off in the first place.

'Everything okay?' she said, gently prompting him.

He nodded. 'Albert's working on a comprehension test. I wondered if we could talk.'

Alice nodded, swallowing down the tears that were already building. Leo closed the door gently and sat down opposite her.

'I was thinking,' he said, then stopped, cleared his throat. 'I was thinking that maybe I could cook you dinner. I know we can't really be seen in public but I'd really like it if we could have a proper date. I mean, I know it's quite difficult for you–'

'I'd love to,' Alice said.

'Yes?'

Alice laughed, relieved. 'Of course yes. I thought you were about to finish with me.'

Leo looked confused. 'Finish? I'm crazy about you. If anyone's finishing anything I'm sorry but it's going to have to be you.'

Alice looked at Leo, stood up and kissed him. 'All this sneaking about isn't good for you. Or me for that matter.'

He smiled. 'It does add a certain element of unanticipated excitement.'

'And nerves.'

'That too.'

They stood against each other, silent. Contemplating.

'Leo! I'm done!' Albert called from his room.

'On my way, buddy!' Leo replied. 'So I don't know what night is best for you but I was thinking Thursday or Friday?'

'Thursday? Seven?' Alice said, wiping the lipstick from the corner of Leo's mouth.

'Sold.' Leo trailed his finger down her cheek. 'I can't wait to have you all to myself again.'

***

When Enjoy came home from school, she hung up her backpack and pulled out her homework diary. Then she threw herself down on the couch.

'We have to do a family tree,' she said, squinting. 'With photos and everything. Or drawings. But how does that even work when you're adopted?'

Alice saw Enjoy's expression and sat down. 'Well, darling. You're my daughter. So my family tree is your family tree. I think it probably works the same as for anyone else in your class.'

Enjoy scowled. 'That's not what the other girls say. They say a family tree is all about blood connections. So I am, like, a total reject. They said I can only put *myself* on mine.'

Alice bit her tongue, trying not to let her fury show. Little bitches. She put her arms around Enjoy. 'Come with me, I want to show you something.'

Enjoy followed Alice to the bookshelf. There was a collection of photograph albums, all lined up by year. She opened the first one, closed it again. Wedding photos. Then she found the album she was looking for.

'You won't remember much about your bio-mom, Enjoy, but we've never kept her a secret from you. Abigail came to work with us just before Albert was born. So she was like Albert's second mom. She didn't know it at the time but she was already pregnant with you.' Alice flipped through, page after page, until she found Albert strapped to Abigail's back. 'See, here she is.'

Enjoy traced her mother's outline. Her expression was tearful but also wide-eyed. Aware.

'You were born when Albert was six months old, and after she'd recovered from the birth, Abigail asked us if she could come back to work. Your bio-dad, you see, had let her down. Unlike your birth mom, he wasn't a very good person. I heard he took a job in Johannesburg but at the time we didn't know for sure. It was like he'd completely disappeared.

179

'Anyway, we didn't want Abigail travelling back and forth on a taxi with a tiny baby, so we invited her to move in with us. See this photo here? The two of you, the day you moved in? We weren't in the same house as now, of course. After the accident, you know, when your mom fell from the attic, I didn't want to live there anymore. And look, here's you and Albert with Abigail. Look at those smiles. How happy we all were. And weren't you a cutie?'

Enjoy smiled.

'Look at this one.' Alice pointed a photo of Albert cuddling Enjoy, a blissful expression on both of their faces. 'You used to calm him down, even then. He adored you.'

Enjoy studied the photo, her face unreadable. She moved the album closer to her, pulling it protectively to her.

'So I guess what I'm telling you, darling, is that you don't just have one family tree, you have two. And that's what we'll make for you. I bet if we look on Pinterest we'll find all sorts of cool ideas to shut up those awful little cows you go to school with.'

Enjoy laughed aloud. She put her arms around Alice's neck and hugged her so hard that she almost squeezed out Alice's breath. The album tumbled to the floor. 'You're the best.'

Alice kissed her daughter on her head. 'I'm so glad you think so, because actually I think the same about you.'

Later when Enjoy was settled at the dining room table with glue, and scissors and printed photos of Abigail, Alice went through Enjoy's adoption file. She found as many names as she could. Enjoy's dad, whom they'd managed to track and who'd been willing to sign away responsibility on the day he was contacted. Abigail's parents and their wedding photo, which Abigail had always had in a frame next to her bed. Of course, she'd seen all these things before, but now their existence had more significance than ever before. Perhaps, one day, they would have to go to the Northern Cape and trace Enjoy's roots. But only if she wanted to. Alice didn't want to force anything. And Abigail's parents had died not long after her, so she wasn't sure there were many roots left. A few radicles perhaps.

As Alice packed away the albums she'd scanned, she realised a photo had fallen from one of them and leant down to pick it up from its place under the couch. She turned it over and her heart swelled like a balloon, then burst. A very young Alice and Bruce stared back at her. They were both wearing swimming costumes standing on a beach somewhere.

But it wasn't really just 'somewhere' for Alice. She recalled that day precisely. Bruce had just passed his driver's licence and had driven them both along the coast to Llandudno. It was the first time ever they'd sat side

180

by side in the front of a car, and Alice's parents weren't at all convinced about the 'long' drive for a new driver. Alice's dad had made Bruce chauffeur him around the neighbourhood for half an hour before he would even let her step in the car with her boyfriend. But when they'd finally departed – the freedom! They'd rolled down the windows of the Opel Kadett and blasted Hootie and the Blowfish. It was like their lives had just started. In love. Independent. A little indecent. They'd necked on the beach. Drunk beer. Eaten fish and chips. They'd watched the sun descend, then bleed orange and scarlet into the night. The sky was corrugated with clouds and the evening had been perfect. No wind. Balmy. And when it had finally started to get a bit chilly, they'd wrapped their beach towels around their shoulders and enjoyed the dark, pierced by only the minimum of stars. And Bruce had told her he loved her and she had felt the same. She'd thought then that things could never change because they were, then, perfect together.

It hurt to think of it.

She hadn't realised that nostalgia could be so painful.

What's really *going on*

It had been a week and a half since Martini's accident. Lebogang's funeral, he'd heard, had happened quickly. Lots of celeb pics and various pieces online about her tragic but stellar career. Though he'd never known her, or even spoken to her, Bruce kept on focusing on the image of her elegant ankle twisting in her expensive shoes. The broken heel. Martini helping her into the car.

A life cut short. And for what. More champagne?

That snapping shoe seemed to be symbolic of everything in his life currently. Although perhaps that wasn't quite true. His life was like a slow unravelling. A running shoe gradually worn away over time rather than a ruined stiletto.

Martini had left the issue of getting the tanks and everything else he'd ordered from Hing and Nyembe in his court. Nyembe hadn't answered any calls. Bruce knew why not, but the job site was standing idle. Time was money. Anyone knew that.

Why Martini wasn't participating in his side of the deal was also not a big surprise. He was in mourning. And in guilt. His skin had taken on a lifeless pallor, his hair looked greasy and when they tried to pay squash, his attention span was so short, Martini reminded him of Albert. Even worse was that Martini couldn't admit to anything. It must have been tough. Bruce's limited empathy could identify that.

'You left your game at home today,' Bruce tried to joke him back into the spirit of things.

'And you left your manners.' Martini picked up his ball. Smacked it hard, and narrowly missed hitting Bruce in the head.

It wasn't easy to control himself but instead of flying off the handle, Bruce simply picked up his racquet case and started to pack up.

'I'm off,' he said. 'Before I lose an eye. I'm going for a run tomorrow morning. Leaving from Chapman's Peak at six. Come, don't come. In the meantime, why don't you hit a few balls on your own. You seem to need the practice.' He ducked before he got a clout over the head.

And then when they set off on their run the next day, they didn't talk. A grunt of acknowledgement. A nod up the hill towards the lakes. Enjoy, as always, sprung ahead, keeping them within eyesight, as per their agreement. Malawi was with her, diving into the bushes to roll in shit and chew on old branches. Bruce and Martini were evenly matched, the dull thud-thud of their tackies in the dust. But this time, Martini seemed to be trying to separate from him, his arms like rotors. He was sweating profusely, clutching at his side every so often like he was trying to hold in his intestines.

'Struggling, mate?' Bruce asked, a little concerned.

'Fuck off. Just keep going,' Martini said but then stopped, puffing so hard Bruce thought he might explode.

Bruce slowed. 'You know, Martini. You may as well tell me what's really going on. You haven't been yourself since the night you stayed over.'

'Nothing to tell.'

'I know about Lebogang,' Bruce said, trying to sound reassuring.

'Who?' But the micropause before the answer was a dead giveaway.

'Lebogang. The model you were shagging.'

'I've no idea what you're talking about.' And with that Martini picked up the pace. Bruce wondered then if he might be sending a helicopter up the mountain to rescue Martini when his heart gave in. It certainly looked a possibility.

***

They made it back to the cars without incident. Enjoy's shirt was wet through, but she was smiling triumphantly, leaning against the car as she stretched. Malawi's tongue was hanging out and she lay in a patch of grass, eyeing him expectantly.

'Let's have a greasy fry-up at mine,' said Bruce, trying to cajole Martini into a different mood. 'Start the day right. It's still really early.'

'Alright,' Martini nodded.

When they got to the house, Leo's Honda Civic was parked in the street, the door to Albert's bedroom closed, Bruce knew better than to disturb class. Albert needed a very specific routine and if Bruce were to disturb it by coming in, God help him. Who knew what behaviour it could trigger? He just wasn't strong enough for that.

Instead he watched his daughter disappear down the passage.

'Enjoy?' he shouted.

She turned.

'You eating?'

'No time, Dad, I'll just grab a health bar or I'll be late for school.'

'You need me to take you?'

'Nah. I'll take my bike.'

'It's just us, then,' Bruce commented to his friend, knowing that Alice would be at the gym like she always was at this time.

Martini shrugged. He walked to the cupboard and pulled out two tall glasses, and filled them with cold water. Once he'd handed one over, he slugged his down in what seem like two gulps. Bruce busied himself at the stove. Actually, he was pretty shit at cooking. Last time he'd made breakfast, he'd burnt the toast. And the eggs had had a brown tinge to them. But everything tasted okay. The way Alice had been acting lately he'd had to supply himself with several meals – something he'd rarely done previously. He could only get better with breakfast. He took some bacon out the freezer, cut up some tomatoes.

'Want to make the coffee, so long?' he asked Martini.

'Alright.'

Ten minutes later, Enjoy was out the door, her backpack already strung over one shoulder. He could hear her bike being wheeled down the drive, the side gate slamming hard shut behind her.

Sliding the only slightly overdone eggs and crisp bacon onto two plates, he handed Martini his portion. They ate quietly. The silence was so loud, it made him shift. Finally, when nothing had been said for five minutes, he capitulated.

'Listen, Martini. Unfortunately for you, mate, I know the truth about this chick of yours. This Lebogang. The night you were at the Toad, the night she died, I was at the Toad too. I saw you there. I saw her yellow Ferrari. I saw you get into it.'

Martini forked his egg around his plate, but it was clear that the colour had drained from his face.

'Is that so?' he said.

'Yes, it is bloody so. How else would I know that as she was walking to the car, she snapped the heel of her shoe?'

Martini didn't say anything. He chewed on his bacon. Bit into his toast. Crunch, crunching, the only conversation between them.

It felt like a minute before Martini spoke again.

'And what if I said to you, *mate*, that every now and then I have a little flashback to 2009? You remember don't you? Alice and Albert in Edinburgh … A little home entertainment.'

This time it was Bruce who felt himself shrink inside. But he braved it out, stared at Martini. 'You fucking shit. Don't make this about me. Or then. That was a simple shag. Nothing more. Nothing less. You were driving the car that killed that girl and you and I both know it.'

'Do we? Do we know it? I don't know anything about that. I took an Uber. I have the receipt.'

For a moment, Bruce hesitated. That couldn't be right. But he looked at his friend. He hadn't got to where he was without a little deviance, a little bending of the rules. That he knew for sure.

'For Christ's sake, Martini. Why don't you just admit the truth? I'm your friend. Or I thought I was. Yet all you've done over the last few weeks is lie. I know you're upset. I saw you in the bathroom that night, after … after it happened. What I don't understand is why you don't let me help you.'

'You can't help me, Bruce. There's nothing to do. Nothing to discuss. Because nothing fucking happened. On the other hand, why don't we talk about the way you manhandle that son of yours?

'What the hell are you talking about?'

'I've seen the bruises. You're a bully. Hurting your own kid.'

'You know nothing about parenting, Martini. That kid needs putting in line.'

'There's a big difference between beating and discipline.'

'Not in my house there isn't. That kid needs to know who's boss. And I am the one to show him.'

It was then that Enjoy re-entered the kitchen. 'I left my lunchbox on the counter,' she said, a furtive look on her face.

He wondered for a moment how much she'd heard.

Not a mistake

He stood in the kitchen considering the tomatoes. They were still a little unripe and unlikely to peel without being in boiling water for a bit. He scored a cross on top of them with a sharp knife, then dropped them in a bowl. When the kettle whistled, he lifted it and poured the scalding water over the tomatoes.

With four older sisters, and an Italian father, he'd had a lot of experience in the kitchen. Watching. Observing. Copying. Funny, then, that he should be so nervous about Alice coming over to eat. It wasn't like he had to win her over; he thought he'd already done that. More then, that he wanted to show her that he was capable. Together. In control in a way that her home seemed not so much to be. He wanted to be her haven, her oasis.

But he also wanted to seem responsible; able to take care of her. So that she could see him in her future, not just as a distraction through her current hard times. But because of the opprobrium from Chris in particular, he'd told no one in his family about Alice. Nothing, beyond, of course, their professional relationship. Of his sisters, the second youngest, Luisa knew him the best. Recently married and very pregnant, she was not one to mince her words – not that these facts were interconnected. Last time he'd seen her she'd been grumpy, her back aching from the heavy weight she was carrying on her small frame. Her husband, Frans, a helicopter pilot frequently working offshore, was often gone for weeks, sometimes months, at a time.

'I just know this baby is going to come early,' she said to Leo. 'And then what? I'm pushing out a giant watermelon through my lady bits and he'll be rescuing some stupid fisherman who's lost his way in a storm. It'll be days before the baba meets his or her daddy.'

Leo had said it before he'd even thought it through. 'I'll be there, if you want. Like a reserve or something.'

Luisa had looked at him, her eyes glistening with hormones. 'Seriously?'

'Well, I don't know if I'd be any help, but you could squeeze my hand and shout obscenities at me.'

Luisa smiled. 'You don't even know how appealing that sounds,' she said.

'I guess, though, you'd probably prefer Mom or Nicoletta? Or Cat? They have the experience down.'

'You're joking, right? Nicoletta will tell me how much better she did it; Cat panics in a crisis and Mom will cry all the time. I'll end up looking after *her*.'

Leo laughed. 'So it's a yes?'

Luisa nodded. 'But you're not looking until the sprog is out, okay? You stand top-side and tell me how superb I am at childbirth. Can you do that?'

'I think so.'

Luisa smiled weakly. 'Oh God. I'm terrified, Leo.'

'I don't blame you.'

'See? A decent answer. Honest.'

'But not very comforting is it? Are you sure I'm up to the task?'

'Darling brother. You were born for it.'

Now with passata almost done and a fresh salad tossed, he was concentrating on the seafood sauce. Splashing out with garlic, mussels, fish and shrimp. He wondered what Luisa would think about what he was doing with Alice. It was easy to be judgmental about infidelity until you knew the intricacies involved. He should be stepping back, he realised that. But he just didn't want to. He was better with Albert than Bruce was and as for Alice, well, he wasn't quite sure he could move aside now even if he wanted to. Family values were great until, well, they weren't.

When the buzzer sounded, Leo had started rolling out the pasta. He washed and wiped his hands and opened the door. Alice stood outside, looking slightly breathless. He smiled at her, pulled her close, shutting the door behind them. Her cheeks were pink from the cold and her hair a little damp from a slight spatter of rain. She was exquisite.

'You alright?' he asked.

She smiled. 'Would it be okay to say I'm a little nervous?'

Alice didn't have to explain further. He smiled back. 'Me too. But you look beautiful. Really amazing.'

She did. Her hair was swept back, to expose a long elegant neck and her ears dangling with something sparkling. She was wearing an emerald-green dress that clung to all her curves in all the right ways. And a pair of heels that accentuated her tight calves. He pulled her to him and kissed her deeply.

'Good welcome,' she said. 'It smells delicious in here.'

A silence settled between them. And they stared at each other, a fraught tension connecting them.

'You know what?' Alice said finally. 'You're going to have to lead the way here. You may be younger than me, but I guarantee you, you're more experienced than I am. This is the first official date I've had in about twenty years.' Her words were self-deprecating, but her hesitation made him hesitate too.

'Regrets?' he said.

'About this? Us?'

He nodded.

'No. Yes. No. Guilt … I don't really know how to explain it. But what I do know is I want to be here. I've been looking forward to seeing you alone all week.'

'Me too.' Leo took Alice's hand. 'Come inside, then I can pour you a drink.'

In the kitchen, the floury surface didn't allow much space for Leo so he poured her whisky in a glass he placed on the surface next to the stove.

'You've been a busy boy,' said Alice, observing, as she took the glass. 'I didn't even know you could cook.'

'I have all sorts of secret talents.'

'Oh, I know about some of them,' she flirted.

'Well, we can test out those ones after I've fed you. You're going to need the energy.'

'Promises. Promises.' Alice walked around to the fridge. Like the fridge in their holiday home, this one had photos stuck to it. She was pleased to see there were several of her. And one really beautiful one of Leo with Enjoy and Albert. But as for the rest of the photos, she didn't recognise anyone except for Chris, who'd given her the drink when she'd last been in this kitchen. And the girl with the long legs who was definitely a better age for Leo. On the left was what looked like a family photograph.

'Are these your sisters?'

Leo dried his hands on a dishcloth and with his one arm around her back pointed everybody out.

'That's Luisa. Nicoletta. Serena. And Caterina – Cat.'

'Who's the oldest?'

'Serena. We're not as close. Maybe because of the age gap. She was fifteen when I was born. So I was more like a little doll she could pick up and dump when something more interesting came up. Although she did babysit a lot when my folks went out. She got married and I was an uncle by ten.'

'Which is why you're so great with kids.'

He shrugged. 'Maybe.'

'What was it like growing up in such a big family?'

'Only two more kids than yours!'

'You remembered,' Alice said. 'I don't even remember mentioning it.'

'Jake and Claire, right?'

'Now you're just showing off!'

Leo grinned. 'My childhood was both smothering and safe. Someone always to watch out for me. Stop me before I made any mistakes.'

'So I guess they don't know about us then?'

'We are NOT a mistake, if that's what you mean. Now come over here, I need your help with the pasta.'

Leo set the pasta machine on top of a piece of paper towel. Then he attached it to the surface by tightening the clamp. He handed her a ball of dough.

'Hang on, I need to wash my hands.' Completing this task, Alice took the rolling pin Leo was giving her.

He stood behind her and with his hands over hers, they began to flatten out the dough on the floured surface. They pushed and rolled together until there was a decent rectangle.

'This feels like *Ghost*,' Alice said.

'*Ghost*?'

'The movie?'

Leo's blank look made it obvious he had no idea what she was talking about.

'Oh my word. I'm showing my age. You don't know the pottery scene with Patrick Swayze and Demi Moore?'

'No.'

Alice leant back into him. 'Well, she's making a vase on one of those pottery wheels, and his hands are on hers on this wet clay, fingers enmeshed. As far as I can recall she's got this skimpy black top on and he's looking all manly, and they're just so intense.'

Leo laughed and then slipped his fingers between hers. 'Like this?' He started to kiss her neck and he could hear her sigh happily.

'Leo, this is definitely not going to get the pasta done.'

'Are you complaining?' Leo said, between kisses.

'Far from it,' Alice said as she turned around, her lips on his. 'I can eat any time.'

So he took her powdery hand in his and led her to his bedroom.

Don't forget, married

She was happy. Truly and completely happy. She smiled at Leo, as he connected the noodle-cutting attachment to the pasta machine, then began to feed the thinly rolled sheet of pasta into it. She turned the crank at a slow pace and the ribbons began to emerge. Leo held them over his arm and when that piece of dough was done, he dusted the pasta lightly with cornmeal.

'To stop them sticking together,' he said.

'I'm impressed,' she said.

'You have to eat it first, before you can say that.'

'Nope. I'm still impressed. You're just generally impressive.'

He bowed. 'Well, thank you, m'lady.'

Soon the pasta was boiling in a pot and Leo was heating up a heavenly smelling seafood sauce. She picked a carrot out of the salad. 'I'm absolutely ravenous,' she commented. 'You've really made me work for my supper.' Alice extracted a stuffed green olive, then walked to the stove where Leo was stirring to pop it into his mouth.

'Open up!'

He opened his mouth obediently.

'Good boy.' She stood next to him, enjoying the domesticity. Bruce was never a good cook – her fault – she found it annoying when people got under her feet when she was trying to make a meal and so he'd never learnt. But it had been a while since he'd sat at the counter with a beer and kept her company. She couldn't remember when last he had done that.

'Not long now, Allie. Why don't you put the salad on the table and I'll serve you there? Wine or another whisky?'

'Wine,' she said, surprising herself.

As they ate, she thought of all the things she didn't know about Leo. He was always so good about asking her questions that she often didn't have a chance to ask back. Despite this, though, she felt like she *did* know him. Not the details, perhaps, but the outlines and she liked the idea of colouring everything in. The evening had been perfect, and guiltily, she realised she hadn't thought of Albert once. Until now. And Bruce was hovering there somewhere but only in the recesses of her mind.

Since their conversation a few weeks back about her architectural degree left in limbo, Leo had also got her thinking.

'Remember when we were talking about the house I designed?'

'The one with the tree?'

'Yes.'

Leo nodded.

'So it made me wonder, if maybe, I could see what any part of my studies are now worth.'

'Go back to your course?' Leo beamed. 'How awesome. You'd be great at that.'

'You haven't even seen the design I did.'

He shrugged. 'Doesn't matter. You've got such flair. And half of a degree is application; blood, sweat and tears. Grit. Which you have in spades.'

'You think so?'

'I know it. Next time I'm at the house, let's try find your stuff. You'll probably need some sort of portfolio.'

'How did I get so lucky?' Alice said.

'Must be because you're so hot,' he replied, making her laugh.

And then his phone rang.

'Answer it, if you need to,' Alice said. But without looking at who was even calling, Leo ended the call. But the phone rang again almost immediately.

'Who is it?'

Leo glanced at the screen. 'Luisa.' He rejected the call again. When the phone rang yet again, Leo stood up. 'Sisters!' he said apologetically, then answered it. 'Hey Lou.'

'You're my motherfucking birth partner and you reject my call!' Alice heard her from the opposite side of the table.

'I'm kind of on a date, Luisa.'

'I don't care if you're shagging Emma Stone and Jessica Alba at the same time! My waters have just broken and my husband is in bloody Madagascar. Get your arse over here right now.'

'Oh shit.'

'That's right, oh shit. You offered and it's time to deliver on your promise.'

'It sounds like I'm delivering something else.'

'Very funny, I'm cracking up. Oh my God, here comes another one.'

Alice stood up. 'I'll drive you,' she said. 'I've only had one drink and only a few sips of the wine. And my car is already out on the road.'

'Oh fuck that hurts.' Luisa's voice was verging on hysterical.

'I'm coming right over. Just try and be calm.'

'Calm? You're shitting me! I'm not calm in a crisis. You know that! That's your job. You be calm. Bloody hell.'

Alice could hear Luisa panting, loudly. She picked up her keys. 'You direct me and you keep her on the line.'

He nodded. 'Lou, I'm leaving the house right now. You got your bag packed?'

'It's by the door.'

'Good, now just check the house while you wait for me. Nothing on the stove? Windows closed.'

'Yes, yes, yes.'

They ran to Alice's car, Leo's phone still to his ear. Her car connected to his phone's Bluetooth and now she could hear clearly too.

'Okay, sis, we're in the car now. Hang in there.'

Alice pulled into the road, turning as Leo directed. The rain had stopped and the moon had come out. It was bright and full, reflecting on the small puddles in the road.

'Here?' she asked.

Leo nodded.

'Who's with you?' Luisa asked.

'My date.'

'Well, I hope she has a strong stomach. I've just vomited and I can't bend down to clean it up.'

'She'll be fine.'

'Distract me. Tell me about her.'

'Luisa, I can't do that. She's sitting next to me right now in the car.'

'And I've got a baby bearing down through my vagina. Distract me NOW.'

He hesitated. 'It's Alice, Lou. Okay?'

'Alice your married boss? Oh my God, this is good!' Luisa crowed with glee. 'I just knew something was up! You've been so bloody secretive. Mamma's going to kill you.'

'Yes, well, that's why I haven't told her.'

Alice looked across at Leo.

'Eyes on the road,' he muttered, looking vaguely ill.

She smiled, patted his thigh.

'So tell me about Alice, brother.'

'Alice is kind, and compassionate, and brave and beautiful.'

192

'And married! Don't forget married!' Luisa laughed and laughed.

'Will you shut up? This is serious, Lou. I'm crazy about her.'

'I'm sorry.' She cackled again, sounding anything but sorry.

'Left at the next road, then right at the stop street,' he directed. 'It's the house with the white wall and the bougainvillea.'

'Does that mean you're here?'

'Almost. Stay where you are. I'm coming to get you.'

'Oh Christ, it hurts. Frans is going to pay for this. Something with diamonds will be fine. You tell him, Leo.'

'Okay, Lou, I hear you. Now I'm going to disconnect the call. Open the front door. We're coming.'

Alice parked the car. 'Shall I come in?' she asked. 'I can clean the puke up while you get her in the car.'

'You can't do that.'

'Of course I can. I'm a mom. I've cleaned up more puke than I care to remember. Anyway, she can't leave it there. Get her while I deal with it.'

Alice's first impression of Luisa was her beauty. She had curly auburn hair, which ran halfway down her back. Her skin was perfect, which had never been the case when Alice was pregnant. She was wearing a white dress, her baby bump enormous, and no shoes. Her cheeks were crimson rather than rosy. The second thing Alice saw was how frightened she was.

'Luisa, this is Alice.'

Alice moved forward and without knowing what drove her to do it, put her arms around the expectant mother. 'It's going to be okay,' she said softly. 'We're here. Where are your shoes? It's wet outside.'

Luisa pointed. 'I couldn't tie the laces. I'm like an enormous fat blimp.'

'Anything but. You're gorgeous,' Alice said going on her haunches as she manoeuvred in Luisa's feet. 'Here you go Cinderella. It's time for the ball.' She nodded at Leo and he picked up his sister's bag, putting his other arm around her. 'Now where did you vomit?'

'Goodness,' said Luisa pointing again to a sticky, rancid mess near the kitchen. 'I think I might just be in love with you too.'

***

They roared down the road. It was probably close to eleven and the streets were quiet. Alice's fingers clenched. She couldn't see Luisa, but Leo, who was sitting in the back with her, was holding his sister's hand and talking softly to her, she could see. She knew without any doubt that he was nervous, but this is not what came across. He seemed so in control. Reassuring. Solid. He would make a good dad one day. A good husband.

And it made her feel ill. What on earth was she doing here? She couldn't deprive him of any of that.

She just wasn't selfish enough for it.

As if reading her mind, Leo looked up and met her eyes in the rear-view mirror. Then he smiled the sort of smile that would make an iceberg melt. In milliseconds her rib cage was crushing her heart.

'Focus on the driving, lovebirds, I've already vomited once,' Luisa said from behind her.

Leo laughed softly.

'And I for one know where those sorts of glances lead,' she added, pointing at her enormous belly. 'Oh Jesus. Here comes another one.'

'Almost there, Luisa,' said Alice. And they were. She pulled into the Vincent Pallotti parking area, and she drove as close as she could to the main entrance. 'Run in, Leo, and get a wheelchair.'

'I can walk,' said Luisa.

'Yes and if you do, the baby might pop out and land on its head. Just stay where you are.'

'Right. Good point.' She winced, clearly in the throes of a new contraction.

Not waiting to hear more, Leo dashed out the car and sprinted into the hospital reception.

'Breathe through it, lovely. Leo's on his way.'

But it wasn't just Leo. He was accompanied by a nurse or an orderly looking both calm and professional – at this juncture, the best combination Alice could think of. She got out the Audi and walked to Luisa's door to open it. The next time Leo's sister would be in a car, her life would be transformed forever. No warning or explanation could prepare anyone for it.

But there was no turning back now.

Leo and the orderly half-lifted, half-pulled Luisa into the wheelchair. 'Has my doctor arrived?' Luisa asked.

'I have no idea,' Leo said.

'You didn't even ask?'

'Should I have?'

'Don't be a dick. Of course you fucking should have.'

'Be nice, Lou.'

'You promised me I could swear. This is just the bloody beginning.'

'Dr Heynes is parking right now,' the orderly said soothingly. 'We're just going to get you settled.'

Leo turned to Alice, looking a little queasy. 'Are you coming?'

She shook her head. 'Over to you. I'll just be in the way. But don't worry about work tomorrow. I'll take care of Albert.'

Leo moved forward and hugged her. 'I'm crapping myself,' he whispered in her ear.

'You're going to be awesome,' she whispered back. 'Like you always are. WhatsApp me.'

He nodded, picking up Luisa's bag from the middle of the back seat.

Alice touched Luisa on the shoulder. 'Good luck. You've got this. And you've got Leo.' Then she bent and kissed her on her head.

Luisa waved as the orderly wheeled her away, her long hair hanging down the back of the chair. 'Nice meeting you, Alice, Leo's married boss.'

At least she'd still retained her sense of humour.

Surprise, surprise

Once again Alice was distracted after her night out.

'How was Gill?'

'Fine,' Alice said, throwing down her keys rather than hanging them up, a habit that irritated him but for some reason irritated him more than usual tonight. 'And the kids?'

'Albert was a bit wild. He climbed out the window onto the roof. I had to get him down but it was a chore. He's getting harder to handle the bigger he gets.'

'Mmmhhh,' said Alice, clearly not hearing him.

'Alice,' said Bruce. 'I just said your son was on the roof of the house.'

'Jeepers, Bruce. You're supposed to keep an eye on him.'

'I *was*. How else would I have got him off the roof, for Christ's sake?'

Alice took off her shoes, holding them in one hand. 'I need a bath. My feet hurt. And Leo's texted. He's not coming tomorrow. His sister's in labour.'

'What's that got to do with him?'

'What?'

'I said, what's that got to do with him?'

Alice looked at him icily. 'He's her birth partner until her husband arrives from Madagascar.'

'Weird,' Bruce said, summing up both the childbirth situation and his wife's expression.

'So I need to get to bed soon. I'm teacher tomorrow. I need my wits about me,' Alice said.

'Your daughter is fine,' Bruce said spitefully. 'And I'm fine.'

'Sorry?'

'In case you were wondering. Enjoy and I are doing well. We ordered Thai. She tried the green curry. Albert ate panang curry.'

'Good, good,' she said, glancing at her phone. She smiled slightly but it wasn't him she was smiling at.

Bruce thought about following Alice to the bath. In better times, they used to bath together. With bubbles. And candles! It was fun. They used to laugh a lot, blowing the white foam into the air and making beards, like children. But now her frosty gaze made him feel unwelcome. Decidedly so.

He picked up his book. Tried to focus on the Wright brothers at Kitty Hawk, 1903. Their second flight, with Orville at the controls. What impressed him was their courage. Perseverance. Their relentless singlemindedness.

But then they didn't have wives to contend with.

Wives complicated things.

Especially when you loved them but could do nothing, it seemed, but watch them floating away like ribbons on the wind.

***

When Bruce woke, Alice was already up and out of the bed. Since her pyjamas were neatly folded on her pillow, she was obviously dressed too. He sighed, rolled over, listening to the click of Malawi's nails on the kitchen floor. He checked his phone charging next to the bed. 05h42. Christ. He hadn't seen Alice up so early in years. Usually he had to bring her coffee just to help her lift her head.

He stood up, realising suddenly that it was Friday, not Saturday. More dramas to deal with on the building site, no doubt. And Martini was meeting him at ten; chances were, he'd be wanting to offer his pearls of wisdom on how he could stop the delays. Until all the fittings and tanks arrived, they'd all be on a go-slow, which made Martini gloat for unfathomable reasons – his bottom line was being affected too.

It was early enough, however, that Bruce could go for a quick run on the mountain before getting to work. It had been a few weeks since he and Enjoy had run together, so he decided to nudge her and check if she was keen. Enjoy was bunched up, a sheet over her head.

Usually quick to respond in the morning, and today was no exception.

'Want to go for a run, Joy?' he said, sitting on the edge of the bed.

'Now, before school?'

'Why not? We can stop at Andy's on the way back and get you a smoothie.'

Enjoy yawned and stretched, her long body elongating even more. 'Sounds good.'

He nodded. 'Meet you in the kitchen.'

That's where he found Alice, an apron around her waist, her hair tied back in a low ponytail. Despite the fine lines around her eyes, Alice was still a beautiful woman. Now, unguarded, a pancake pan on the stove and a few splatters of batter on her face, she was even more so.

'You're up early,' he said.

'I couldn't go back to sleep. I forgot to switch the sound off on my phone. A message woke me up.'

'Who was sending messages in the middle of the night?'

Alice's eyes flickered. 'Spam. I guess they just programme to send them out when the rate is cheaper.'

There was something jumpy about her now. He suspected she was lying. But why? With a bit of reflection, he might be almost certain this wasn't the first time either. Alice had never been very good at deceit, but it seemed she was acquiring a knack for it. He just wasn't sure why.

'And the baby?'

'Which baby?'

'The one Leo was helping deliver.'

'Oh yes. A little girl! Faye. Three point four kilos.'

Bruce rather thought this was actually the message that woke her. But why the fuck lie about it? And why the feigned nonchalance? She knew which bloody baby he was talking about.

'What time was it born?' he said, trying to sound casual.

'Two? Three? I don't know. I haven't spoken to Leo yet. Sure he's fast asleep after all the excitement.'

Bruce had half a mind to check the message and see when it came in. He added this to his mental to-do list. He'd have to crack her phone code first. Easily done.

'Want a pancake?' Alice asked, flipping a new one onto the plate next to the stove.

'Probably not. Enjoy and I are going for a run, then a smoothie. Thanks though.'

Their daughter entered the kitchen, her braids tied up in a bun on her head. 'Let's do it, Dad,' she said, positioning her finger and thumb in an 'L' on her head. 'Second is the first loser.'

***

Martini cancelled on him.

'Listen, mate. I just can't make it this morning. Can you come to mine? Tonight? Five o'clock?'

On a Friday? He hated being summoned, yet again, but actually this time it suited him. He had a few client meetings and a quote he needed to prepare for a green project in Botswana. This would give him the time to get his presentation together before he flew to Gaborone on Thursday. It would be good to spend some time in the office. Especially if Albert and Alice were on their own today. It could get noisy. Inevitably Alice would lose control and there'd be shouting.

And that would be a good day.

The hours flew by. He didn't even have a chance to eat, so the thought of Alice's pancakes made his stomach roar. Pulling into the driveway, he noticed that Martini's car wasn't parked in its usual spot under the carport. Late. Again. Typical.

He walked up to the open front door where Elaine was standing. She was holding a glass of red wine, her light brown hair newly done in a short style, some strands curling around her face. Barefoot, wearing a cotton button-down top and a pair of tight black leggings, she was looking very relaxed. And actually, he conceded, *very bloody* attractive. There was also something different about her that he couldn't quite put his finger on.

'Hi, Elaine,' Bruce said. 'Not in Elgin tonight?'

She smiled. 'It's raining tomorrow. I decided to stay where it's going to be cosier. Come in.'

He stepped inside. There was a fire burning in the grate, sending blasts of warmth into the room.

'What can I offer you? Your friend is late. Surprise, surprise,' she added conspiratorially.

'That wine looks good.'

'It is.'

She gestured towards the lounge, walking cat-like into the kitchen to retrieve the bottle and a glass. Standing, Bruce shifted from foot to foot. Despite knowing Elaine for more than twelve years, he could count the number of times he'd been alone with her on one hand. He drank the first glass a lot faster than he might normally have.

'You're thirsty,' said Elaine.

'Sorry, I rather gulped that down, didn't I?'

'Nervous?' she said.

'What about?'

She smiled, then leant forward to pour him another glass. As she did, the top two buttons of her shirt popped, exposing a very ample cleavage in a lacy black bra. He tried to look away, pretend he hadn't noticed.

But as he raised his eyes, his glance caught Elaine's.

'So what do you think?' she asked.

He cleared his throat, wondering what she was asking him. It couldn't be what he was thinking, surely?

'My new boobs,' she prompted. 'Here,' she took his hand, 'feel how real they are.'

The situation was more than a little weird. 'I'm not sure–'

'Oh come on, Bruce. It's just us here. You don't want just a little squeeze? Our little secret?'

But she'd already pushed his fingers against her body, her breast weighty in his hand.

'And?' she asked.

He realised that she was not entirely sober. 'Elaine.'

'Try the other one. Use both your hands, put the glass down.' She pulled so hard on her top that the next two buttons flew off, her floaty top now exposing her lithe body, toned from years of horse riding. And no childbirth.

He tried to picture Martini in this situation. Ironically, he knew that if Alice offered herself up to his friend on a plate, Martini would have no compunction in having a taste. A whole meal if it was offered. But he wasn't Martini. He also hadn't had sex in weeks. Alice had barely touched him lately, never mind look him.

'You look great,' he said.

She pouted. 'Great is such a bland, boring word.'

He smiled. 'I'm not used to *this* version of Elaine. Where did she come from?'

'I'm not sure you ever knew me, Bruce. I've always just been Martini's wife. Martini's wife who talks too much about herself.'

Bruce looked away, a little embarrassed.

'That's true, isn't it? That's what you and Alice say behind closed doors? So why don't we just start again?' Elaine said, as she opened her shirt, exposing her bra completely.

'I'm not sure that right now I'm in a suitable position for small talk.'

'Who said anything about talking?'

Bruce laughed self-consciously. 'I didn't know you were so ... feisty.'

'My husband,' she said piously. 'Asked me to entertain you. I'm just doing what he asked. Besides, it's not like I'm getting any. He's still pining after that model he was screwing. The one who died?'

Bruce blinked.

'Oh,' she said. 'So you knew about her too?'

'No,' he said. 'But I suspected.'

'Well, I *knew*. And if he hadn't been with you that night, I would have thought he had more to do with the whole crash thing than he's saying.' She leant forward, her ample tits swinging. 'We have at least an hour to make the most of it. Last chance, Bruce. What's it to be. Yes, or a no?'

A family

He snuggled the newborn against himself, feeling the emotion of the night welling inside him. There were moments in your life of before and after. This was one of them. How could you remain unchanged after witnessing something as unfathomable, as magical, as the entry of a new life into the world? He knew this was a turning point.

Beside him, Luisa was stirring. She opened her eyes and when she saw her brother cuddling the little bundle, she smiled.

'We did it,' she said.

'Well, I think you did it,' he said. 'I was just the punching bag.'

'I wasn't that bad, was I?'

He smiled. 'You were awesome. But I do have a sore hand.'

'Liar!' His sister raised her eyebrows. 'So have you heard anything from Frans?'

'Nothing new. I've checked the flight. He still lands at two. He's getting an Uber straight here. And no-one else from the family is allowed to see Faye until he does.'

'So for now it's just us then? You and me.'

Leo nodded, a silence settling between them.

'So, brother,' Luisa said eventually. 'What are you going to do?'

'What do you mean? Do about what?'

'You know exactly what I mean. About Alice. This isn't like you.'

He shifted, feeling the snuffle, snuffle of the baby against his chest. 'It's not like I planned it. I'm not a monster.'

'Of course I know that. That's what I'm worried about. I saw the way you looked at her. You've got it bad.'

Leo didn't deny it. 'I should bow out, I suppose. That would be the morally correct thing to do. I just don't want to. I don't. I love her.'

'If that's the case, at the very least, Leo, you need to let her and her husband try and fix it. There are kids involved.'

'Don't you think I know that? I'm more a father to Albert at the moment than Bruce ever seems to be.'

'But you're *not* his father.'

'I know that too, for fuck's sake.' Leo raised his voice uncharacteristically, startling the little baby awake. She began to mewl.

Luisa sighed. 'Here,' she said. 'She's probably hungry. Or terrified. Pass her over and if you don't want to see my boobs, better look away now.'

When Leo looked again, the baby was latched contentedly. 'I was worried about this,' Luisa confided. 'There are all these horror stories about breast feeding and I thought I'd be terrible at it. But look at her. She's perfectly happy.' She bent her head, studying her daughter's auburn fluff. 'You know, maybe you and Alice should talk about it. The thing is, if you carry on, you have to be all in. You don't break up a family for a fling. It's all exciting now. Clandestine. Hot. Don't you want a family of your own?'

'I want Alice.'

'You'll find out at some point, that she isn't going to be enough.'

'You don't know that.'

She sighed. 'You're right. I don't. I'm just worried about you, Leo.'

'I can see that. But you mustn't. I can take care of myself.'

***

Leo left the hospital when Frans rushed into the ward, his shirt untucked. His chin was covered with dark stubble and his eyes were puffy, but he looked delighted.

'Oh, *skat*,' he said. 'I'm sorry I wasn't here.'

When Luisa handed the baby over to him, his cheeks flushed, and a smile almost too big for his face emerged.

'She's gorgeous. Isn't she perfect? Just look at these fingernails! Aren't you clever!'

'Everybody's dying to meet her,' Luisa said, looking pleased. 'And you can thank Leo. I broke his hand instead of yours.'

'Dankie, boetie,' Frans said. 'I was so relieved you were with her! Couldn't sleep on the plane worrying.'

Leo smiled. 'I'm going to give you guys some privacy, but let me take a family shot first.'

'A family!' sighed Luisa happily.

202

He took out his phone, snapped a few times. 'I'll send you the best ones. For your announcement.'

'And one of the godfather and his niece?' Frans asked Luisa.

'Godfather?' said Leo.

'Well, don't you think you earned it?'

In his car, Leo leant his forehead on his steering wheel. He was tired. Exhilarated. Nervous. He wanted to go straight back home to sleep and also to see Alice so her could tell her everything. But he was booked off for the day. Would it be nuts if he just arrived?

He pulled out of the parking lot, debating. But the car was driving him forward and he knew there was no way he would be able to sleep now. Without thinking more about it, he headed towards Alice.

***

He was going to buzz at the front of the house when he saw Albert. He was perched in a tree in the front garden, his legs flopping down in front of him. For a moment, Leo's heart stopped. *What was he doing?* But then Leo saw him and beamed.

'I thought you weren't coming today,' he said.

'Couldn't keep away. I missed you,' Leo replied.

Leo grinned. 'Missed you too.'

'What are you doing in that tree?'

'Thinking.'

'I like a good place to think.'

'You should try it.' There was a moment of silence between them. 'I'll let you in,' Albert decided. 'Just wait a moment.' Albert opened the gate and Leo followed him into the garden. 'I want to build a tree house up there,' Albert said. 'A platform. I could sleep out here in the summer.'

'We could do it together,' Leo said. 'Build it and camp out.'

'Really?'

'Sure, why not? And your mom could design it. It could be a homeschooling project. Calculations. Measurements.'

'And art. Because it's going to be beautiful. Like a sculpture.'

'Okay.'

'Climb on up,' Albert said. 'Follow me.'

And Leo did. When they were both comfortable on the thick branch of the oak, Leo grinned at the tween. 'It *is* a good place to think. I feel like a bird.'

'Right?'

'The most amazing thing happened last night,' Leo confided.

'Really? What?' Albert didn't look at Leo, but his body altered slightly and Leo could see Albert was interested.

'I watched my niece, Faye, being born.'

Leo pulled a face. 'Wasn't it gross? I mean, it came out–' He waved in the general direction of his crotch, making Leo laugh aloud.

'I didn't look there.'

'Oh, good,' Albert said. 'Because, she's like, your sister.'

Leo looked out towards the mountain. 'I held a baby that was seconds old. In my arms. It was like a magic trick. Slightly unbelievable.' He was saying this to Albert, but also, in a way, reminding himself that it had really happened.

'So you feel different now?' Albert said with uncanny, adult-like perception.

'I do,' Leo nodded. 'I really do.'

'In a good way?'

'I think so.'

'Cool,' Albert said, swinging his legs.

Do it for you

Alice walked to the kitchen window. She thought she'd heard the gate open but she must have been mistaken. Albert had seemed calmer today. Perhaps, for the first time in months, he was in a good place. The constant changes in medication had wreaked havoc on all of them but teaching Albert today had been, not easy, perhaps, but achievable. His focus seemed different. More targeted. The boy had quizzed her on states of matter. Not the states of matter she was used to – solids, liquids and gases. Now, suddenly, she was dealing with plasma and Bose-Einstein condensates, which Albert had explained to her like *he* was the teacher.

'So they were only really created in a lab in the 1990s or so. You make them by cooling atoms to almost absolute zero. At this temperature the atoms are sluggish. They can hardly move relative to each other. It's like they have no free energy, see? So they begin to cluster together. And then they act, you know, like they're a single atom. Because from a physical point of view, right, they're identical.'

Her face must have registered her bemusement.

'It's like a group of kids. You put them all in the same environment. Peer group pressure, makes them cluster. Then they all begin to act exactly the same, yes? Like they don't have energy or minds of their own. After a while they're so like each other, you can't even tell them apart.'

Alice had looked at her son, his description both insightful and tragic. But she understood what he meant.

Now as she washed her hands at the sink, she could see his feet dangling from a tree. *How many times had she asked him to keep his damn feet on the ground?* Yes, he was still a little boy, but one who was a constant danger to himself. If he needed to climb trees, couldn't he do it with his father around? Or at least tell her where he was so she could watch him. But then she saw a second pair of legs, and her heart clenched. She knew those legs. *What was he doing here?*

Alice dried her hands and walked out the back door to the oak.

'Room for one more?' she called up.

'Leo's here, Mom,' Albert said from behind a clump of leaves.

'I see that.'

'Is that alright?' Leo asked, his voice uncertain.

'Of course it is. Maybe instead of my coming up, you guys should come down. I was going to make that lemonade you like, Albert.'

Albert's head popped out the foliage. 'Two minutes, Mom. We're talking.'

'Alright then. Leo? Lemonade? Coffee? Beer?'

'Whatever you're having, Allie. Thanks.'

It was incredible how Leo could affect her like this. She found her fingers were shaking and she dropped onto the floor the lemon she was about to cut. She leant to pick it up. Enjoy was in her bedroom listening to Spotify; she could hear the music banging against the walls. Usually the noise would irritate her, but now she just felt like cranking it up and dancing. She'd thought she'd only see Leo next week, but here he was. And Bruce was going to be late – a meeting with Martini. They could have a fun family supper. An evening free of tension and accusations. And when the kids were in bed, she and Leo could be together, alone. The thought animated her, and when she turned to see the guys entering the kitchen, she couldn't hide her smile.

***

When the kids were put to bed, Bruce was still not back. Alice looked at Leo, wondering if he would stay.

'Would you like a coffee?' she said.

'Please.'

The kitchen looking onto the front garden had no curtains, and she was aware that any moment Bruce came into the drive, he would be able to see them. She'd always felt exposed there and wondered, not for the first time, why they hadn't installed blinds after they'd chopped down the part of the hedge in front that used to shield a view from the road. The milk frothed and Alice poured it into the mugs, feeling a silence hanging heavily between them.

'You must be tired,' Alice said to Leo. 'You were awake all night.'

'I guess all the adrenaline is beginning to dissipate.'

That was one of the things Alice loved about Leo. Bruce would never use a word like that. Dis-si-pate. 'But you came here,' she stated.

'I did. I wanted to see you. You and the kids.'

She smiled, handing him the coffee, then picked up her own mug. She began to walk to the lounge.

'Luisa is worried,' he said as they sat down.

'About us?' Alice glanced at Leo, feeling already that her world was tipping over.

'She thinks we need to have *the talk*. That we're not the only people affected here. Albert. Enjoy. Bruce, even. Obviously.'

'And what do you think?' She sipped her coffee, trying to seem measured. Collected.

'I don't know. I don't want to ruin things.' He stopped for a moment, reaching out for her hand. His touch steadied her but only for a moment. 'It's just that seeing Faye born–'

'Has made you think about the future.'

He smiled. 'I guess so.'

'Well,' she said, pulling him by the hand to a couch. 'I'm listening. What do *you* want?'

Leo was silent, as though building courage. Alice studied him; the anxiety obvious in the way he sat. He didn't answer.

'No, really, Leo. Maybe Luisa's right. Maybe we do need to talk. What do *you* want?'

He gulped in breath, then let it out in a torrent. 'I want you. And the kids. But I don't want Bruce. I don't want you in his bed. I don't want him touching you, or sitting down for dinner with you, or watching Netflix with you, or asking you how your day was. I want to be *that* person. And I want a baby of our own. Not now. But when we're ready.'

'A baby?' Alice thought she kept the bemusement out of her voice, but probably didn't succeed. *A baby, for goodness sake?*

'I want to be a dad. Is that so strange?'

'Of course it's not. You'd be a wonderful father,' she replied honestly. *But what did she know really? She'd chosen Bruce, and he certainly wasn't. Not for Albert, anyway.*

'I know we've only been "us" a short while. But I also know that I can't imagine my life without you. I don't want to.'

Alice sat back. 'I don't know, Leo.'

'Well, you asked what I want. I want to keep having this hot sex. I've never fitted together with anyone the way we do. But that's not only what I want. I love you. But I don't want to share you. It's just not who I am.'

They sat. The silence between them hanging heavily. Despite how horrible her marriage to Bruce had been lately, for years even, Leo's meaning was clear. Alice picked up her coffee, playing for time as she sipped.

'Look, I get it. You need to think. I'm not asking for a small thing.'

'It's kind of mind-blowing, Leo.'

'Sure, I can't deny that. I also can't deny that your life with Bruce is financially very comfortable. I'm probably a step back. Definitely a step back. But I have plans. And if you're willing, I want them to include you.'

Alice studied Leo's serious expression. She reached for his hand and squeezed.

He continued, 'I don't expect an answer tonight or even next week. I just think that we should be clear on how I feel. And I guess what I'm saying too, is that because I love you, if I'm standing in the way of a marriage you can repair – one you want to fix – then I need to do the right thing.'

'You mean leave me?'

'Bow out.'

'You make it sound like a theatrical performance.'

'Well, I can promise you, I'm no good at theatre. The thought of separation makes me sick. But I would do it for you. To ensure your happiness.' He attempted a smile, but his eyes were watery and he looked away instead. He raised his fist to one cheek, slid away the wetness. Then he stood up. 'I think I need to go. I have a reputation to uphold.'

But Alice pulled him back onto the couch. 'What about Albert?'

'We have two weeks of school left, then the holidays on the twenty-ninth. Maybe you and I need to think about spending time apart so we can make clear-headed decisions. I could fetch Albert on Monday morning. I'll set my spare room up as a school room. Maybe the change of scene will be good for him.'

'And then?'

'And then I bring him home, or you come to fetch him. I won't be in your space, clouding your thoughts.'

Alice bit her lip. 'I think it might be a bit late for that. You're in my head every second of the day.'

He touched her face, leaning forward to kiss her on the forehead. 'Then I hope it will be an easy decision.'

Leo stood up, retrieving his car keys from his pocket. 'I'll fetch Albert on Monday at eight. I'll make the room nice for him. It'll help focus me.'

'Hey,' Alice said as he began to walk to the door.

He turned.

'I love you,' she said.

Leo smiled. 'Got to go now, Allie. Not sure I can keep it together much longer.'

Then the garage door began to rumble.

Oh great.

Bruce came in through the kitchen door. 'Jesus,' he said, observing Leo. Then he held out his hand. 'Have you decided to move in or were you just leaving?'

Leo shook. 'Just going.'

'No you're not. I hear there's a new baby. Time to crack the cigars.'

'Um. Well, it's not *my* baby.'

'Close enough. Come on onto the patio. Cognac and cigars, matey. And I won't take no for an answer.'

Hospitality

Bruce was feeling expansive. Adrenalised. He pulled out three Cohibas from the humidor. He clipped their ends with a quick, strong motion to avoiding tearing. For the better smoking experience. Alice stood uncertainly, then shrugged. 'I'll get some glasses,' she said.

'And the Courvoisier XO Impérial.'

'Of course.'

'And see if you can dig out some more matches. We're running low, darling.'

His wife nodded. Her back was stiff and he wondered what was biting her in the arse tonight. The last time he'd been a little offish with Leo she'd complained. And now he was welcoming him with true Louw hospitality. So she had nothing to carp on about.

He lit the first match, holding the end of the cigar above the flame.

'You had one of these beauts before?' he asked.

'Sure,' Leo said. But Bruce seriously doubted it. He looked so clean living. So … young. And besides that, he was holding the fucking thing all wrong. What a waste.

'Well, I'd like to give you a few tips if I may. Watch how I spin the stogie around, getting an even burn all around the end. You don't want the cigar directly in the flame, right? It wrecks the taste.'

Leo took the matches, struck a flame. His hand was unsteady and Bruce had to resist the urge to do the bloody job right. Eventually, they both had an even orange glow.

Of course the young man inhaled. Obviously. He coughed and hacked, growing crimson.

Bruce glanced at him. 'It's better if you suck on it, like you're sucking through a straw. Don't use your diaphragm.'

Leo held his chest, his eyes wide. But he recovered quickly enough, his eyes watering a bit.

'You okay?'

Leo nodded.

'Now fill your mouth up with the smoke. Let it swirl around, then release it slowly. See, like this?' Bruce sucked and after five puffs, his Cohiba started making a plume of thick white smoke. 'Now the cigar is properly lit. So I don't need to puff for a few minutes.'

Alice walked outside carrying a tray.

'Thanks, babe,' Bruce said, noticing a glance between Leo and her. He couldn't decipher it.

'We're having a cigar-smoking lesson,' Leo commented in an ironic tone that put Bruce on edge.

'I didn't know that was even possible,' Alice replied, pouring them each a cognac.

'Oh, come on,' Bruce said. 'I taught *you* didn't I?'

Alice shrugged, lighting her own cigar. 'Well, let's see what sort of student I was.'

As bad as each other

This was just too much. Bruce moving his cheeks like a toad and the smoke curling in front of his face. Alice was, as always, impressive. The cigar twirled in her fingers as she lit up, an expression of grim determination settling into her features. This felt like a challenge. And though she was doing impeccably, it was as if he were a pubescent teen waiting for approval. He didn't even *remotely enjoy* the taste of the cigar. Neither was the effect relaxing, or soothing. It set his teeth on edge. The cognac, on the other hand, was masterfully smooth. And before he knew it, the glass was already empty and Bruce was filling it up again.

He needed to go home. This place wasn't good for him. Not with this toxic atmosphere. He tried to put his hand over the glass before the older man could pour, but he just wasn't quick enough.

'Oh relax, bru,' Bruce said and Leo felt his neck hairs rising, but he took the second glass. That would be it. He couldn't stand the supercilious sonofabitch much longer. Alice and his lives would certainly be a lot easier if Bruce wasn't in them. And the sooner, the better.

Leo sat back a moment, dark thoughts crossing his mind that made his own skin crawl. He tried to sip quickly, but the cognac was strong and he was already feeling nauseous. When he heard a little voice behind them, he almost shot out of his chair in surprise.

'I can't sleep,' Albert said. 'I'm feeling weird.'

'Weird how?' Bruce asked, dismissively.

'It's like my heart is racing too fast.'

Leo took off his Garmin, placing it around Albert's wrist. 'Come here, Albert. Let's check your pulse.'

Alice put her arm around Albert. 'Maybe you're having a panic attack. Try breathe in like I taught you, darling,' Alice said. 'Remember the yoga breathing?'

'Oh, for Christ's sake, Albert,' Bruce said, standing up. 'Stop being a bloody drama queen. We're trying to have some adult time here.'

This only made Albert breathe more erratically. His wide eyes darted from Alice to Leo. He seemed unsteady, whirling.

'Look at me, you little twerp. They're not going to help you. You need to do it yourself,' Bruce said, his voice becoming both rougher and louder.

'Hey, Bruce,' Leo attempted. 'Give the boy a break. I'll take him inside. You guys carry on.'

But this only seemed to enrage Bruce more. 'My house. My rules. Go to your room, Albert. Enough of this horseshit.'

But Leo could see it in Albert's face. This was more than a panic attack. The boy's pupils were so dilated they clogged up his eyes. Albert began to cackle, the way he sometimes did when he was really high. It was maniacal, a little scary perhaps if one hadn't heard it before. He moved forward and without much thought, it seemed, bent his head and rammed it hard into Bruce's chest.

Ouf.

Bruce stumbled a little and before he could right himself, Albert charged him again. He connected right with Bruce's solar plexus and Leo couldn't help but be impressed by both his speed and accuracy. He was like an enraged bull. Alice shrieked uncharacteristically and tried to jerk her son away. But Leo was in a better position to extract him. He put his arms around the boy, holding Albert's back against his chest, pinning his elbows against his side. But then Bruce righted himself, and without any hesitation punched Albert in the face. Whether Albert's nose was broken, Leo didn't know, but the fist hit hard enough, and Albert, with his arms caught by Leo, was unable to defend himself. Leo let go immediately.

'What the hell are you doing, Bruce?' he demanded. 'Hitting a little kid who doesn't even have his hands to defend himself? Are you insane?'

But Bruce looked not in the least bit ashamed. He glanced at Albert almost scientifically; his son's nose was streaming blood, spurting like a new borehole. And Bruce said nothing. Did nothing. Albert was howling now, holding his face. As he stepped back, he knocked the tray, Bruce's special cognac cascading all over the tiles. His crystal glasses shattering.

This changed Bruce's expression a lot more than the blood. From near nonchalance to fury. 'Fucking waste. Fucking waste!' Bruce said icily, making Leo wonder if he was talking about the booze or the boy. Bruce began to lift his fist again but this time, Leo stepped forward.

'Would you like to rather pick on someone your own size?' he said.

'No. I'd like to beat the little shit and teach him the world doesn't revolve around his hysterics. Get out of the fucking way.'

Leo looked at Alice. 'Get Albert out of here.'

She moved quickly, trying to gather the bloody kid against her.

'You listen to the tutor over your own husband?'

'Oh, shut up, Bruce. I listen to myself.' Alice moved forward, cupping her son's chin with her hand.

'Get out of the way, Leo, I am his father and I discipline *my* child, *my* way.'

'That's not discipline, Bruce. That's–'

'What's going on? Why are you shouting?' Enjoy popped her head around the door, and this only made Bruce angrier.

'Go to bed, Enjoy. This isn't any of your business.'

'Why is Albert bleeding, Dad? What's happening? Did you hurt Albert? Dad?'

Bruce grunted. 'This is my house, Enjoy. And you are my children. Go back to bed. Fuck off.' And with that he threw a wooden sculpture from the side table at her. It bounced near her head as it hit the door. 'You heard me. Scram!'

Enjoy shrieked. 'Dad?'

'Listen to you father,' Alice said quietly. 'Go to your room and close the door.'

But instead, Enjoy walked forward, and stood next to Albert. 'You're not hurting my brother, Dad. Leave him alone.'

'Come on, Bruce,' Leo said, fearing this was going to escalate even more. 'Just step away.'

'Oh bugger off, Leo, you're the one who needs to leave. And what the fuck are you doing here anyway? A Friday night?'

'You invited me in, Bruce. If you recall it correctly, I was bloody leaving.'

Leo's heart was booming. The last time he could remember ever being in a fisticuffs was in Grade 6 – over a mobile phone that he shouldn't have sneaked into school anyway. But now he was burning, like hot milk about to boil over. He'd never felt so incensed. And when Bruce moved towards Albert again, Leo lifted the boy to the side, taking the punch to the side of his head instead. He was on both feet still, his head reeling.

'Stop it!' Alice was screaming. He could hear her only distantly; his head hurt but even worse was how much it would have hurt Albert. The kid didn't deserve this. And now it wasn't really about Alice, or even Bruce.

It was just enough. And he'd had enough. As Bruce came forward Leo feinted, then knocked him solidly with an uppercut in the jaw.

Bruce roared.

'Stop it, both of you. Stop it!' Alice shrieked.

But now they were both so hyped, they were at each other, their arms swinging. Fists on flesh. Knuckles on buttons. And Bruce knew this wasn't just about Albert. It was about so many things. The disappointed tiredness in Alice's eyes. His own jealousy. The knowledge that Alice was still with this dickhead and didn't instantly choose him. Even as Bruce's solid punch hit his eye, he was unsteady, beginning to tumble, overbalance. No ways was he going to allow a man fifteen years older beat the shit out of him. He lifted his arm and moved in again, his feet back in a solid stance. But then he saw Alice's face as she shoved herself between them.

He wouldn't hit Alice. He wouldn't touch Alice. He lowered his arms.

'Get out, I want you both out this house. What's the matter with you?'

Bruce grimaced. 'You can't kick me out of my own house,' he sneered.

'Get out, right now, or I'm calling the police,' she said. 'Enjoy and Albert, go to the kitchen and get some frozen peas out the freezer for Albert's face. Then you go to my bedroom and lock the door. You don't come out for anyone but me.'

The kids scampered away, and Leo felt himself deflate. What was he thinking? He wasn't. Of course not. He sighed. His eyes sought Alice's but she wouldn't meet his gaze.

He stood. Powerless. Bleeding. His right eye already beginning to throb and swell.

'Bruce,' she said.

Alice's husband straightened. Picked up his keys from where he'd put them on the table outside. 'We're not finished with this, Alice,' he said. 'I'll go tonight. But don't think for a moment Albert has won.'

Alice sighed. 'You just don't get it, do you? You don't get to win against a small boy. Please just leave. I can't stand the sight of you. You make me sick.'

Leo silently begged her to look at him. But she didn't.

'Alice,' he said.

'Get out of here,' Alice said coldly. 'You're both as bad as each other. And look what you've subjected my children to. You should be ashamed of yourselves.'

He was. He wasn't. What was he supposed to have done? Just let it all happen? He didn't understand her.

Leo strode to the front door, pushed down the handle. Outside, he watched the automatic gate slide open. His life unfolding on a mechanical arm.

Behind him, he could hear Bruce's Porsche Cayenne roaring to life.

He slipped into the driving seat as Bruce's car careered down the road. Overwhelmed, he felt the tears rising from his throat. He gulped deeply, trying to suck in air. He was exhausted. Dead inside.

His life was out of control. And he didn't know what to do about it. He sat, trying not to cry. This was a total screw up.

When a small knock echoed on his car window, he started. Turned. Albert was holding a slightly bloody bag of frozen peas in his hand. Leo rolled down the window.

Albert handed it through.

'You're supposed to be locked in your mom's room,' Leo said, trying not to smile. Anyway, it hurt his face. He patted the cold packet against his face. 'Thanks, buddy.'

'Gotta go,' Albert said, going back to the bedroom. That Albert had recycled the peas for him was touching, despite the gore. And God they felt good. He started his car, put on his flicker, and turned into the road.

All miserable

She dialled Gillian.

'What's it, doll?' Gill said. 'I'm like two glasses into the vino by myself, the kids are both on sleepovers … Alice, are you there?'

Alice sniffed loudly.

'Alice?'

'Hey.'

'What's up, babe? You sound like you've been drizzing.'

'I'd like to change the code on my gate and alarm. And replace the front door locks. I wondered if you knew anyone? Doesn't that boyfriend of yours, Tony, do that sort of thing?'

'Ex-boyfriend. Oh God, I'm telling you from personal experience he wasn't very good with his hands. Know what I mean?'

'Oh. Okay,' Alice said, not much in the mood for *double entendres*.

'But I am. So very good. I am a computer engineer by training. You know that, don't you? Sure I can rejig your codes. Give me a few minutes. I'm coming.'

'You can? Oh you're wonderful.'

'I know.'

'Shall I send an Uber for you?'

'Oh please. It's like five minutes. I'll pack a bag. We're having a sleepover, right? With booze?'

'I'm not great company, Gill.'

'That's why I'm bringing the alcohol, Liss. What do they say? *Wine a little. You'll feel better?*'

'Do they now?' Alice said, beginning to smile.

'Five minutes, honey. Keep the doors locked.'

***

It wasn't five minutes, more like twenty, and Alice found herself pacing up and down, her shoulders hurting from the tension. After she'd knocked on the door and let the kids out, she was even more shocked by how Albert's nose had swollen. She didn't think it was broken. But how did she know? Apart from Dr Google? And besides that, what could she do about it? If she went to the hospital, she'd have to drag Enjoy out of her own bed, where she'd just settled, and then what about Albert? If he said something about what Bruce had done, surely her husband would be arrested? She hated him for his violence, but it was more complicated than that. They relied on him financially. And he wasn't a terrible person, just an angry one. Besides, in Albert's current state, he couldn't stand an interrogation. It could set him off even worse. She'd wiped his face down, asking him where he'd put the peas.

He shrugged. 'Forgot.'

In the end she'd crushed some ice, and placed it inside a dampened, folded-over dishcloth. She held it against his face, watching it turn pink.

'Does it hurt?' she asked.

Again, he shrugged. 'You were mean to Leo,' he said. 'He was helping me.'

'Darling, sometimes there are adult things you don't understand.'

'Oh please, Mother. I even understand what *fermions* are. There are two categories of these elementary particles: quarks and leptons. I know that quarks are the basis of protons and neutrons in the nucleus, whereas leptons include neutrinos and electrons. They're different because while leptons don't react to a nuclear force, quarks do. A fermion has an odd half-integer spin.'

Alice tried to straighten her face. 'I'm not sure that's entirely relevant in this particular situation, Bertie.'

'It's all about the spin-statistics theorem.'

'I'm talking more about the theorem of family dynamics.'

'Bowen's theory?'

'Excuse me?'

Albert made air quotes with his fingers: 'Often people feel disconnected from their families, but this is more feeling than fact. Families so profoundly affect their members' thoughts, feelings, and actions that it often seems as if people are living under the same "emotional skin".'

Alice sighed. 'Do you even understand what that means, lovey?'

'Sure, when Dad shouts and hits, it makes us all miserable.'

She couldn't fault that interpretation. She sighed, patting again at Leo's face. 'How does it feel?'

'Sore.'

She rummaged in her first-aid kit for a few Nurofen. 'These will be okay with your other meds. Take two.'

He popped them in his mouth, threw back his head and swallowed. 'Water?'

'Don't need it, Mom. I'm fine.'

She was tucking him in his own bed when the doorbell rang. Albert stiffened immediately. 'Who's that?'

'Gillian. She's helping me with something.'

He nodded, settling back into his pillows.

'Try to go to sleep, Bertie. You'll feel better in the morning. And you're safe now.'

'What about Leo?'

'What do you mean?'

'Is he still my teacher?'

'Sweetie, stop worrying. Everything's going to be okay.'

'I can't just switch my mind off, Mom. It's not a light bulb.'

'I know. But do your best. Things will seem calmer tomorrow.'

And as she turned off Albert's lamp, kissing her son on the forehead, she only wished she could guarantee it would be.

That bad

Lying in Monk's spare room, he tried to forget the night before. Naked skin. Fistfights. An unhappy, distressed wife. And the email he'd sent in a rage to his son from his phone because it's not like he could speak to him.

"You'd better rein yourself in, kiddo. Or I am going to do it for you. I don't care if you're high or low. You're not sick, you're just a fucking waste of space. I'm not tiptoeing around you anymore. You're not in charge. I am. Me. ME! You think the way you're behaving's okay? The way you're wrecking my marriage? My life? Your mother won't have sex with me because of you. She won't come near me. No longer, I'm telling you that right now. We'd be better off without you. And I'm going to put you in your place. Just wait for it. Be ready, Albert. This isn't over."

Yes, the mail was juvenile. Hurtful. He regretted it now but it wasn't like he could recall it. He'd deleted it from his phone but he would have to explain himself. Apologise. He'd made so many mistakes but he didn't think he was completely to blame. She'd denied him for weeks now. He deserved to be touched too. To be loved. He wondered if she still felt for him. It wasn't too hard to recall the first time he saw her… spectacular. Those legs!

Now, with crow's feet and her often harried look, she was, surprisingly, still beautiful. But she wasn't soft anymore. Not in the way she used to be. Responsive to *his* needs. Understanding *him*. She was gritty, clenched.

Of course, Albert had triggered this change. Not Bruce. It was all his fault.

What a different person she had been before motherhood.

Lighter. Happier. Spontaneous.

Fun.

Everything had begun to go downhill the moment Albert had burst through her womb. She was all touched out, resenting his need to press himself against her.

Can't you see I'm busy doing Bert's nappy? Not now, Bruce. I'm exhausted.

Oh God, I'm so tired, please just go to sleep.

Oh for goodness sake, just sort yourself out; I've just got home.

It wasn't easy to endure constant rejection.

But he loved her and he kept on trying. And her submission was grudging. Work. Another tickbox, ticked. But it was better than nothing, he supposed.

He thought, now, though, that they were at their end. She'd given up. And actually, he was beginning to think he had too.

He had enough self-confidence to realise he was still attractive. Fit.

Elaine had certainly shown him that. He allowed himself the vision of those breasts. Gravity defying and full. It was enough to make him hard. He moved his hands down to his groin. Used to the quick and easy manipulation of his own body, it didn't take long.

He wiped his sticky hands on the sheet, unsatisfied.

It was so obvious that a change was needed. A rupture or a reconciliation. With Albert constantly in the way, he had an idea of where it would go.

Alice was a mother first. A wife second, despite the order in which the events had occurred. Sometimes, when he was at his lowest, Bruce wondered what it would have been like if Albert had never ... been. And if Abigail hadn't died that day ... no Enjoy either. Or would Abigail even have been working for them without Albert? They hadn't needed someone around every day until he'd come into the picture. They'd managed with a char twice a week.

Now though, everything seemed to be coming to a head. Martini's deeds. His own. The intolerable antics of his son. And, perhaps more concerning, the heavy silences and black insinuations from Nyembe and Hing. He'd thought at the time there was something shifty about them. And now he was trapped. Money paid. Nothing delivered. Yes, he knew the connection now with Martini's dead lover, and that made him worry even more. Martini thinking with his dick instead of his head had sent him into this downward spiral.

He'd trusted him, for Christ's sake.

If none of the order arrived, how would he defend himself to his investors? He couldn't, of course. The final decision, however misguided, had been his. He'd have to take the hit. And the hit was enormous. Back-breaking.

Now, with icy silences between him and Martini, there would be no rescue boat. It was sink or swim. But entirely on his own recognisance.

In better times, he would have talked this through with Alice. Exposed his vulnerabilities. But now he was on his own.

Outside his bedroom he could hear the sounds of Gabriel and Michael waking up.

Gabe, the early riser, would be the one making coffee. Mike had never been good at mornings and had always needed a double shot of caffeine even to open an eye, preferably intravenously, as Gabe always recounted. It was Saturday morning, so no real rush, but Bruce's head was already thudding. He'd hardly slept, watching his world unravel in his mind. For the first time in his life, he felt completely alone, cast out like a leper. Although Gabe had let him sleep in the spare room, he knew there was a time limit on staying. There always was with guests, even brothers.

So the knock on his door was surprising.

Gabe balanced a tray as he stepped into the room. 'I thought you might need some sustenance,' he said. 'To fortify yourself.'

Not only was there coffee – thank God – but scrambled eggs on toast.

'Thanks,' he said, surprised.

'Want to talk about it?' Gabriel asked.

'I don't even know where to begin,' Bruce said. 'I guess I'm sorting things in my own mind.'

Gabriel nodded. 'Makes sense. And if Alice calls?'

'She won't.'

'That bad, huh?'

'It's all a total fuck-up, actually.'

'Well, you're going to have to sort something out. You can't avoid her forever.'

'It's been *one night*, Gabe. One night.'

'I know that. I'm just trying to help you.'

Bruce sighed. 'I do need help. I just don't know where to start, though. On top of all of this shit at home, there's the two fuckwits I'm dealing with, who promised me the moon and seem, at the moment, only to be able to deliver cheese. Or nothing at all.'

Gabriel looked blankly at his brother.

'So the first delivery. Just taps, right? So I pay the bill and the taps arrive. They're beautiful. Shiny. Great quality. The mixers are just as good. So I think, well, fantastic. A slightly longer process than local but the saving in the thousands. Multiple thousands. Then Nyembe says–'

'Nyembe?'

222

'My supplier.'

'So he says, okay, Mr Louw. Bruce. Put your money behind this and I'll get all the solar gear and the heat pumps for the entire complex. Same low price. Same impressive quality.'

'Like the taps.'

'Exactly.'

'And he talks the talk. Walks the walk. He's wearing Armani. Hugo Boss sunglasses. The whole nine yards. And I have to say, I'm already on the hook. So I'm out of breath, gagging for this amazing deal. My share of the pie is doubling and in my mind I've already spent it. Flights to New York, flashy speedboat, the works.'

'And then?'

'And then Nyembe says he's got to go. His shipment for another client has arrived. He's giving me a week to decide. And after that I'm the loser. But I'm already convinced and I do the EFT right there on the building site.'

'Everything?'

'No, the rest I have to get transferred from one of my other accounts. It takes a few days but I get the cash together.'

'And now?'

'Absolutely nothing. No tanks, no solar. Zilch.'

'Have you spoken to Martini about it? Isn't he your partner for this project?'

'I wanted to, but the conversation didn't go as planned.'

'What do you mean?'

'He threw me out the house on Friday.'

'Jesus, Bruce. Burning down a few bridges, much?'

'It wasn't even my fault.' Bruce watched the slight arching of his brother's eyebrows. 'No, Gabe. I mean it.'

'Alright,' Gabriel said. 'So what's the plan today?'

'I'm meeting Nyembe at the site. Tomorrow morning.'

'On a Sunday? But why? How's that going to help? Why would he even bother to come?'

'You know that model, Lebogang whatever her name was? The one who died in that car crash near Constantia?'

'Vaguely. I think I read something about that.'

'Well, she was Nyembe's sister. But I know something about her death. I saw her the night of the accident.'

'Oh Bruce. Sounds to me like you're playing with fire.'

'The arsehole has my money. And I have information. Isn't that how it works?'

'Right. You pay twice and he gets in for free.'

'Don't worry so much.'

'Do you want me to come with you?'

'I'll be fine, Gabe. I know what I'm doing.'

'Just like you knew what you were doing when you shelled out all that cash for the solar and tanks that don't seem to be coming?'

'Don't remind me! Anyway, Martini was the one who built the foundations to this particular house of cards.'

'How?'

'He made the introduction. He guaranteed their work.'

Gabriel let out a whistle between his teeth. 'Seriously, Bruce, is this really the best solution? Bringing Nyembe's dead sister into this? It's kind of – well – sick.'

'I'm not going to say anything if I don't have to. For all I know, he tells me the delivery is happening next week and we both leave happy.'

'Or you don't.'

'Yes, well,' Bruce commented. 'Let's hope *that* doesn't happen.'

Poisoned

Her head pounded. She felt like her whole body was encased in concrete, with holes only for her nostrils so that she could breathe. Her chest hurt, as if a very heavy dog was lying on her. And her pillow was wet. Clearly she'd been crying in the night. She remembered dreaming but not what she'd dreamt. But she knew whatever it was had left her heart racing. And she was beyond exhausted, wiped after a marathon all night. The light was pouring in the window and even though her curtains were closed, the streams coming through the gaps made her realise how late it was.

She checked her watch. 10h30. How was that even possible? Where were her children? Her dog? By now Malawi would have jumped into the bed and settled herself under the blankets, a child should have demanded food and she should have been wide-eyed and alert. Yet today she didn't really care. The previous evening had been too horrible. And then Gill. Those glasses of wine. Three? Four? With whisky she would have been fine but she just about never drank red. Her mind flitted to Leo. Then Bruce.

Oh God.

She rolled over to check her phone but found it wasn't next to the bed. She needed to get up. Shower. Get dressed. What kind of an example was she setting for her kids? Alice tried to move. Swing her legs over the edge onto the carpet. But that's as far as she got. She felt frozen. Shell-shocked. Poisoned.

When the door opened, she was still sitting there, her head in her hands.

Gill swung in, wearing a pair of running shorts, a luminous green crop top, and Nikes. Her head was in her pineapple style, cascading around her face. She was sweaty and smiling; she was also carrying a huge mug of coffee.

Alice moaned softly.

Gillian handed her the mug and sat down next to her. 'That awful, huh?'

'Worse.'

The Panados she slipped into her palm went down instantly.

'I've been bonding with your beautiful children. Enjoy and I did a ten kay.'

'Show-off.'

'And young Albert looks like he's been in a bar brawl. I took him to a doctor friend. Very discreet. The nose isn't broken. But I've taken photos. To document. You know? I took a few last night as well.'

'Yes, I remember,' Alice lied. 'How is he?'

'Upset. About Leo.'

'Me too.'

'He's tried to ring you. Five times. I took your phone so you wouldn't wake up.'

'And Bruce?'

'Nothing. Tosser.'

Alice nodded tiredly. Malawi entered the room, and leapt onto the bed. She stank of dog, the rancid odour of dust and sweat. 'Get off, you smelly hound,' Alice said.

'Ah, poor baby,' said Gill. 'Be kind, she ran the whole way.'

'Oh rub it in, why don't you? So where are my kids now?'

'Watching TV, something suitably PG-13.'

Alice tried to smile. 'Want a job?'

'Already have one. Alice's friend,' Gillian said, grinning.

'Oh God, I'm a job now? I'm going to have to work on my skills!'

'Perhaps you should start with a shower. I don't want to be mean, but you smell worse than Malawi. *Parfum de* distillery.'

'Hilarious.'

'And you should eat something. I'm making bacon and eggs. So clean yourself up, doll, and then I'm going to feed you.'

Pinned

Sunday.

Luckily he and Gabe were of similar stature, but Bruce was pleased to be the one with more hair. Bruce's jeans were still workable but the T-shirt he'd slept in yesterday needed a good wash. His brother had tossed a few items on the bottom of the bed.

'See what you want to wear, but I'm not giving you my jocks.'

'So much for brotherly love.'

'It's all about setting boundaries.'

'Thanks, I think.'

'Of course thanks. You're going to be the best dressed you've been in years, with or without my jocks.' Gabe smirked. 'And there's a spare toothbrush under the sink, in case you didn't find it yesterday.'

Bruce showered and dressed quickly. He wanted to get to the site before Nyembe and Hing. Easier to dominate if you were in place. He pushed Martini and his family situation out his mind. One issue at a time. And compartmentalisation was always something he'd been good at. Alice had always *hakked* on at him about it.

He got out the car, greeted the two labourers who were digging a trench nearby. Took a photo of the site. The development was beginning to show character. He took a photo. Posted it. #progress #goinggreen #off-the-gridliving

He walked to the back of the property, enjoying the fresh air. Then his phone rang.

'We're not coming.'

'Excuse me?'

'It's Senzo. Nyembe? I'll give you the address.'

'For fuck's sake, Nyembe. We arranged to meet here. And *I'm* the client. I'm already at the site.'

227

'Do you have a pen and paper, or do you want me to send you a pin?'

Bruce sighed. 'WhatsApp me. But I'm warning you. I'm sick of these bloody games.'

'Come on now, Mr Louw.' The voice was condescending. 'We want to all get what we need here, don't we?'

'You have my money, I think you have what *you* need.'

Bruce's phone pinged. It seemed he was going to some industrial area near Epping. He looked at the screen for a moment, frozen in hesitation. Normally he would phone Martini for backup. Something was screwed up here. And he was all alone. His own fault. He considered letting Gabe know. But Gabe was a pussy and Michael wasn't much better. He was going to do this and finish this off for good.

But even as he drove, he could hear his teeth working against each other. At this rate, he'd be grey by next week. He dug in the glove compartment at the stop street. Sometimes Alice kept pepper spray in there. But not today it seemed. *Dammit.*

The warehouse was behind another gate. A security guard opened it, studying Bruce impassively. He handed Bruce a clipboard with a form to complete. Bruce signed and when Bruce drove in, the security guard looked away disinterested. Bruce parked, reversing into the space for a quicker getaway. Not that that would help exactly with that massive galvanised entryway all locked up.

Gingerly, Bruce stepped out of the vehicle. He would sort this mess up and then, when this was done, he would think very, very hard about how to fix his family. And explain to Martini exactly what happened with Elaine.

But one thing at a time.

He looked around. This place was creepy. Everything locked up with chains on some of the doors. There was a bit of lime-green graffiti on one of the walls, the barbed-wire fence at the back covered in bird shit. He could hear a low hum. If it hadn't been in the middle of winter, he might have suspected it was the aircon. He shivered. What the hell was he doing here?

In front of him, a metal door swung open. Voices. But indistinct. The only sign of life beyond the pigeons, which were hopping about nearby.

He could turn around now, and just go back to Gabe's. But there was a lot of money hanging in the balance here. His reputation. His bloody profits. And yes, he could leave, but this would still be hanging over his head like a guillotine. Best just to get it over with.

He pushed his shoulders back, stabilising himself.

***

The door was heavier than he expected, more like the weight of a safe door than an entryway. He had to really shove to open it. Walking inside, he couldn't see anybody, but there was a sweet smell in the air that reminded him of a hunting trip. He sniffed. Forced himself forward. The cement floor was slightly damp, freshly mopped, maybe, but more likely a leak coming through the MDF roof.

'Hello?' Bruce called, feeling increasingly uncomfortable as no response came back. A corridor in front of him. The light on. He walked towards it.

As he moved through, the door to the passage slammed behind him. *Click.* Like a key in a lock. He bolted around, the hairs on his neck rising. *Shit.*

'Mr Louw,' he heard.

'What the fuck, Nyembe?'

'Oh calm down, just come through.'

With little choice at this point, Bruce forced himself forward. Nyembe was standing on the other side of a counter, a white but bloody plastic apron covering his clothes. On his feet, black wellington boots. But perhaps, more disturbing, the animal carcass hanging behind him, its entrails removed and dumped in a bucket below. But the body still dripping any remaining gore onto the floor. Bruce, who usually had a strong stomach, felt the bile rise in his throat. It was perhaps more out of fear than disgust. He wasn't totally unfamiliar with dead animals. And then, of course, there was Nyembe holding a meat saw, his teeth gleaming in his dark face.

Bruce tried to make his stance erect, his frame taller. He'd never been the victim of bullying. As one of the sporty kids, he'd never battled to hold his own, on or off the field. But now he was unarmed. Taken by surprise. But he knew even that wasn't true. This wasn't a revelation. He'd just been stupid enough to ignore his own sense of self-preservation in favour of the money. Bruce held onto the other side of the counter, trying to steady himself. His fingers pressed down, anchoring him. But then he let go quickly.

Nyembe had turned on the saw, beginning to carve a leg off the carcass. He was clearly experienced. An icy shiver traced its way up Bruce's spine. He tried to control the muscles in his face, adopt an impassive expression. But he wondered if he was achieving it. The sound of the machine drilled into his ears. He slid his hand into his pocket. If nothing else, he had his cell phone, which at least offered him a route to the outside world. He pulled it out, keeping his hands below the level of the counter. Martini's was the last number dialled. He tried to push he recording button in the WhatsApp button, then surreptitiously slipped it back into his pocket. He wondered if it was recording or not.

Nyembe put the saw down, wiping his hands on a towel. 'Excuse me that I don't shake your hand.'

'I'd rather you didn't,' Bruce said shortly.

Nyembe laughed. Bruce didn't.

'Listen, this charade is all very well but I have work to do, not watch you slice and dice an impala.'

'Springbok.'

'Who the fuck cares? Right now, I want my money back or the goods delivered. It's that simple.'

Nyembe clicked under his breath. 'I've been wondering about that daughter of yours.'

'My daughter? What the hell has she got to do with it?'

'I've always wondered. These cross-cultural adoptions. A bit of social investment? Brushing up the CV?'

Bruce bristled, despite the fact he knew Nyembe was achieving exactly what he wanted – to get a rise out of him. 'I love my daughter.'

'Oh come on, Bruce. There must be some other, shall we call it, advantages?'

'For Christ's sake, are you insane?'

'She's a good runner. Tall. Very tall. I've seen her. Up and down the road. Long legs. Tiny little shorts.'

The sweat beaded his forehead. This was getting out of control. 'You keep away from her.'

'So sweet. Innocent, even. She always goes the same route. Five kilometres usually, but then there's the ten-kay route as well. You know it?' Not waiting for an answer, Nyembe lifted the saw, buzzing again. As he sliced the meat, Bruce felt his heartbeat intensify. Was this man threatening his family? And for what? The measly money that he already had? Measly in comparison to Enjoy's life, anyway. Or more?

Nyembe switched off the saw.

'And your son. A little strange. Gawky, isn't he? Awkward age. And that wife of yours. Spending quality time with the tutor. But you know about that, I'm sure.'

Bruce's jaw dropped. Then he closed his mouth very firmly. Of course this man was a fucking lunatic. He saw what he saw. Alice was a frigid bitch at the moment, but she was as pure as the driven snow and all the clichés that went with that.

The man washed his hands under the tap of a huge metal trough. 'Walk with me,' he instructed.

'I'm getting a little tired of these games, Nyembe.'

'Oh don't be such a spoilsport, *Louw*. We're just getting started. I'll give you a tour.'

'I don't want a fucking tour.'

Nyembe looked at him. His eyes piercing. 'You'll take the fucking tour if I tell you to take the fucking tour. Are you hearing me?'

Bruce gulped, then nodded. They walked to another thick metal door, where the hum he'd noticed when he arrived was the loudest.

'Come on, Louw, open up.'

Bruce did; shoving the door handle down with a violence that seemed to be rising in him like damp. Inevitable. Insidious. The adrenaline whooshed through him, making him dizzy. His hand, he realised, was clammy with sweat.

Once inside, Nyembe pulled the heavy door shut. Here there were pieces of meat drying. Row upon row hanging from the ceiling, like desiccated black tongues. The smell was overpowering, and Bruce held his hand to his mouth.

Noticing this, Nyembe smirked.

Bruce said nothing, however, and followed behind him.

'Am I locked in here?' he said suddenly. 'This charade has gone on long enough. Tell me what you want and just let me leave.'

'Maybe I don't want you to leave. Maybe you're just going to stay here and chop meat.' Nyembe laughed but his deep voice sounded crazed, reminding Bruce of his son. Is this is what Albert was going to be? A psychopathic maniac? Bruce tried to control his breathing, to keep his head about him. And at least he'd said *chop*, rather than *be* meat.

They passed a massive fan – the slightly warm air enveloping them. An exit door. He was about to run towards it, but already the man had gripped his wrist hard. 'I have a knife and I *will* use it, Bruce.'

'Okay, you've got me. Just spit it out.'

'You don't have much patience, do you *Mr Louw*?'

'No,' Bruce said. 'I actually don't. Never been one of my qualities.'

Nyembe laughed good humouredly. But the laughter made Bruce's blood freeze. He should have trusted his instincts that first day. But he hadn't. And now …

They reached the end of the room. To the back, meat hooks hung down, their sharp metal points exposed like bare necks. As Nyembe pushed the exit door open, the vacuum seal whooshed. And now they were in another compartment of bloody corpses. It wouldn't be that difficult to hide a human body here, Bruce thought, the anxiety clenching into his guts. He wanted to vomit. He could taste the bile jetting up his throat. But he swallowed hard. This was the point, he knew. To terrify him.

'Okay, Nyembe,' he said. 'You've made your point loud and clear. What do you want me to do?'

LEO

Worth it?

Once he'd set up the office – not knowing really if Albert would ever use it – he spent the rest of the weekend with his family. Apart from that long escape on the mountain on Sunday morning, alone and sore where Bruce had hit him. When he'd arrived, his mother, seeing his swollen eye, was typically business-like. She removed two ice packs from the freezer and made him lie down on the couch while she tended to his face. It felt good to be looked after, even after she handed him a pair of pink panties she'd found in the jeans he'd mistakenly left at her house.

As she placed the silky material in his hand, she said, 'I washed the jeans for you. And when I checked the pockets for tissues, I found these. They have anything to do with the state of your face?'

The ice packs hid his blush. 'No kissing and telling, Mamma.'

'I'll take that as a yes. I hope she's worth it.' And when she removed the packs, and wiped down his face, she looked hard into his eyes. 'The last time you had a shiner like this was from rugby. An elbow in the face I seem to remember.'

'Water polo. Not rugby.'

'Mmmhhmm. Well, you look awful.'

'Thanks.'

'I'm going to put a little concealer around your eye, so you won't scare the baby.'

'What?'

'We're going to visit Luisa. I need to cuddle my granddaughter. And you're going to drive me because I feel like your company, even if you're distracted.'

Leo's heart sank. All he needed now was to have another sisterly lecture. Especially with his mother there.

'I don't think so, Mamma.'

233

'Did I say I was asking you? Get your car started and stop messing about.'

Leo sighed, hesitating. He had an enormous headache. He looked like a brawler. And he was exhausted. But his mother simply picked up her handbag, an enormous thing that could probably hold a toilet seat, and marched him to the front door, thumping him gently on his backside. 'Get that butt in that car seat, *caro*. You know I have absolutely no patience with dithering.'

He climbed into the car, looking across at his mother, who was anything but the stereotypical Italian mamma. For one thing she was a truly average cook and her thin angularity testified to that. His father had always been the feeder, the nurturer, the emotional one, while she was the practical parent, the problem-solver, the person with the screwdriver, the light bulbs and the budgets. He knew, without questioning it, that he was now the problem she was solving.

'Well?' she said, settling her bag at her feet. 'What are we waiting for?'

***

In the hospital, they signed themselves into the neonatal ward. One of the nurses recognised Leo and squinted at his face. But she said nothing, apart from, 'Your baby's a little pumpkin!'

'She's not my baby,' Leo muttered under his breath, feeling exposed.

Leo's mother marched ahead of him, into Luisa's private room. 'Where's my *bambinella*?' she said.

'Hello, Mamma.'

'Ah yes. Ciao! Now where've you hidden my granddaughter?'

'A hearing test. I was asleep, so they took her.'

'You let them take our baby?'

'Mamma, it's a hospital. I was fast asleep. Why don't you go see what's going on? I'm a little sore.'

Their mother left the room, her voice loud down the corridor. 'Where's my Faye? Where's my granddaughter?'

The siblings looked at each other, beginning to smile.

'So, little brother. Wall. Husband. Or windscreen?'

'What?' Leo said.

'I guess husband. Am I right?'

'I don't want to talk about it.'

'Bull's eye, then.'

'If you must know, I was protecting Albert from Bruce. He punched him in the face.'

'My God.'

'And I asked Alice to choose. She hasn't spoken to me since Friday night.'

'Come here,' Luisa said, patting the side of the bed. He didn't move. 'Come here, I said, Leo,' more forcefully this time.

He sat. As she put her arms around him, he finally let himself cry. He thought about Bruce. And Alice. Albert and Enjoy.

He had so very much to cry about.

Stone-cold sober

Nyembe stood opposite him, seeming even more intimidating than he had by the hanging meat.

'You'll be accepting the deliveries – all the deliveries – without question.'

Bruce said nothing. His breath was catching in his throat and his heart clenched tight and hard. He wondered if he was having a heart attack but a panic attack was more likely. Christ, he was turning into his kid. He focused on evening out his breathing. He heard Alice's voice in his head, the way she spoke to Albert when he was losing it. Recalled the relief on the boy's face as his breath returned. Then he directed his gaze at Nyembe, keeping his eyes directly on him.

'And what, may I ask, will the deliveries contain?'

'You may not ask.'

'Is it drugs? Weapons? Children? Pornography?'

'You're asking, Bruce.'

'So fucking what?' he said, trying not to sound intimidated. His voice shook, betraying him.

'What does it matter to you? You protect your family, you do what you need to do.'

'Surely there are limits, even for that?'

'You're not very loyal then, Bruce. Shall we just cut you loose? That daughter of yours? That wife? Your autistic kid?'

'He is not autistic.'

'Weird then. Very weird.'

'You don't get to comment on my family, you arsehole.'

'Mind yourself, Bruce. I don't think you're holding any cards here. Let's just say you don't touch those water tanks until I say so.'

'Yes? And what about the stuff I fucking bought?

'Ah, Bruce. Don't worry about it. You'll get what you paid for.'

***

Bruce drove fast through the open gate of the industrial estate. The security guard was nowhere to be seen – it was him, most likely, who'd locked the door behind Bruce as he'd gone in. And now, the warning over, he wasn't needed any longer. Bruce shivered; his nerves tight and his stomach pulsing from the experience. The bile rose up and he stopped the car to vomit on the grassy verge. A car close behind hooted. They probably thought he was drunk.

But he was stone-cold sober, imagining himself hanging from that meat hook. That sharp butcher's knife at his throat. Nyembe knew too much about him, too much about his family.

He cursed Martini. He'd clearly used Bruce to get in Nyembe's sister's good graces. And then he'd killed her. It was manslaughter, sure, but Martini *was* responsible. He wondered how to untangle the mess he was in. Inside, his guts roiled once more. How did he end up being so fucked up?

He'd temporarily forgotten the incident with Elaine. He found Martini's number in his contacts and called, but when his friend didn't answer, he remembered again.

It was another day of the silent treatment. Now, when he really needed help. Martini always used to have his back. Always.

Did a lifetime of friendship disappear just like that? One stupid drunken mistake? He couldn't believe what had happened with Elaine. Elaine, of all the people on this earth. She'd planned it; that was certain. The way she'd ripped her blouse open, the buttons popping onto the couch.

But why? He just couldn't fathom it.

Why try to screw him knowing Martini was about to come home? What purpose did it serve?

Bruce picked up his phone, scrolled for her number. So many of his bridges were burnt. What difference did it make if he lit another match?

At first she didn't answer. It was obvious she was disconnecting every one of his calls. But finally, she picked up. She sounded breathless, a gust of wind rocketing around her. Obviously she'd gone outside.

'Hello,' she said, her voice icy.

'Why?' Bruce said with preamble.

'Oh please, Bruce. You're all hurt now?'

'You've never shown the remotest interest in me. At all. Ever. Then the night you know your husband's on his way, you pop out your boobs and I'm supposed to jump you?'

'You *did* try to jump me, as far as I can recall.'

237

'Well, what the hell do you expect, Elaine?'

'Nothing. You did exactly what I wanted. So predictable. And now your precious Martini has lost the person he loves most in the world.'

'You're leaving him?'

'Don't be ridiculous, Bruce. Not me, *you*. Now he's lost *you*. Because no man with even the slightest bit of self-respect will stay friends with a guy who tried to nail his wife.'

Without another word Bruce disconnected.

He hoped to God she was wrong.

Never in his life had he felt so alone. It was like the entire word was conspiring against him. His wife. His clients. His children. His friends. He'd go back to his brother but he couldn't stand the self-satisfied smirk of a too-happy perfect life.

He'd have to turn this all around. He just didn't know how.

His phone pinged and he glanced at it.

The next time I see you, I hope it's in a coffin.

What the fuck? Nyembe? Martini? Alice? The list was certainly piling up.

Pulling his car to the side, he looked at the number. Number withheld. Of course it was.

Maybe he should be getting used to this. It was just another threat. But he wasn't stupid enough not to feel threatened.

He could do with a run. Brush out the cobwebs, calm the spirits. Make a plan. And fuck it, if he had to do it alone, so bloody be it.

Done

Nyembe's voice was crisp and businesslike. 'It's done.'

Martini hesitated. 'Done how?'

'You told me to take care of it, and I have. If you wanted to know the details, you could have done it yourself.'

Martini felt a cold chill come over him. He wasn't built for this. *Done it himself?* Sure, the whole thing with Elaine had made it easier to swallow but once this debt was paid off, he would dispense of Nyembe and Hing. He regretted the day they'd ever hooked up.

'Are you saying he's dead? Or domesticated?'

Nyembe chortled. 'He's not a dog.'

'Cowed then?'

'Excuse me?'

It was almost comedic. Almost. These animal references. 'You know what I mean, Nyembe.'

He could virtually hear the shrug across the phone connection. 'What do you care, Webster? Just take it from me that it's done.'

'I do care, if you must know. Where are you now?'

'What the hell difference does that make? In Epping, at my offices, finishing off something.'

Or someone? He almost choked.

Martini wasn't responsible for this. It wasn't like he'd ordered a hit, or anything. And Nyembe was just probably teasing him. His humour had always seemed off-colour. Growing up in a butchery business might do that to you.

When things had died down, maybe, he thought, maybe he would even bring his friend back into the fold.

But then he thought about Lebogang, her body bleeding, the quick adjustments he made as he left the accident.

Bruce knew. He *knew*.

It would hang over them forever. And if Bruce ever told Nyembe, well, he knew *he* would be the one lying at the bottom of a ditch somewhere with his head carved off. Nyembe didn't mess around. He should have worked that out at the beginning. But self-preservation was a slippery thing. *Wasn't it?*

And Bruce was a loose cannon at the moment. Unpredictable. Unreliable.

So it didn't matter that when Martini went to sleep at night he dreamt about him and Bruce as boys. Arms around each other in a scrum. Boozing illegally on a beach. Sleeping on a river bank, tired out from an all-day hike. Their trip to Yosemite, and their Las Vegas jaunt drinking free shots and playing the slot machines until they'd made enough coin to buy dinner.

This friendship had reached its sell-by date. *Or had it?* His heart jack-knifed.

Maybe it was actually Nyembe who needed to be dealt with now. And Martini could finally get his own life back on track.

That, he supposed, could work too.

Liberated

He was tying his laces. The weather was shit. So shit. But he wasn't going to melt and maybe if he was lucky, lightning would zap him and the problems would incinerate with the rest of him. It would be a glorious way to go!

He didn't mean it. Obviously.

But life, its vagaries, seemed pretty insurmountable. And there was something pure about it. Pure as vodka. Which he could do with a shot of. To start.

A car guard was standing nearby wearing a bright orange bib. They nodded silently at each other. Bruce's crimson rain jacket was already sticking to him. The rain. And the sweat pouring from him. Stress sweat. He was going to give himself a heart attack. Orphan his children. Finally, he'd make the little shithead happy.

And who said parenting wasn't all sacrifice?

Bruce's phone rang. He almost didn't answer it. He couldn't face another encounter with his waste of sperm or anyone else for that matter. The bust-up at his home a few days before was more than enough. But maybe this was the turning point. Maybe the little squirt would finally know who the alpha male really was.

'Dad?' It wasn't his son though. Thank God for Enjoy.

'Hello baby.'

'When are you coming back?' Her voice was strained. Pitchy.

'I don't know.' He sighed. 'I guess it just depends on Mom.'

'Mom's asleep.'

'Now?'

'Yes. For hours and hours.'

'Well, I guess she's wrung out. It's been a stressful time. For me too.'

'Mmmhhmm,' she said non-committally.

'I'm at Newlands Forest. Going for a run. Maybe up to Ledges. You loved that last time. Want to come?' He waited, wishing he hadn't asked.

The silence from her was deafening.

'Enjoy, are you still there?'

'Yes. But I'm not sure.'

'Well, I'm going.'

'I don't know. The weather's really muck … Nah. Not today. Another time, hey Dad?'

Bruce sighed. 'Fine then, stay at home and be bored. I can't make your fun for you. Read a book. Watch TV.' He disconnected, relieved she'd said no. He could do without a handbrake.

It felt liberating, like cutting a string to let a balloon rise up into the air and fly away.

***

As he ran up the path, he passed a group of runners. Nobody he knew, but they all looked exhausted. A German shepherd ran behind them, his long tongue lolling. His fur was wet through, and caked with mud. Bruce's shoes sank into the soft sand. Streams of water ran off into the gulleys next to him, draining away untrapped. The city was drying up and the water sinking away. A bit like him. His energy was low. He should have eaten something other than the muffin he picked up at the SuperSpar. The really bad coffee that came with it. He sucked on the outlet from his CamelBak. He was saving his biltong and energy bar for the view from the top. But there were a few jelly babies in a packet in his pocket. He stopped for a few seconds. Unwrapped the crumpled plastic. The sweets were a bit old. Hard and dusty. But he ate them anyway.

He felt more cheerful as he started up the hill again. His legs burnt and it was a good feeling. Lactic acid. A distraction from everything else. The pain was better than thinking.

He ran faster.

He hadn't gone much further when he bumped into Tim Herd, an engineer he sometimes used for projects. Always garrulous, Tim was already speaking before they had both come to a standstill.

'Only heading up now?' he asked. 'I've been on the trail for two hours already. Training for a marathon. You know the one in Ceres? Newish.'

Bruce didn't. He hadn't run a marathon for years. He preferred triathlons anyway. More varied.

But Tim didn't seem to care for an answer anyway. 'And where's your dog today? Usually she's nipping at your heels. My dog, you know Rocky? The black lab I had? Died. No warning. Probably a heart attack. Keeled

242

over in the garden. My kids were there. My daughter tried mouth to mouth. Not much help. But sad, hey. Sad. Thinking of a puppy. But you can't just replace a pet, just like that. Part of the family. Devastating. And how's that wife of yours? Still so beautiful? You're a great couple. Great! My wife's on sabbatical. Going to some art theory thing in Florence. Abandoning me for six weeks. Granny moving in. Not sure that will be fun. But good for her, hey? I've always thought that my wife could–'

'Listen mate,' Bruce said before Tim could continue. 'Nice to see you, but I've got to go. Catching up with someone. Fallen a bit behind. You know how it is.'

'Sure. No problem. Really good to catch up. Nice to hear your news.'

Bruce grimaced slightly. 'You too,' he noted, beginning to run before Tim could start talking again. It was enough to spur him on at speed.

Breathing again

On Monday, he arrived at Alice's house, as he'd promised. Alice hadn't called him back and his heart was so sore that the pain well exceeded the swelling of his face. And now he was outside her house with no idea of whether his life without Alice had just begun. He tapped the steering wheel nervously. Should he get out or just sit there? Then as he made a move to exit the vehicle, he saw Albert emerging from the house, a bag slung over his left shoulder. As always, he was wearing a hoodie to cover most of his face and tracksuit pants that were holey from overuse, especially at the knees. On his feet were a pair of tackies, the laces tucked rather than tied. Leo found himself smiling for the first time since Friday.

Seeing Leo looking at him, the boy waved shyly and grinned. Leo unlocked the doors, and Albert slid in. What a pair they made. Their faces both discoloured by vibrant bruises. Leo and Albert knocked fists together and Albert said excitedly, 'I thought you might not come. I got up really early, like at five, and I thought, if Leo doesn't come I'm going to get on my bike and ride to you.'

'Why wouldn't I come, buddy?'

'Well, Dad promises stuff. You know, like an ice cream or something and then he doesn't come home in time. Then we wait all night for our treat and when he gets back he's forgotten. And he says he's sorry, next time he'll remember, but he never does.'

'I'm not your Dad.'

'I know. I wish you were.'

Leo warmed, starting the car with a quick turn of his wrist. 'Your mom know you're with me?'

'Yeah, sure. Look, she's at the window.'

Leo looked up, seeing Alice, her face expressionless. He didn't know what to think. But then she lifted her hand and waved, her eyes reflecting back his uncertainty.

He waved back.

***

They worked all morning. In their breaks, Albert petted Rascal and told him that they hadn't seen Bruce.

'And I don't miss him,' Albert confided. 'He sent me an email, you know? I showed it to Enjoy.'

'An email?'

'Yes. Look, I have it here.' Albert pulled out a well-thumbed piece of paper.

Leo peered over his shoulder. His heart sinking at the damage this terrible man was doing. He scanned the text quickly. ... Rein yourself ... waste of space ... wrecking my marriage ... she won't come near me ... better off without you ...

'Jesus,' Leo said. 'You need to show your mother, not Enjoy.'

'Enjoy was so flipping mad! Now she knows he hates me for sure.' Albert shrugged. 'Anyway, I don't care. It's peaceful in the house now. No fighting. It's like there's more space, you know? I can really breathe!' Albert puffed out his chest as though pulling in as much oxygen as he could fit. 'I like being here,' Albert confided. 'In your house. It's like crawling down an escape tunnel.'

Leo smiled. 'I'm glad.' Yet the tone of the email still worried him. The man sounded unhinged. Dangerous. He tried to focus on what Albert was saying.

'... you know? But I think Mom is worried. She cried a lot on the weekend. She pretended she was fine but she's a really shitty actress.' He tasted the word, waiting for Leo to correct him. Leo didn't. 'Anyway, her eyes were all swollen up. Like massive strawberries. And on Friday, after you and Dad left, she called Gillian. And Gillian stayed the night. And now we have a new code for the alarm. And I'm not supposed to tell anyone. But you're not just anyone, right?'

'Right.'

'And you can keep a secret? Hey, Leo?'

'Sure, buddy.'

'So I was thinking, if it's okay, maybe I could meet that baby. Faye? Because I haven't met such a tiny baby before and I think I would like to. But we need to do it soon. Because babies lose seven to ten percent of their birth weight in the first week and I want to see what she looks like now.'

'They do?'

245

'And if your sister is breastfeeding, Faye will feed eight or more times in twenty-four hours, so that's at least every three hours, so she's probably tired and maybe we can help.'

'You're very informed, Bert.'

The boy shrugged. 'So can we? I think it's a good homeschooling topic, because I can track her from now until she's one, and then we can do a chart and graphs and stuff.'

'You've certainly thought it through.'

'Also. I want to meet your sister.'

The mountain

Dassies had begun to emerge to bask in the sun, which had appeared brightly from behind a cloud. Bruce was further up the mountain now and he was going to have to start clambering soon. He liked this part of the trail, mainly because he could slow down and focus on his steps. His breathing. Keep his grip firm, direct his attention. Listening to his own heartbeat pulsing in his head, he thought about Nyembe. Martini had said that the man had fingers in a lot of pies, but he didn't realise it meant the actual ingredients.

Bruce had thought briefly at the meat factory about how it would help him to tell Nyembe the real story of his sister's death. Gabe's warnings had rung true at the time and anyhow, Martini had always pulled through for him. Bruce was many things but he was never a snitch. It wouldn't achieve anything. If he was going to pull this friendship back – and he was – it wasn't going to start with another betrayal. It only occurred to him now too, that his incident with Elaine would hurt Alice too. If she heard about it.

But why would she? He wasn't proud about it and he didn't see Elaine as a total bitch. She was messing with him and Martini but Alice had never hurt her.

You couldn't tell with people though.

Bruce was beginning to feel light-headed. Slightly unhinged. Like his blood flow had thinned in his head and thickened at his feet.

But when he looked down, he saw a familiar figure coming up the mountain.

It couldn't be …?

What the hell?

This person was faster than he was. Lithe and limber compared to his own lumbering gait today. Long legs, easily buoyed forward. Un-fucking-

247

believable. Escaping the world for a few hours clearly wasn't on the cards today.

He slowed as the new arrival rocketed towards him, hair hidden under a yellow Nike cap.

Milk

The next day, they arrived at Luisa's door. Her hair was flowing around her face unbrushed and wild and she was wearing a white blouse with buttons, and a long skirt, looking beatific. Leo expected Albert to be shy, to hide behind him, but instead he pushed past him and held out his hand.

'I'm Albert. And you must be Luisa and I'm very pleased to meet you.'

Luisa smiled, and shook the proffered hand. 'Well,' she said. 'What a gentleman. Do come in.' She swept her arm in a flowing motion and Albert walked in.

Leo caught Luisa's expression and shrugged slightly. 'How's my goddaughter?'

'You know what I've noticed, Albert,' Luisa said. 'Since I've had Faye I've become invisible.'

Albert nodded knowingly. 'It's like all you're good for now is to provide milk.'

Leo's jaw dropped but Luisa smiled. 'Exactly, you're so perceptive.'

'Well,' said Albert. 'Where is she then?'

Luisa's brow funnelled a little, but then she laughed. 'I'll show you.'

And she walked into the lounge where a tiny baby was lying in a bassinet. Her eyes were open, watching them seriously.

'Faye,' Luisa said. 'This is Albert.'

'Newborns aren't pretty, are they?' Albert said. 'Don't worry,' he added. 'I'm sure she'll improve over time.'

Leo tried not to laugh. 'I told you, Lou, she looks more like her dad.'

'So can I hold her? Please?'

'Alright,' Luisa replied. 'But you need to sit down.'

249

'I've googled it,' Albert said. 'I should support the head. And I don't have any flu or other diseases. Apart from mental ones. Which aren't contagious. And I took all my pills this morning. So I'm not a danger to her.'

'Right,' Luisa said, glancing at Leo once again.

'Bert, you'd never be a danger, with or without the pills,' Leo said reassuringly.

'Right,' he replied, echoing Luisa.

'How about I make us some tea or some juice?' Luisa suggested.

'Sugar-free?' asked Albert. 'My mom will kill me if I have sugar. Or maybe we can cheat?'

'Sure,' Luisa said, glancing at Leo. 'Why not? Don't tell her, okay?'

Luisa and Leo sat next to each other on the couch, Albert and Faye in the tub chair. There was an expectant silence in the room and Leo knew that Luisa was gagging to ask what was going on with Alice. But she said nothing, and all that could be heard was the sound of sipping. Leo asked where Frans was and Luisa sighed.

'Some oil rig or other,' she said. 'At least he got to meet his own daughter.'

'How long is he gone this time?'

'Not sure, maybe three weeks?'

'And you're managing?'

'You know me – the manage-r. Dutiful wife and mother.'

There was another silence, and as though to fill the quiet, Faye let out a huge ripper on Albert's lap. His face was a picture, and Leo began to laugh.

'I think she's pooped, seriously right through her Babygro,' Albert said matter-of-factly, touching the wetness on his lap. 'When you change her, you must wipe away from her bits not towards. Or she could get an infection.'

'Well,' Luisa said. 'Aren't you just a mine of important information? Want to help me?'

'I think,' Albert said. 'I've seen enough for one day. But thank you for the generous offer.'

Leo tried to not grin by how controlled yet sarcastic he sounded.

Chicken

When Leo and Albert drove up she was getting out the dinner. Chicken fillets and wraps. Something quick and easy. She still hadn't spoken to Leo, frozen like the chicken she was, the chicken in her hands. As if saying nothing would be enough. She was working hard to keep herself together. Bruce had not come back. He hadn't even phoned and she wondered if she'd been a little extreme by changing the alarm code, the code for the gate. Legally, she wasn't even sure she was allowed to do it. It was his house too, after all. Gillian had dismissed her concerns.

'Oh Alice, haven't you learnt anything from me? Possession is nine tenths of the law.'

Even more concerning, though, was her inability to keep track of her own kids. Waking late on Sunday as well, she'd found Enjoy had gone for a run, nowhere to be seen. Alice hadn't heard a thing. She'd been horrified.

'Why didn't you stop her?' Alice had asked Albert.

'Why would I? Anyway, I was still asleep.'

And since Enjoy didn't own a phone, she couldn't get hold of her. It was many hours before her daughter returned, dripping with sweat, an indecipherable expression on her face. She didn't react to Alice's anger either, shaking her head and walking to the bathroom.

'I'm here, Mom,' she said, before she closed the door. 'So don't freak out.'

'Next time, please take the emergency phone.'

'Why? No emergency?'

'Yes, but there could have been.'

And now she was 'freaking out' again. Her son was stepping out the car and she could let Leo leave again, like she had before. Because she was a coward. Weak. Pathetic. But instead she threw her shoulders back and walked outside quickly.

She waved tentatively at Leo who looked at her, not moving out the car. He didn't wave back either, so now she was caught with indecision. And the ridiculousness of it all. So she pushed the remote, opening the gate, indicating for him to drive inside.

As Albert climbed out the car, he smiled at Alice. 'I met the baby today, Mom. I met Faye. And I held her!'

'Was she cute?'

'Of course. And she liked me. I could tell.'

Leo smiled.

'Anyway, why can't Leo come in for a drink like he used to? I'm thirsty.'

'Sure,' Alice said, trying to keep herself neutral. 'I didn't say he couldn't.'

'Come on, Leo. I want to show you my new algorithm. For my Rubik's cube.'

Alice leant down to peer into the car where Leo still sat. 'Now how,' she asked, 'can you refuse an invitation like that?'

***

As she stood pouring the drinks, a whisky for her, a beer for Leo and a lemonade for the kids, she could hear Albert and Leo chatting. She longed for Leo to come into the kitchen, to hold her, his body tight against hers. Instead, when he came in, he sat on the other side of the counter.

'How have you been?' he asked, in a dispassionate tone.

'I didn't call you back.'

'I noticed.' His mouth twitched a little at the corner. 'You didn't reply in any way.'

'I was a mess.'

'Me too.'

'How's your eye?'

'It still looks worse than it feels. Any sign of Bruce?'

'We haven't been in touch since Friday. You know, since he left.'

'Since you kicked us both out, you mean.'

She smiled. 'Not letting me off the hook, then?'

'Do you think I should? I was protecting Albert.'

'I know.' She sighed, wiping her wet hands on a tea towel.

'Are you going ...' His voice petered out but Alice caught him.

'Going?'

'Going to have him back? Bruce, I mean?'

Albert and Enjoy walked in, grabbing their glasses without thanking Alice. She flicked the nearest child with her drying cloth.

'Ouch,' Albert said.

'Thanks Mom,' Enjoy said, diving out the way before she got flicked too. There was something different about Enjoy today. Alice could sense it.

'You okay, Enjoy?' she asked.

'When are you going to phone Dad?' she asked.

'I'm not, for the moment.'

'I think you should phone him.'

'I'm sorry, lovey, but that's none of your business. I know you miss him, and you're welcome to phone him yourself if you want to speak to him.'

She tried to hand her daughter the phone but Enjoy wouldn't take it. Instead she burst into tears and ran into her room.

Alice glanced at Leo.

'Leave her, she's entitled to be upset. He is her dad, after all.'

Alice nodded uncertainly.

'When can we visit Faye again?' Albert asked Leo, oblivious to Enjoy's mood. 'She's so cute. Those fingernails!'

'Isn't she?' Leo said, smiling.

'Mom, she's so adorable. She was even cute when she farted.'

'Nice, Bert,' Leo said.

Alice laughed. 'Well, I think we'll have to make sure it's okay with Luisa. It's hard having a baby. You get really tired and grumpy. Maybe we can bring her some food so she doesn't have to cook.'

'I could help,' Albert said.

'Sure you could, buddy,' commented Leo.

'Anyway,' Alice said, her eyes meeting Leo's. 'I love babies too. Especially *my* babies.'

'Do you now?' Leo said, casually but his voice broke slightly.

'Absolutely,' she said smiling, then clinked her glass against his.

The beginning of something

Did this mean what he thought it did? He wanted to pick her up, drag her to the bedroom and ravish her, but instead, here they were as Albert explained his latest algorithm, in great detail and with very little pause for breath. The Rubik's cube spun back and forth. He had to admit; the kid was impressive.

As Albert gabbled on, Leo could feel the slight pressure of Alice's body against his. Except it wasn't slight, it felt like he was being scalded down his side. Their hands grazed and Leo's breath caught like Albert's. Like a landed fish. He hoped the kids would lose interest in them and go and find an iPad or something. But that wasn't really Albert's way. He knew that. Bert would be on this topic until he'd extinguished it. Finally, it wasn't the children's abandonment of them that altered the evening.

It was the doorbell.

The policewoman and man, parked outside the front gate.

Alice's brow furrowed. 'Do we let them in? How do we know they're even real police?'

'Mom. They're in a cop car. You listen to too much Cape Talk,' Albert commented. 'Get them to flash a badge or something.'

'Right.'

'Let me go,' Leo said, 'Before you open.'

He walked out the front door, and waited for the passenger to get out the car. 'What's this about?' he said, taking a wild guess in his mind.

'You live here?' the man said.

'No, I'm just visiting.'

'Well, we need to speak to the owner of the house.'

'Do you have identification? Alice asked me to check. She's the owner.'

The man shrugged, extracted a badge and waved it at him in a way that he was completely unable to read it. But it looked genuine. Leo felt suddenly nervous.

'Can I ask what this is about?'

'We'll speak to the owner, dankie.'

Rebuffed, Leo nodded towards the kitchen window. And the gate shuttled along.

No good could come from this sort of visit. It was, inevitably, the beginning of something horrible.

Missing

They were Warrant Officer Boesak and Constable September. She was tall, extremely thin. Almost skeletal, with slightly pockmarked cheeks, a thick dusting of freckles over her nose, and beautiful teeth. She was wearing bright red lipstick, almost incongruous with the blue uniform and rather stern manner. Her nails were long and pointed, like talons. He was shorter than her by at least three centimetres, a receding chin, with a thick head of hair, already greying at the temples. She was clearly the one in charge, although he looked older.

Alice led them to the lounge, sent the kids to their rooms, their ears flapping wildly to hear.

'Should I go?' Leo asked her.

'No. Please stay.' Then she looked at the police officers. 'Can you tell us why you're here?'

'Do you own a red Porsche Cayenne, registration CA 459 213?'

'Well, my husband owns a Porsche Cayenne. I can't remember the registration number offhand, but I can check for you.' She stood up, opened a file on the bookshelf. As she was about to read it off, Albert popped his head out his door.

'That's Dad's registration. CA 459 213.'

'Is that what you said?' she asked.

Warrant Officer Boesak nodded. She studied Albert. And then looked again at Leo. 'Do I know the two of you?'

'Who?'

'You and the young man. You both look very familiar. I never forget a face.'

'No, I don't think so.'

'Oh, I disagree. We've met before. Don't worry, it will come to me.'

Alice pulled her knees up behind her on the couch. She thought it would make her look relaxed, but now she felt unbalanced. 'Albert,' she said. 'Please go back to your room and close the door.' She waited for the door to close, before she asked again. 'Can you please tell me what is going on? Why are you asking about my husband's car?'

'It was found abandoned at Newlands Forest.'

'Abandoned?' Alice said blankly. 'What do you mean?'

'When did you last see your husband, Mrs Louw?'

'On Friday evening. Around seven, or eight. I don't remember exactly.'

'And did you speak to him since?'

'No.'

'Why not?'

'What has that got to do with the price of eggs?'

'Pardon me?'

'Why is that important? Please tell me about my husband's car.'

'It's been parked in the same place for two days, possibly longer. We were called because someone tried to break into it. The alarm was going off. One window broken. The car guard claims it's been there since ...' she checked her notes, although she clearly didn't need to. 'Since Sunday. Or maybe Monday.'

'Well, what is it?' Leo asked. 'Sunday or Monday?'

'Sunday then. Two days ago.'

'Maybe he's hiking overnight or for a few nights,' Alice murmured. 'He's been known to do that.' *Not,* she recalled, *since he was a student, but you never knew.*

'Yes, of course that *is* possible.'

'I have to admit, though,' Alice mused, 'that's probably unlikely.'

'Why do you say that?'

'He's in the middle of a big building project. It's not like he has heaps of spare time. And I can't see him doing an overnight hike alone. He always runs with a group of friends.'

'How do you know he's alone?'

'I guess I don't. We could phone his best friend.'

Constable September took a small notebook out of his breast pocket. 'Please give me the details.'

She picked up her phone and scrolled through the numbers until she found Martini. As she rattled off his number, a thought occurred to her. 'You do think he's okay, don't you?'

'Ma'am, I hope so.'

'Have you tried to ring Bruce's number?'

'Yes. No answer.' The woman studied Alice pensively. 'Why?'

'I don't know. Something's definitely not right. Shall I try him again?'

She didn't wait for an answer and rang. Nothing. And her WhatsApp didn't go through either. Edgy, she scrolled back to Martini's contact entry. 'Why don't I phone Martini now? Perhaps he knows something?'

The cops both nodded.

'Alice?'

'Hey Martini. Have you seen Bruce?'

'No. Why?'

'He's missing. We haven't spoken, since. You know.'

'Know what? I haven't seen him since Friday.' There was a deathly silence between them. 'And he was acting fucking weird. Try Monk.'

She did.

Gabriel answered immediately. 'Yeah, he's bunking with me for a bit. But he didn't come back Sunday. I thought you guys had kissed and made up. Some of his stuff's still here. Tried to ring him but he didn't reply. Supposed you were all loved up.'

'Seriously? With two kids in the house?'

'How do you think a second kid gets made?'

Silence.

'Although, I admit. Not in your case.'

Alice sighed, sick of the stupidity of Bruce's friends. And his brother. Thinking about it, she'd never really liked any of them, although Gabe was marginally better than some of them. 'Okay, well, please just ring me if you hear from him. Immediately, Gabriel. Okay?'

As they disconnected, Alice looked at the police officers. 'Nobody knows where he is. It doesn't sound *right*.'

'We're going to have to move the car,' the woman said. 'It can't stay there.'

'My husband is missing. I think that's more the concern, isn't it?'

'You didn't exactly seem to be missing him before we arrived.'

'Excuse me?'

'Who are you?' She eyed Leo, her glance jabbing him viciously in the chest.

'I'm Leo, Alice's son's, tutor.'

'Ja, and I'm your domestic worker.' The sarcasm was so thick it could have coated the walls. 'Nice little evening together, without the husband, hey?'

'I was dropping Albert home,' Leo said defensively. 'Then Albert asked if I could come in and have a drink with them.'

The policewoman shrugged. 'I tell it like I see it.'

'And I'm telling it like it happened. Not that I have to explain myself to you,' Leo said, his nostrils flaring.

'If we have a missing person here, maybe you do,' she disagreed.

Alice stood up, neither denying, nor confirming. 'The point is here, Warrant Officer, that nobody he is close to has spoken to him since Sunday. And it's Tuesday night.'

'Tell me again why you haven't seen him since Friday.'

'I didn't tell you.'

'Tell me for the first time why you haven't seen him since Friday.'

'We had a fight.'

'People do,' the constable said, reassuringly. 'We see it all the time.'

'What was it about?' the policewoman asked.

'Parenting styles.'

'Pardon?'

'He hit our son. I was furious. I told him to leave.'

'Mmmhmm. And you, Albert's teacher. Why do you have a black eye? Car accident? Judo? Woodworking project mishap?' she asked, the tone of her questioning becoming more menacing.

Leo kept silent, but looked at Alice.

'My husband hit him. He was protecting Albert.'

Warrant Officer Boesak sighed, slammed the notebook shut. 'You'd better come to the station. It seems we have a lot to talk about.'

'But what about Bruce?' Alice asked.

'Who?'

'My husband, Bruce.'

'Well,' the policewoman said. 'I think we've just confirmed your husband is missing, don't you?'

Burning

He paced the house. The kids were fast asleep, and here he was in Alice and Bruce's home. His nerves jangled. The gradual unravelling of his life, and Alice's, was almost visceral, like his own body detangling. His head hurt. His stomach cramped.

How often had he wished that Bruce would simply … disappear? And now he had and it was a horrible, horrible reality to face. If something had happened to Bruce, something … terminal, how would Alice and the children ever rebuild?

How would Leo?

And what about the secret hope building up in him? That Bruce was now taken care of?

He'd never felt so uncertain. Or guilty. He'd called Luisa but she didn't answer. He'd thought of calling Chris but knew already what he would say. *I told you so*, even if not in those exact words.

Leo wanted to be in his own home, curled up in his own bed. But what was he meant to say when Alice asked him to stay with the children?

Bruce wasn't his responsibility. The marriage had clearly already been in danger long before he and Alice had even met. But Leo was the catalyst. He'd increased the reaction rate of this particular combustion, and now they were all going to have to try put out the engulfing flames without any third-degree burns.

~PART III~

Everybody lies

When he walked into the police station, the jacket of his tux was hanging over his arm, and his bow tie was loose at his collar. He was a tall man, angular and despite being on the wrong side of forty, he was fit and slim. His startling blue eyes, he knew, were framed by a craggy face, weathered by almost thirty years of climbing and rescue.

Leaving events like the one he'd just abandoned was not something he necessarily liked, but over the years he'd got used to it. His daughter, however, performing on the piano at Artscape, was no small thing, and he wondered how much longer he was prepared to do this.

Miss out. Walk out. Let people down while picking others up.

The first time he'd seen a rescue, he'd been twenty, climbing near the cableway – the old one of course, because the upgrade to Rotairs – the cars with revolving floors – had only happened in 1997. He'd watched the swinging load of the stretcher, the tense descent of the injured person, and thought, *I could do that.*

It was a volunteer position, and therefore unpaid. A giving-back to society in his own way where others might run soup kitchens or knit blankets. But there was also the adrenaline rush, the close-to-the-edge suspension, the chance of bringing someone home.

The danger.

Recently, on average, there had been eight deaths on the mountain annually. Search and rescue was different in Cape Town, than it might be, for example, in the American wilderness. There was no possibility of grid search, where people hold hands, and march through tracts of land, the middle people responsible for keeping the line straight. Everybody looking for a clue: a piece of material, a dropped cell phone, blood.

The mountain terrain didn't allow for that, with gulleys, crevices and sheer rock faces; it was complicated, also, by its proximity to the city.

People made use of its pathways all the time, confusing the police K9 rescue team by the preponderance of human scents wafting from hikers, and joggers, cyclists and the Sackcloth People, who – arrayed in hessian – venture into the City to hawk their gatherings of medicinal herbs, roots and plants.

They'd had very limited success with the dogs. But they kept trying. It was better than not trying at all.

Nevertheless, this terrain was criss-crossed with paths. Equally there were unreachable areas – unreachable without the use of helicopter – an endeavour that often required budget and begging. Search was not a well-financed area of the Metro Emergency Services. But then, what was?

And now he was once again on the trail of a missing person. Sure, he'd moaned to his wife that he should have switched his phone off, but actually, he could feel the rise of his heartbeat, the slight clamminess of his palms brought on by the chase. The dark art of the interview. Everything hung on the information people would give him. Over the years, he'd got better at it but one thing that he knew for sure was that everybody, in some way or another, was going to lie. It was a matter of finding enough truth to establish where to look.

Just his wife

She leant forward. The man in front of her was about her age, maybe a little older, greying slightly at the temples, fair-skinned with unnerving blue eyes. His face had grooves and crevices, like the mountain. He seemed too close. Disbelieving. His manner indicating, ever so slightly, that he didn't credit anything she was telling him. She held the cup of coffee between her palms, feeling chilled right to her bones.

'So what happens now?' she asked.

'We need to get a sense of Bruce. His state of mind. Our aim is to establish the POA and then, from that work out a possible scenario.'

'POA?'

'Probability of area. Where your husband is most likely to be.'

'That's easy enough, isn't it, if his car is parked near the Newlands fire station.'

'Perhaps. Tell me about your husband.'

'What do you want to know?'

'Any health issues?'

'Not that I know of, but it's been a stressful time. He was running and exercising a lot. It's how he copes.'

'So it wouldn't be unusual for him to be on the mountain?'

'Unusual? No. But not normally on his own. He has this pack of buddies he runs with.'

'Not you?'

'No. I'm usually watching the kids.'

'And when was the last time you saw him?' he asked.

'That was Friday night. We had a fight. I told him to leave.'

'Was it a bad enough fight for him to want to harm himself?'

'Are you talking about suicide?'

The man nodded.

'What you have to understand about Bruce,' she said, 'is that he is never wrong. He will always lash outwards not inwards.'

'Has he lashed at you?'

'He hasn't hurt me, if that's what you're asking. Not physically. Recently we just haven't been on the same page.' *To put it mildly.*

'Is there anything you need to tell me about this that is relevant to his disappearance?'

'I guess I should have called him. I didn't. The only reason I knew he was even missing was the report of his parked car – the window broken.'

'Mmmhhmm. And why, do you think, Bruce went onto the mountain on his own?'

'I have no idea.'

Trouble

He wrote down her phone number. As she left, he could hear the wife speaking to somebody in the corridor. He didn't trust her. She was clearly hiding something. Unable to meet his gaze, the pauses between her responses were just too long to be natural.

The lies that people told. The dishonesty wasn't always malicious. Sometimes they lied to protect themselves. Sometimes they lied for the missing person, to make him seem more likeable, rescuable, worth saving. But he couldn't put his finger on this one. It just seemed like she wasn't quite, well, upset enough. He was probably wrong, but she seemed, how could he express it, relieved?

Knock! Knock!

'Hans?'

'Yes?'

'This is Gabriel Louw, the missing man's brother.'

Hans nodded at the policeman. 'Thanks.'

The two men shook hands. Hans was immediately aware how rough his own hands felt from years of climbing in comparison with the other man's soft touch.

'Will he still be alive?' Gabriel asked, by means of introduction.

'I don't know enough to say, I'm afraid. I was hoping you could help me with that.'

'Shoot.'

'What was he wearing when he left your house?'

'I only saw him Saturday but he didn't have a lot of clothes, so doubt it would have changed much. Bright blue puffer jacket, jeans. I think a T-shirt, white. Tackies. I also lent him a few things. Not sure if he had those items with him.'

'So he wasn't really dressed for hiking?'

266

'No. But he had all his stuff with him when he arrived. Not that he had much. A gym bag, I think. I had to give him a toothbrush and shampoo, though. There are still a few odds and ends at home. On Sunday morning he left my house in quite a hurry. He didn't even say goodbye.'

'Why?'

'Honestly, I thought he was going home to make up with Alice.'

'Did he talk about the fight?'

'Not much. He's not exactly touchy-feely, my brother. I'm the sensitive one in the family, or so he tells me. But the situation with their son hasn't been easy. I think it was something to do with that.'

'What situation?' he asked, surprised Alice hadn't mentioned a 'situation' of any sort.

'The boy tried to hang himself earlier this year. It's been rough on all of them.'

'And what about Bruce?'

'What do you mean?'

'In my role in search, I have to establish a scenario. It makes sense to categorise our missing person. Hiker, runner, climber, despondent–'

'Despondent?'

'Anyone in a fragile mental state.'

'He wasn't suicidal, if that's what you're thinking. Bruce and Albert couldn't be more different.'

'Who is Albert?'

'My nephew. If anything, Bruce would have been running. That's how he's always dealt with any issues that come up, especially those over which he has no control.'

'What time did he leave your house?'

'On Saturday? Or Sunday?'

'Sunday.'

'Maybe seven? Seven thirty?'

'Did he say anything?'

'No. He didn't. On Saturday night Mike and I ordered pizza and we were in bed by nine thirty. So we didn't actually talk at all. He came back in the evening. Late. I heard the keys. The alarm. Early Sunday morning, he wasn't there.'

'What work does he do?'

'Currently, he's working on this green complex, totally off-the-grid.'

'Anything about that I should know?'

'I've no idea. Except that Bruce was dealing with some plonkers who were promising but not delivering. Water tanks or something. And he'd paid. A whack of money.'

'Where did he like to run?'

'I just know he mostly parked at Newlands Forest, or sometimes Constantia Nek. Actually, sometimes he also left from Rhodes Mem.'

'His car was at Newlands Forest.'

'Sure, but sometimes he would run to the Cableway or something and then catch an Uber back to his car.'

'So basically he could be anywhere.'

'Didn't anyone see him?'

'That's what we're trying to establish.'

'Well, I wish I could be more help. I don't know what else to say. I guess my brother and I have a rather superficial relationship. I was pretty surprised when he arrived and asked to stay a few days.'

'Why?'

'Why? Because Martini's his best mate. They've been joined at the hip since primary school. His real name is Oliver though.'

'Oliver who?

'Webster. I've got his number if you need it. But nobody calls him Oliver. He goes by Martini now.'

***

When Martini entered the room, Hans studied him thoughtfully. He seemed jittery, on edge. Not all that unusual with the family and friends of missing people but … Hans pulled his shoulders back. He needed coffee. It was almost midnight and they didn't seem any closer to any real idea of where Bruce Louw might be. Of course that meant he wasn't sending a team out to walk randomly in the dark on the mountain. He had to narrow their search area. It was just too vast and whatever the circumstances of the missing person, which, admittedly were most likely dire right now, the safety of his team had to come first.

'So why did Bruce not stay with you?' Hans asked, trying to knock the friend off his guard the moment he sat down.

'Excuse me?'

'Gabriel was surprised Bruce didn't escape to your house after the fight.'

'What fight?' Martini shifted a little.

'The disagreement with his wife.'

'Alice? *Really?* I can't picture it. She's a bit of a mouse. Never heard her roar before.'

'Are you saying there wasn't a fight?'

'No. I'm simply saying it's a bit of a bombshell, that's all.'

'She told me he'd been at your house before the argument.'

'So what? We've been working on this project together. It was work.'

'The green complex?'

'You know about it?'

'I'm trying to find Bruce. I need as much information as I can get to establish his state of mind.'

'The fucker was about to screw my wife when I got home. So perhaps he was horny still.'

'Excuse me?'

'That's why that dickhead wasn't staying with us. I sent him home with his tail between his legs – if you know what I mean.'

'He was having an affair with your wife?'

'No. He was trying to nail her. Not the same thing, I think. I told him to get the fuck out of my house.'

'Did you speak to him again? After he left?'

'He phoned once or twice. I didn't answer him. I wasn't feeling all that charitable.'

Hans sighed, rubbing his stiff neck with his right hand.

'How are you feeling now, then? Charitable enough to guess where your friend might be on the mountain?'

'Well, did anyone see what time he parked?'

'Is that relevant?'

'His favourite run and hike combination is Ledges. But he generally only does it when he runs in the morning. You don't need to have equipment but it's a bit of a scramble to the top. A lot of bouldering. Not great in the dark, even if you're fit. Dangerous. But I could show you. We weren't there all that long ago.'

'And if he left later?'

'The Blockhouse maybe? Sometimes he also does a loop on the Contour Path above the Blockhouse around the front of the mountain; it's a bit longer than just up and down from Rhodes Mem. Maybe nine kilometres? But he could do either route in his sleep. Unless he had a heart attack or something, he'd have been down within two hours. And that's including taking time to enjoy the view.'

Hans wrote this down. Martini's answers seemed perfunctory. Not those of someone who'd been friends for so long.

'Have you checked his Facebook or Instagram accounts?' Martini asked suddenly.

'No. Why?'

'He does like to post from the mountain. Maybe you'll get some clues. The photos all look the same to me, but maybe you'll recognise something.' Martini took out his phone but his nose twitched like he'd smelt something awful. 'That's really odd. Not one thing from his run. Last time he posted was Sunday morning. Look here. That's the site where we're building. The tanks are going to go there, like a wall.'

'What time was that?'

'Eight, eight thirty? Not sure why he was even there.'

'Look carefully. There's somebody there with him,' Hans said. 'See the shadows there? Two other people, maybe?'

Martini grimaced. 'Strange. Maybe Nyembe and Hing? Before our disagreement Bruce mentioned he was having trouble with them.'

Oh my God, Hans thought. *How much trouble is this guy in?*

'Why was that?' he asked neutrally.

'They hadn't delivered the equipment we ordered. Bruce was irate. That's why we were supposed to meet on Friday but due to – circumstances – we didn't even discuss it.'

'Can I have their numbers, please?'

'I'll give you Nyembe. Private-school boy. Hing can barely speak any English; he definitely won't understand a word on the phone.'

There was another knock on the door. 'Any progress?' It was the policewoman, Warrant Officer Boesak. She was holding a mug.

'I really hope that's coffee,' Hans said.

'Well, it's Ricoffy. No fancy-pants blends here.'

'I'll take it. Thank you.' Hans sipped deeply. He was beginning to think it was time to retire. He was getting too old for this shit. The coffee. And search and rescue.

'Do you want to make a call to this guy?' He handed the policewoman the number Martini had given him. 'Maybe he knows something we don't.'

Hiding something

Alice drove tiredly into the garage. Leo's car was still parked behind the gate, but the former high she'd experienced when making the decision to leave Bruce was gone. Bruce could be dead and how would this look? Like she'd killed him? Or Leo had? Especially as she had no idea what Leo had been doing the whole weekend. Was Leo capable of hurting Bruce? She didn't think so but she knew how protective he was – of her and Albert.

She hated herself for the thoughts effervescing. The distrust. The suspicion. It was late and things always looked worse in the dark. But what about Bruce – up on that mountain? If that's where he even was?

How easy would it be to park his Porsche and leave it there for someone to find? To punish her and make her worry.

Alice slipped out the car. Instead of finding Leo asleep on the couch in front of the TV as she'd guessed he might be, he was sitting at the dining room table, a laptop in front of him.

He looked up as she walked in, the keys jangling as they hit the hard granite of the kitchen counter.

'Hey,' he said. 'Any news?'

She sighed. 'No. Nothing. Honestly, I'm not sure what to think. This kind of behaviour isn't like him.'

'Have they sent a team out?'

'To the mountain? No, they don't have a search area identified yet. Right now he could be anywhere. It isn't safe for the search team. I feel like I have my hands tied.'

'Well, you don't. I've had some ideas.'

'Like what?'

'Albert said I could use his laptop. I've been on the Pink Ladies site and it seems we can report Bruce missing to them if you have an AB number? I guess that's the case number?'

'I thought the Pink Ladies only deal with missing kids?'

'Not according to the site. There's a document you can fill in. We'll need two recent photos.'

Alice nodded.

'And then I thought you should post on Facebook. If we boost the post, which will cost a bit, we can target the specific area around Newlands Forest to see if we can find anyone who might have seen him. Leaving the parking lot. Or even on the mountain. I've been googling and this guy in the US, he's been using geotagging to solve murders and missing persons by crowd sourcing.'

Alice looked at Leo's serious face. This didn't *sound* like a man who'd hurt her husband. 'I have no idea what half of you just said even means. But we need to find Bruce. So just tell me what I must do.'

Leo typed into the computer. His face was serious, full of concentration. Then he pushed the computer towards Alice. 'Fill in your log-in details and then we can set up the post. We can tag Bruce in it; that way, any of his friends will see it as well and then people can share.'

'So it'd be out in the open?'

'Sure. Why not?'

'Leo, my husband has been missing for at least two nights and I didn't even notice. How does that make me look?'

'Allie. Bruce needs to come home. We can't move on with our lives if he doesn't.'

'So a little embarrassment–'

'Is worth it. Besides, people don't need to know the details. They just need to see that you're looking for him.'

'You're right. It's just that that search guy, well, I could see he didn't trust me. He clearly thinks I'm hiding something.'

'And you are.'

'Excuse me?'

'You're hiding me. But he doesn't know why you're less than forthcoming. It's got nothing to do with him and everything to do with us.'

She nodded. Resolute. 'If we scroll through the photos in my profile, we should find a few of Bruce we can use.'

Facebook post

Have you seen this man any time between now and Sunday 17th September? Bruce Louw has not come home to his family. His car has been parked at Newlands Forest Fire Base since Sunday morning. Last seen, he was wearing a blue puffer jacket, white T-shirt and jeans. We think he may have been running on Table Mountain, so he might have changed his clothes. Bruce is 44 years old, six foot two, with brown hair, hazel eyes and last seen, was fit and healthy.

Please respond to me in the comments or direct message me with any tips.

Priorities

He'd interviewed everybody who knew Bruce and remarkably, it seemed he still knew very little about the man. Nyembe hadn't answered his phone – but it wasn't that surprising – it was the middle of the night. Martini had called Hans several times. So had Gabriel. Both eager just to get on the mountain and search with their running headlights. But he'd talked them down. He didn't need two more people to rescue.

And the wife, Alice, had set up a Facebook post, which was beginning to gain traction. Every few minutes, she was forwarding tips. So many insomniacs trying to be helpful in the night hours. Many of the leads were idiotic. But now and then the odd message stood out. Enough to isolate Bruce's run away from the Cableway and closer to the eastern face of the mountain. The problem was that some of the messages were contradictory. It was frustrating; people weren't always as observant as they thought they were.

- I saw Bruce at his car on Sunday at around seven thirty. He was wearing a blue vest top, black shorts and black running tackies. I was in my car, so I didn't speak to him. We just waved.
- Bruce was wearing white shorts and a lime-green top. He was standing next to his car with a black guy I didn't know. (Nyembe? Hans thought. 'Bruce doesn't have a lime-green top', Alice told him.)
- I saw Bruce at the SuperSpar on Rosmead Avenue on Monday morning. I think I did, anyway, I saw his car. I recognised the number plate. ('Impossible,' said the tall policewoman. 'The car guard said the car didn't move. And his feedback seems more feasible anyway.

274

Below the car is completely dry, and it rained on Sunday afternoon.')

It was dispiriting. As the tips came in, they seemed to fall flat just as quickly. And as the night went on, it seemed very unlikely they were going to get anything useful to go on. Really, what did they have? Bruce parked. He was wearing shorts – either black or white, from the various contrasting tips that came in. A blue running shirt – most likely. Possibly a red tracksuit top. He'd got out his car, and one person at least had seen him standing there for a few minutes as though waiting for someone, or possibly he was on his phone.

Finally though, with the first traces of morning – not light but human activity – the people going to the gym or leaving early to beat the traffic, they got their first confirmation. This time from a colleague of Bruce's and someone Alice knew quite well. Tim something or other.

- Bruce was on Newlands Ravine. We didn't speak long as he said he was trying to catch up with someone. He didn't say who. There was a big gap between them. But he was definitely on Newlands Ravine.

'Bingo,' Hans said to the policewoman. 'We have our LKP.'

Warrant Officer Boesak looked at him quizzically.

'Last known position? Time to get the team out.'

Hans asked Alice over the phone to confirm with this person if Bruce was carrying anything that would be seen easily – a tracksuit top around his waist? Maybe a water bottle? Or a CamelBak? He waited while she typed.

'A blue CamelBak, actually, if it's the one I'm thinking about, it's a bit faded, or maybe a red jacket?' Alice said after she'd received a reply.

'Well, it's something to look for, at least,' Hans said.

'Yes,' she said softly, then, 'It's been two nights, almost three now. In *winter*. Is he going to be okay?'

'Honestly, Mrs Louw, I can't say either way.'

'You'll find him?'

'We'll do our best.'

'It's really cold up there. And the rain–'

'Yes.'

'Can I help in some way?'

Hans considered for a moment, thinking how he could keep the family busy and out of the way. 'We're going to set up a command centre at the Newlands Forestry Centre. We'll need sustenance and hot drinks for the team. Everybody is volunteering. They'll appreciate it.'

'Okay, I'm on it.'

'But Mrs Louw–'

'Alice.'

'Alice, I must warn you that we'll try to keep you informed but your husband is our priority now.'

'I understand.'

'And dress warmly. We don't know how long it will be. And if Bruce requires any specific medication for any conditions then make sure you have those with you.'

'Alright. Anything else?'

'Bring a set of dry clothes for Bruce – something comfortable. A tracksuit or something like that.' Hans sighed as he disconnected.

His stomach windmilled. Three nights was a very long time on the mountain, even in summer. If Bruce was still alive, he'd be hypothermic at the very least. Into WhatsApp Hans keyed the message he was well used to typing after all these years: Searchers needed for missing person Newlands, if available please respond to the Ops group.

He was glad now that they'd had better sleep than he had.

Knowing that

The kids were still asleep and Alice was in the kitchen, making piles of sandwiches. He walked up behind her and put his arms around her waist. She leant back into him for a millisecond, he could sense it, but then she pulled away.

'I don't feel right about it,' she said softly.

He understood. But he noticed it. How she was leaving him, disengaging like a bad internet connection. He wondered, now, if they would ever get back on line.

'Let me help you, then,' he said. 'What shall I do?'

'Can you boil the kettle? And the coffee machine? I have some thermos flasks. They all need to be filled.'

He nodded, picked up the kettle to run the water into it. 'What are you going to tell Albert and Enjoy when they wake?'

'I think we just need to keep it like a normal day. Enjoy must ride her bike to school. Albert to do the usual with you.'

'Here or at mine?'

She shrugged. 'You choose.'

Leo looked at her. 'I haven't seen Bruce since Friday, you know that, right?'

Alice nodded.

'I was with my mother and with Lou, and the baby. I *wanted* to be with *you*.'

Alice pulled out two more slices of bread from the packet. 'You didn't have to tell me that,' she lied.

277

Conflict

She wanted to lean into Leo. She wanted him to take her into his arms and kiss the hope back into her. It was all so screwed up. How could she expect him to reassure her – about her own husband? What could he really say?

Whatever happens

'I love you, Allie,' Leo said as she piled the last things in the boot. He handed her the tog bag she'd packed of Bruce's warm clothing. She lodged it in between the basket of food, and flasks, coffee, tea, sugar and UHT milk. This time he did kiss her, but softly on her forehead. 'Be safe,' he whispered, then, 'Can I call you for news?'

Alice cupped his chin, her eyes meeting his. 'I'll call *you*,' she said. 'Whatever happens.'

Searching

They'd managed to get a room inside the station to run the operation from. This was preferred, if not the norm. He was more used to the truck Metro sometimes sent to act as command centre. Metro 1: with an enclosed back, inside of which was a radio setup, whiteboard, bench to sit, and a place to plug in a laptop. The power supplied by generator. It was adaptable, because it could be parked anywhere but it wasn't nearly as warm as standing inside, while he still could.

Here, at least, there was electricity, lighting. Running water. In the still-dark morning, all of these were luxuries. A relief. It was clearly the same room that the Volunteer Wildfire Services used. It was in times like this that co-operation with Table Mountain National Park and other organisations like the Cape Metro helped. Ultimately, they had the same goals. The focus was the rescue. For most people, anyway.

Until the confirmation of Bruce actually having been on the mountain, Hans had not been able to arrange anything. But now, the WhatsApp group was lighting up. The pinging of arriving messages more reassuring than irritating.

Hans had already kitted up. His usual rescue volunteer rain jacket for really crap weather already on, his branded red rescue T-shirt underneath several other layers for warmth and insulation.

Like many volunteers, he had a backpack always ready to go, either in his car, or next to his front door. It weighed a solid fifteen kilograms but he was used to that. And he didn't resent it anyway – survival gear combined with technical gear allowed him to operate in any mountain terrain under any weather condition – including the downpour that was the Cape Town winter this morning. So much for a drought. He'd manage forty-eight hours on the mountain before he'd need to return.

Often, he sympathised with the officials from Metro and other departments. Their gear was far from waterproof. Half the time they looked as miserable and cold as the people they were trying to rescue. Drowned rats. He could only hope they'd find this man quickly.

Once again, he'd let his daughter down. The video his wife took of her performance a speck on the screen of his iPhone. He'd ask her to do it for him again, privately, at home. But it wasn't the same. It wasn't Artscape. And he knew he'd be paying for putting the rescue before her. How many times in her life had they had this conversation? He could, in retrospect, he thought, have ignored the original call for help. But, actually, rescuing was FUN. A high without the drugs. Especially when they brought someone home, alive to their family. This time, however, he doubted this was going to happen. It was too wet and too cold.

Chances were, they were bringing a body back.

***

It wasn't long after that he saw Alice lugging the basket into the room. But he neither greeted her nor went to assist. He was already focusing in. One couldn't control everything or everyone and he knew what his job was. And it wasn't cosying up to the relatives. He just didn't have the emotional capacity for that. The team was assembling and when it was lighter, if they hadn't had any luck on the ground, a chopper might be secured. But as always: budget. He noticed the arrival then of a familiar face, a Metro EMS chap he'd worked with before. Dressed in his green jumpsuit, a luminous yellow waistcoat flapping over it, the man marched towards him, his hand out.

'Rademeyer.'

'Paddy,' Hans replied. Manoj Padayachy was always known by this nickname. It made him seem friendlier, more jovial than he actually was. In the times that Hans had worked with Paddy, he had generally found him to be serious and studious, more suited to accounting perhaps, than emergency work. But this was also what made him good on the scene as Incident Commander. He was pernickety; his attention to detail sometimes exhausting.

'Long night?' Paddy said, studying him.

'I haven't slept,' Hans admitted. 'We were trying to get to the bottom of where the man might be.'

'But you've narrowed it down, I heard. How many searchers do you have?'

'Thirty-two. So far.'

Paddy nodded. 'You think he's alive still? It's been freezing the last few nights. Colder up there.'

'Honestly, I doubt it. One night, maybe. But three?' Hans looked over to where Alice was putting her thermoses. 'That's the wife. Alice.'

Paddy cocked his head in her direction. 'I'd better introduce myself then.'

Waiting

She held out a cup of coffee to the small, sallow man. Despite being so early still, his chin was patched with a newly arriving stubble.

'As Incident Commander, IC,' he explained, 'I have authority on the scene. Hans Rademeyer will be on the mountain with his team. And over there is Christine Kruger. She's non-Metro but knows the mountain, so she'll act as rescue manager and advise me on the scene. We'll be located at the JOC until we find your husband.'

'JOC?'

'Joint operations centre.'

'Right. And when will they go up?'

'Now.'

Alice bit her lip. 'Okay then.' She hesitated before asking, 'And how will we know what's happening?'

'We'll communicate by radios. The field teams will have handhelds. Sometimes, if it's possible, we'll use WhatsApp.'

Alice bit back a tear. 'Thank you,' she said.

Paddy patted her arm. 'Keep busy if you can,' he said. 'The waiting can be the worst part.'

Difficulties

Like Albert, he was having difficulty concentrating. The boy refused to write out the workings for his sums, complained that their setwork was 'more boring than usual' and kept crawling under the table so that Leo found himself craning forward to try meet the boy's eyes. When he *was* sitting on his chair at the desk, Albert was banging his pen or his ruler on the wood, to the point that Leo's head began to pound. Administering an ibuprofen, Leo thought about Bruce and the last time they'd seen each other. Whatever the search team discovered, Leo knew he was going to have to keep away. Half-made plans with Alice would simply disintegrate. How could they not, with responsibilities unfolding beyond her normal time and capabilities. Despite his wish for Bruce to be out of the picture, the whole thing had turned to shit. Leo's life had turned to shit.

He washed his face, then went back to where Albert was meant to be working on his character profiles. Instead he was hanging out the window, a deadly drop below him. Hearing him, Albert turned and smiled. 'It's stopped raining. The sun is coming out.'

'Please get inside, Bert.'

The legs dangled for a moment as the boy hesitated.

'Now!' Leo said, raising his voice in frustration.

Sure

Paddy turned, obviously seeing someone approach. Alice turned too.

'You could have called me, babe,' Gillian said. 'You don't have to do this on your own.'

'But I'm not alone,' Alice said, waving vaguely at Paddy, who was already stepping past them.

'You know what I mean.'

'Thanks for the coffee,' Paddy called back, walking away as he spoke into the radio. 'Yes, they did mention the rain was clearing …'

'How did you even know?' Alice asked softly, when Paddy had retreated far enough away.

'Lover Boy, how did you think? He said if he couldn't be with you that I should be.'

Alice smiled.

'He's a gem, that boy.'

'Yes.'

'Bruce will be alright, Alice, I'm sure of it.'

Alice sighed. 'I wish I had your confidence.'

Focus

He wondered if Enjoy had made it to school in the rain on her bike. He'd tried to give her a lift but she'd insisted on going on her own. She was jittery this morning. Unsurprisingly. And he didn't want to push her over the edge.

Now he glanced at Albert, who hadn't written a thing.

'Let's just give up,' Leo said. 'Neither of us is concentrating anyway.'

'A movie?'

'I don't think I could even focus on that.'

Albert stretched his gangly frame out. His back cracked as he did. 'I could eat,' Albert said.

'Again?' Leo commented.

The boy shrugged. 'Or we could visit Faye.'

Leo checked his watch. 'Okay,' he said. 'But not for long.'

Albert smiled. 'Then pizza.'

Leo sighed as he willed himself out of his thoughts and into the car.

Climbing

The sun shot bright filaments through the heavyset clouds. It was going to get easier and warmer through the day. He'd seen very few trail runners; most people were sensible enough to stay in bed on a day like this. So when a young man in lumo-green rain running jacket approached, he stopped him.

'Morning,' he said.

The man hesitated, steam puffing airily from his mouth and nose. His dog, a King Charles spaniel, panted next to him.

'We're looking for a man. Forties. Brown hair. Possibly a red jacket. Blue CamelBak. Missing for three days. You seen anything?'

The man frowned. 'To be honest, mate, most of my run was in the dark.' He gestured to his running headlamp. 'But I've only seen people on the path. And no one in trouble. Everyone was in a group.'

Hans nodded. 'Thanks. And nobody said anything to you?'

The man shrugged. 'Nothing of importance. Just that the trail was slippery.' He whistled, calling the dog, which had disappeared down a path. He swung his arms, as though to start himself up. 'Good luck,' he said, as he began to run.

Hans continued up. His right knee ached from surgery years before. He wasn't going to be able to do these rescues much longer. Today, especially, he just felt *old*. And the path *was* slippery. Pools of water everywhere. Rivulets cascading over rocks. Maybe the drought was finally beginning to break. Hans's radio crackled and he lifted it to his ear to hear better. 'Anything?' he asked.

'Spoken to a few mountain bikers. They were up near the Blockhouse. Quite a few of them and no one has seen anything. But–'

'It was dark. I know. I know.'

The next time he heard the radio buzz, it was Christine Kruger. 'Listen, Hans. The best friend is here. Martini? He wants to come up. Join you. Says he knows the exact path that Bruce always takes. He's fit. Says he wants to come up. Says he can help.'

'What do you think?'

'Well, his kit looks used but well kept. And he's strong. You're not far up yet are you?'

'No.'

'I think he'll do more good than harm.'

'Okay, then. Tell him to move it, though. And we can't afford to babysit. If he's not up for it then he mustn't waste our time. Every minute we wait Bruce is in jeopardy.'

***

They shook hands.

'We used to do this hike once every two months or so. But since the kids …' Martini said.

'Yours?'

'No, Bruce's. He has two. We haven't been so lucky.'

'So when was the last time you were up here together?'

'A few months ago.'

'Any special reason?'

'I can't remember. Problems at home. Both of us. We needed a distraction. To de-stress.'

Hans didn't need to ask about the issues. He just needed to find Bruce.

'We need to move fast. You can fill me in on anything I need to know while we go up.'

'I'm fit. Let's go.'

'And keep your eyes peeled for a red jacket. That's what we're looking for.'

'I remember it.'

'Your climbing experience?'

'Oh don't worry about me. I'm adept.'

A natural

Albert passed Faye back to Luisa. She was fast asleep now, and even the slight movement didn't jolt her.

'You're a natural,' Luisa said to Bert as she placed the baby gently into her crib.

Albert smiled. 'I know, right? One day I'm going to be a great dad. And my children will never feel like they're not good enough.'

Dangerous

Now that the rain had cleared, Alice had begun to pace outside. Her boots were splattered with mud, and she was glad for the jeans, her stockings below. She was warm enough. Gillian, wearing a tracksuit and puffer jacket with fake-fur trim around the hood, looked exhausted. Her mascara had run slightly, so her eyes were dark rimmed; smudged.

Paddy came outside and they hurried to speak to him.

'Is there news?' she asked.

'Nothing yet, they're at Knife Edge. No updates about seeing anything.'

'So there is visibility now?'

'The mist is gone.'

Alice nodded. 'I don't even know where Knife Edge is. But it sounds dangerous.'

'Well, it's on the east face of Table Mountain. Above Newlands Ravine. They know what they're doing, I can assure you.'

Alice shrugged. 'Okay then,' she said.

Seeing red

He climbed upwards. Although this was a site that didn't actually need rope, they were helpful, allowing them to ascend the larger quartzitic sandstone boulders more quickly. It was slippery work as the rain still poured between crevasses and gaps from the craggy mesa. Martini didn't say much, but he did indicate where he and Bruce had last climbed.

'Which way did you usually go up?'

Bruce's friend pointed. 'Up there towards Sloping Block, then that difficult pullup at Giant's Step.'

There were tufts of fynbos poking up between the rocks, the green almost lurid against the grey rocks. Some of the first spring flowers were even beginning to pop out. The odd yellow or cerise splashed around them. He liked colour. Always had. The contrast was even more evocative of happy times climbing, hikes on the West Coast, Postberg.

Then Martini gasped.

He stopped. His hand outstretched.

'What is it?' Hans asked.

'Can't you see it?' He pointed. 'There's something red there.'

Hans took his binoculars out his bag. 'It looks like a jacket or a top. It's material of some sort.'

'Can we get there?'

'I should think so. Let me radio down first, give them an update.'

Confirmation

Paddy beckoned to her, and gripping Gillian's upper arm for strength, they walked quickly over to him.

'They've found him?'

'No. But they've found a waterproof jacket. A red one. Folded on one of the boulders.'

'Folded?'

'Yes, like maybe someone had been sitting on it. The way it flattens seems to indicate that.'

'Can I see it?'

Paddy produced his phone. Showed her the photo on WhatsApp.

She expanded the image on the screen. 'It's Bruce's,' she said, uncertain if this news was good or bad.

'You sure?'

'See that patch at the collar? He ripped the jacket hiking through some thorn bushes. I mended it. Not my best repair job. Actually, I've never been a very good seamstress.' She was babbling and tried to stop herself. Alice bit down hard into her lip until she could taste her own blood.

Paddy nodded, then spoke into the handheld radio. 'It's Bruce Louw's,' he said. 'Confirmation from his wife.'

Then she spoke carefully. 'If that's his jacket, then where the heck is he?'

Blue

The jacket was not good news. That meant their missing person was not just missing but very, very cold. Martini tried to pick the jacket up, but Hans stopped him. 'I'm afraid we'll need to treat this like a crime scene. We don't know where Bruce is yet and–'

Martini paled, stepping back. 'You think he's dead, don't you?'

'I didn't say that,' Hans answered matter-of-factly. 'But this does change the Last Known Position. And we do need to preserve the site in case of any … issues. Now I'm going to locate the other searchers. We can narrow down where we're looking now. I can't think he'd have gone intentionally far from here. Not with the rain we've experienced.'

But of course he thought Bruce was dead.

It was inevitable.

***

They clambered over the rocks. From above, they would have looked like ants mounting a pile of sugar or biscuit crumbs. They levered themselves up over rocks and while some of the areas lower down were easier to navigate, there were frequently drops that, if accessed accidentally, could certainly mean more than a few bumps and bruises. And perhaps they already had. Even the most experienced climber could make an error here, especially in bad weather.

They accessed the gnarled perimeters of the mountain. It was like climbing a tree; the bark rough under your hands, but sometimes it was slippery as wet tiles. Hans stopped once to eat a box of Smarties. He did what he always did, starting with the pink ones then the yellow, then the brown. Never the same colours at the same time. It was his way of bringing order to his life. But not much sustenance really. He remembered his dinner from the night before – a long time ago – before the piano performance. An Ouma rusk at seven. He didn't offer any to the friend. He could bring his own bloody Smarties.

Putting the binocs to his eyes, he realised they should be looking down rather than up. In all likelihood, Bruce had fallen.

Some of the boulders below him were rugged and uneven. Some had narrow gaps between them, but others had larger ones, man-sized yet also deep enough to shade a person inside them. His heart was beating hard. He could hear it in his ears. From the ascent perhaps, but more because he sensed Bruce was close by, below the bushy ledge where he and Martini now stood.

'If the jacket is here,' Martini said, 'then it makes sense we're not looking for red anymore.' The CamelBak was blue, Alice had said so.

'You could be right,' and he probably was. Blue wasn't nearly as obvious. It could make their job harder. As if it weren't already hard enough.

On not blaming Leo

'Excuse me, ma'am?'

She turned to see a policewoman walking towards her. It was Warrant Officer Boesak. She nodded, not sure what to say. She hadn't even known the woman was here.

'I found a teenager on a bicycle in her school uniform skulking outside near your car. She says she belongs to you?' The disparagement or disdain in her voice were obvious. Like Alice couldn't keep tabs on either her husband *or* her daughter.

'Enjoy?'

'Excuse me?'

'That's my daughter's name.'

Alice rushed outside, where a rather bedraggled tween stood, her bicycle now leant against a wall. 'You're meant to be at school,' Alice said.

Enjoy nodded, not looking even vaguely guilty.

'Does Leo know you're here?'

Enjoy shrugged.

'For goodness sake, my girl, is that a yes or a no?'

'No. I told him I was riding to school.'

'In the rain?'

'I told him I was going. And I did. But then I left. I threw my bike over the wall and climbed after it. Don't blame Leo, Mom.'

'I'm NOT blaming him. I'm just stressed. How'd you even know where to go?'

'I heard you talking.' But the girl didn't meet her eyes.

'Well, I'd better phone the school. They'll be searching for you.'

'Just leave it, Mom.'

Nevertheless, Alice dialled the receptionist, explaining the situation in clipped tones. She could hear the strain in her own voice, which was pitched and shaky. Her speech dripped with apologies she didn't entirely feel. But as she put the phone back into her pocket, she realised how selfish she was being. Her daughter was worried too.

Alice put her arm around Enjoy, pulling her close. But the tension in Enjoy's shoulders made her stiff as rigor mortis. She wasn't easily comforted.

Alice wanted to reassure her. But everything she'd say right now would be false. They stood together, then, staring up at the impenetrable hulk of a mountain, and waited for news.

Crevices

The police always had jurisdiction for missing people like Bruce. Equally for body recoveries. So whatever happened, they were involved. It was better that way. He was good at the climbing, good at the search. But after that, it got messy.

And now as he rappelled down the mountain to reach below the ledges, he felt he was close. He had a sense about it. Like a bloodhound. He looked up to where Martini peered over the edge of the hard rock. He was scowling. The tension furrowing his face, an etching of apprehension.

If they found Bruce here they'd need help getting him out. You couldn't access this place without technical ropework. It was beyond the scope of most, or even all forensic pathology services and SAPS. And the police would need photographs. Evidence. Able now to get his feet lodged in enough to let go of the rope, he edged forward. It was then that he noticed how the rocks were disturbed, and a patch of colour on one of the sharper rocks. Blood? He approached. It might have been, but the rain had washed most of it away. It was more of a discoloration. Like rust. He sniffed it. Unsure. Took a photo. Took another of the displaced rocks.

Below him was another deep crevice. He reached for the rope, careful just to hold on for leverage. Another substance on the edge of the deep rock slit. He'd seen this before, a while ago, but he remembered it like it was yesterday: a woman fell from an overhang, her brain smashed as the skull cracked open like a nut. The grey matter a mess of neuron cell bodies and glial cells. Deeper, the fat of the myelin sheath making the exposed brain seem white. She was dead, of course. No one could survive a fall like that.

And if he was right, and Bruce had tumbled in between these rocks, hitting his head on the way down … Then he had, without a doubt, no longer needed the red jacket folded on the rock above to keep him warm.

Don't have to say it

Paddy the Incident Commander walked over to Alice, the handheld against his ear. She could see the slump of his shoulders, the erect stance of his back, weighed down. Defeated.

He didn't have to say it, but he had, without any words.

'Mrs Louw.'

'Alice, yes.'

'Will you come with me please, we have news we'd like to discuss with you on your own.'

***

She watched as the helicopter rose up above the trees. The slope had been so steep, the ways down so treacherous, but now her husband's body was up there in the clouds. The rotor blades chopping at the sky and Alice, her hand in Gillian's, her other in Enjoy's, down below. The rescuers were still hiking back down the mountain. Martini too. They could be a while still and she should thank them. They'd brought Bruce home and everything that had preceded this no longer seemed to matter. Her husband of almost twenty years was dead. She tried to recall their last argument and it trickled into her brain, rather than gushed.

She was going to have to tell Albert soon. *How was she meant to do that?* Enjoy hadn't needed her to say much, she'd also seen Paddy's expression when he'd walked towards them, then. What she feared perhaps more than telling the news, was that Albert might, in fact, actually be happy about it. Her heart tightened. Her daughter's face was flooded with tears, and when Enjoy started to sob, there was nothing she could do but hold her.

Paddy was waiting for the team to descend. The debrief was the final step in the search, but it no longer mattered to her so much. The thought that most occupied her was what Bruce was doing up in the mountain all alone. Was he dying there without her?

Her mind spun with all that Paddy had said to her. Bruce's body handed over to the Forensic Pathology Services, to be removed to a local mortuary for a post mortem. Some Inquest Act or other, which determined that all deaths on the mountain or at sea were from unnatural causes until proven otherwise. How a magistrate would be assigned to "their case" as part of the inquest. The red tape to get his body back.

Paddy looked at her and it took all her effort to focus on him. 'We understand if you need to leave immediately. We can help you get your thermoses and everything packed up. And perhaps your friend should drive you. You're in shock.'

'No, I can drive myself. Maybe you can help put my daughter's bike in my car. What'll happen to my husband's car?'

'The SAPS will have a look at it. I don't think you'll get it back today at any rate. Perhaps not this week even.'

'Right,' she said, not really hearing him.

News

He picked up immediately.
'Is Albert nearby?'
'Um, yes.'
'Can you find a spot to talk? Keep him busy with something?'
'Give me a minute,' Leo said. 'I'll call you right back.'
He stood outside his front door and held the phone to his ear.
'Allie?'
'Bruce is dead.'
'Jesus,' Leo said. 'How?'
And then she told him what she knew.

ALICE

Knowing

She put the phone back into her handbag. The irony wasn't lost on her. Her seeking comfort on the death of her husband from her lover. She felt eviscerated. Empty. Her daughter's big brown eyes were reviewing her, almost scientifically. But when Alice tried to catch her eyes, Enjoy jerked her face away. Her daughter shook silently as though she was iced through.

'Leo is going to bring Albert home,' Alice said. 'So I can tell him myself.'

Enjoy gulped. 'Oh Mom, he's not an idiot. He knows.'

'Not in so many words he doesn't.'

Better from here

He walked back inside.

Instead of sitting at his desk and working on the timeline he'd set him, Albert was holding Rascal close to his face, allowing the vibrating whiskers to tickle his skin. Leo studied Albert's expression. It was blank.

'I'm thinking we need to teach Rascal a new trick,' he said.

Leo nodded. 'I need to take you home, Bert.'

'I know,' Albert said. 'Everything will change now, won't it, Leo?'

'Life is always changing, buddy. It's really how we deal with it that matters the most.'

Albert eyed him suspiciously.

'That doesn't make it easier, though, does it?' Leo added.

Albert shrugged. 'I actually think it gets better from here.'

~PART IV - AFTER~

Last messages

The medics had discovered Bruce's phone in his shorts pocket. And miraculously, though the screen was slightly cracked, it was still functioning. Even the rain hadn't destroyed it. Alice had been brought into the police station again. This time, Warrant Officer Boesak placed a print-out in front of her. It was covered in highlights.

'What's this?' Alice asked.

'Bruce's last messages. Sit.'

One in particular was highlighted in bright yellow.

The next time I see you, I hope it's in a coffin.

Alice baulked. 'Who was this even from?' she asked.

The policewoman frowned. 'The number is registered in your name.'

'*My* name?' she repeated dumbly.

'Yes.'

Alice baulked at the accusation in the woman's expression. 'Like I told you before,' Alice said quietly, 'I didn't speak to Bruce again after our argument. Do you know how that feels? Every morning I wake up, and it's the first thing I think about. How virtually my last words to him were that I couldn't stand the sight of him. That he made me sick. It was a tiff. A big one but ...'

The officer sighed. 'The phone is in your name.'

'Impossible.'

'It's in your name.'

'I don't care. It's not my message.'

The policewoman lifted the paper to her eyes like she was slightly nearsighted. '084 312 6792.'

'Excuse me?'

'The number in your name.'

'It's not my number,' Alice insisted.

But Warrant Officer Boesak stared at her coldly. 'I remembered how I knew you,' the woman said suddenly as she leant forward into Alice's space.

Alice sat back, caught off-guard. 'And how was that, exactly?'

'You came to collect your son from the station. He was with his tutor. Your kid had done a little streak in the park.'

Alice felt a shiver escape up her back.

'Oh,' she said.

'I knew it!' The woman sounded gleeful. Triumphant. 'I told you. I never forget a face.'

'How lucky for you.'

Not picking up on the sarcasm, the woman nodded. 'Yes. Very useful in my line of work. So where's the phone?'

'Which phone?'

'084 312 6792.'

'For goodness sake, I've no idea.' But then something niggled at her. A twinge of ... what was it ... doubt?

The policewoman cocked her head. 'See, you've thought of something! I can tell!'

'We have an emergency phone the kids use. We keep it at home. We don't have a home line. So it's just for ...'

'You said. Emergencies.'

'I don't know what the number is. But it's programmed into my own phone. Let me check.'

She took her phone out her handbag, scrolled through it quickly.

Bingo.

Someone in her family was in a lot of trouble. And she knew without doubt who it was.

Nothing to complain about

Alice was tense on her return from the station. She was coiled – like a spring. The slightest noise made her jump and when she walked into Albert's room where they were working on geography, it was as if Leo wasn't even there.

'Did you send your dad that text?'

'Which text?' Albert said innocently. But it was obvious to Leo that even though he didn't know what Alice was referring to that Albert certainly did.

'Albert!'

He shrugged. 'So what? He's in a coffin now, so I guess that's my good luck.'

'Albert!' Alice repeated.

'He was the idiot who fell off a bloody mountain. It's not like I pushed him. Unfortunately I didn't get that pleasure.'

Albert's voice was cold. Calculating. The lack of emotion unnerved Leo. For an instant he wondered if Albert had actually managed to secure Bruce's untimely exit but dismissed it almost just as quickly. Albert wasn't fit enough to reach Newland Forest by foot.

'You know you don't really mean it, buddy.'

'Right,' Albert said, nodding, clearly knowing exactly what he meant.

But the acknowledgement filtered through gently to Alice. And it was obvious she wanted to believe him.

'That's what I told the cops,' she said firmly.

***

Since Bruce's death, Leo had worked on his thesis and taught Albert. He didn't know how to support Alice but she'd curled away from him and wouldn't allow him close.

He guessed it was over. But she hadn't said so. Not in so many words. Not yet.

Albert, however, seemed delighted with his new father-free life. It was grotesque. Macabre. Even more fascinating was his ability now to concentrate. To sit still. Like the loss of his father had cured him of his illness. It was impossible, but it was what Leo saw.

Leo felt caught. Between moving forward, and staying exactly where he was. It was purgatory; something a Catholic family like his would understand. Yet, what was he to do? Complain? *He* hadn't lost a husband or father.

He had nothing real to complain about.

Except that he felt really, really lonely. Not long now and Alice would push him away completely.

Unravelling

She sat once again in the police station. This time with a detective. So many people criticise the cops, but in the short time she had *really* had to deal with them, she had found them efficient. Relentless. They'd gone through Bruce's phone and its contents, placing the pieces side by side until they finally had a picture. It was blurry.

But it was enough.

She looked at the man across from her, the detective. He was broad shouldered; his nose stubby. His hair was thinning along his parting and greying at the tips. He looked weather worn, and tired. But his onyx eyes were fiery when he began to explain.

'The pin WhatsApped to your husband's phone led us to an industrial estate in Epping.'

'Epping?' Alice repeated, sounding stupid, even to herself.

He nodded. 'Yes. And it was there that we discovered a man's body.'

Alice sat back, the shock hitting her viscerally.

'What do you mean a body? ... Who had died?'

'The man who sent the pin to your husband. He was identified as Senzo Nyembe, the brother of recently deceased actress and model Lebogang Dinangwe.'

Alice's head spun. She presumed she was supposed to know who this Lebogang person was but she really had never heard of her. Didn't recognise her from the photo the detective placed in front of her either. But the brother. That name she had heard, many many times before from Bruce. And never with any complimentary associations.

'What happened to him?' she asked, realising the detective was staring at her, trying to gauge her reaction.

'He died of hypothermia in the walk-in freezer. The door had been blocked from the outside, with a large metal filing cabinet, most likely wheeled from the main office. Of course all walk-in freezers are equipped with buttons to unlock the door from the inside but with the door wedged closed ...'

'He was murdered?' Alice gasped.

'That is what we presume. He had bruising on the back of his head. Occurred ante mortem. Probably a hard object. We questioned Mr Nyembe's wife about his movements. According to her, she last saw him Sunday morning. They're not on good terms. A divorce looming. From his side more than hers. They had an argument about future maintenance and then he left. She didn't know where he'd gone and it seemed she didn't care at the time. Too angry. But from these timings we assume Mr Nyembe had been hit over the head and left in the freezer some time between Sunday morning and Wednesday, when the police searched the building.'

'But surely that gives her motive? Isn't the spouse always the suspect?'

'Of course we considered that but she flew to East London shortly after the argument. She had a business meeting the following day, and the timing of her departure was too tight for her to have been responsible. Her mother dropped her at the airport, with both her children in the car. And we have confirmed she boarded the plane for the 8h30 flight. She just made it. Mrs Nyembe was still in East London when the body was discovered. Her reaction – one of extreme disbelief. And grief. She kept telling us we were wrong. It's my feeling that this wasn't a woman who wanted her husband dead. Also, it wouldn't makes sense, ma'am. He was the main breadwinner. She needed him to pay the bills,' the detective responded.

'She could have got him killed to keep the family money all for herself. An insurance policy, maybe?'

'No. We've checked. Nothing like that. He was more useful to her alive. And according to her mother, she wanted to reconcile.'

Alice felt a little spasm of tension coursing into her neck. 'But then who? You don't think–'

'We can only judge this situation by what we know.'

'Which is what, exactly?'

'We believe Bruce was the last person to see Nyembe alive. A security guard signed him in. Look, this is his signature, is it not?'

She looked at the man's screen on his cracked phone. It was hard to tell. That is, except for his distinctive w, wide and trailing a tail behind it.

Alice nodded. 'Yes, I think so.'

'Also,' he continued, 'the registration number of the car that entered the estate matched that of the Porsche discovered in the parking area near Newlands Forest. Your husband's car.'

Alice studied the man's expression. 'You can't be suggesting that my husband killed Mr Nyembe?'

The detective held up his hand. 'Let me continue. We dusted the filing cabinet – the one lodged against the door – for prints. Nothing. The filing cabinet was empty apart from some old stationery and a few scrumpled pages, no prints inside.'

'Nothing?'

'Nothing *there*,' the detective responded pointedly. 'But, ma'am, on the handle to the large freezer, that's where we found your husband's fingerprints. Clear as daylight. Unmistakable.'

Alice sucked in her breath, glad she was already sitting. 'That doesn't mean he did it. Just that he was there. There could have been someone else–'

'Ma'am, we have to follow where the evidence leads us. And it's leading right to your husband. We call it Ockham's razor, the simplest explanation is usually the correct one. Especially in my line of work.'

'I'm well aware of Ockham's razor, detective. But my husband was not a killer.'

'Then why the suicide up the mountain, Mrs Louw? As far as we can tell there is no indication of anyone else being at that site on the mountain. We think he may have sat on his raincoat considering his options. A guilty person does stupid things. Reckless things.'

'Suicide? Really? That's where we are now?'

'It's a theory. A workable one.'

Alice still couldn't picture it. Bruce was just too full of himself and his own superiority to kill himself. Murder someone else – perhaps in extreme circumstances. But himself? Never. But she sighed, willing this conversation over. 'Okay, so suppose I accept this theory, although I don't. A murder requires a motive. Doesn't it? My husband needed Mr Nyembe alive to conclude their business. For the delivery.'

'This gets a bit tricky of course. But we don't know what documentation he managed to obtain from the filing cabinet.'

'You think he took papers from it? Then why kill himself? If he had what he needed?'

'Regret. Don't you think that's possible? Anyway, we have more. There was a waitress who has linked your husband to Mr Nyembe's sister on the night she died in that car accident.'

'Don't be ridiculous. He wouldn't have known who she was. *I* didn't know who she was. My husband never picked up a *YOU* in his life.'

'Then the fact the waitress who served your husband at the Toad recognised him from his photo in the paper is irrelevant?'

'Why would it be relevant? He likes the Toad. He eats there often. Ate there often, I mean.'

311

'Well, the waitress told us that he was staring fixedly at Lebogang throughout the evening, despite the fact she was clearly romantically involved with the man at her table. An unidentified man who was definitely not her husband. The history in your husband's Google searches point to his knowledge of her. And specifically to repeated searches on her death. He even saved some of the articles relating to the accident in a folder on his laptop. Still a coincidence do you think?'

'Yes. I do think so, actually.' But Alice was a lot less sure than she sounded.

'Give me a little leeway here, ma'am. So what if your husband was involved in Lebogang's death in some way? She was over the limit, yes, but why the sudden swerve? Your husband, perhaps? The waitress maintains he left shortly after her. And he was drunk. Several beers. A brandy. Mr Nyembe finds out about it, somehow. Gets Mr Louw to come to his offices to talk it out. They fight. Fearful for his reputation, Mr Louw gets the upper hand. Hits Nyembe on the head and locks him in the freezer. He take the documents relating to the delivery. Maybe he intends to come back. Maybe not.'

Though the doubt was beginning to creep in, it just didn't ring true.

The detective leant forward. 'Was your husband home that night?'

'Which night?'

'The night Lebogang died. Thursday the 15th? June?'

'I have no idea. I'd have to check my diary.'

But she did know. Because that was the night she'd first slept with Leo. It was imprinted into her memory. She realised she couldn't vouch for one minute of Bruce' movements since he'd left the house in a fury and they'd escaped to the cottage. But what she did know was that Bruce's car was in perfect condition when he arrived the next day. Undented. How could he possibly have been involved in a motor accident? She sat silently, unsure what to say.

'Nothing?' the detective asked.

'If all of that is true, then your suicide theory doesn't work. There would have been no motivation for it. He had the documents. Nyembe was out of the way.'

'You're right. But Nyembe wasn't alone as I recall? Mr Webster mentioned a Mr Hing. Could he perhaps have followed him? Pushed him over the edge.'

'Wasn't he in China? And if he wasn't, would he seriously have left Nyembe to die in the freezer? His partner? And where were the documents? Not in his car or with him. You would have mentioned that. I think you're reaching, detective.'

'Then what about the mundane? An accident? Your husband falls during the hike. Slips over the edge and hits his head? It *was* raining after all.'

Alice sighed heavily. 'I just don't know, detective. Your guess is as good as mine.'

'Well,' the detective answered. These are the only workable theories we have and unless we get more information – a witness, for example – I don't think this investigation is going to move any further along.'

Alice knew he was right. But it didn't make the uncertainty any easier.

'Let's hope for a witness then,' she said, standing up to signal the end of the meeting.

No more

She waited outside the psychiatrist's office. Albert always saw her on a Wednesday afternoon, and with Bruce gone, she'd tried to keep the same routines. Bruce had never been a part of most of their day, so none of that had to change. Now, more than ever, she wanted to keep things stable, for Albert – and Enjoy – but, ironically, also for herself. It kept her getting up every morning. When she slept, the thoughts she pushed to the back of her mind surfaced. Her nightmares, not specifically Bruce, or even anything could decipher, woke her up.

In her most recent one, she and Albert were transporting boxes and boxes of newly laid eggs on a quad bike with a large trailer. There were so many of them, the chickens laying directly into egg boxes, one after the next. Albert had taken the wheel of her car. He was driving too fast. And as they rounded a corner, everything began to topple. She was trying to slow him down, but she couldn't. She woke as everything rose up, just before the quad bike landed on its back like a toppled beetle, legs flailing.

That's how she felt, incapacitated. And she'd realised she couldn't offer Leo what he needed. She should do the right thing and let him go. However much it hurt her.

In the therapy room, Albert's voice rose and fell behind the closed door. She could hear them both laughing. The psychiatrist, Valentina, had Italian heritage like Leo, and two teenagers of her own, also boys. She spoke to Albert in a way that Alice had never quite achieved – understanding, but not chummy. Direct but not judgmental.

Alice cringed at the few words she could decipher through the door – shit and bitch and fuck – words she would never have allowed. But she knew that she shouldn't be listening and would have to pretend she hadn't heard.

This was Albert's safe space, not hers.

When he shoved the door back and called Alice in, Albert grinned at her, his face alive with mischief. And also, she noticed, caked with the barbecue sauce remaining from his lunch. His feet were bare. Shoes were yet another step too far. A social construct. Inwardly she sighed. But her face, she knew, betrayed nothing.

She entered the room, settling herself next to the bookshelf loaded with books like *Child and Adolescent Development* and *The African Textbook of Clinical Psychiatry and Mental Health.*

Valentina's bobbed hair, framing her face, made her look younger than Alice. But Albert had told her that the psychiatrist was at least eight years older. Alice shifted into the wingback, trying to make herself seem relaxed.

'Explain what you told me,' Valentina said to Albert.

Without the expletives, Alice thought.

Albert clicked the magnetic balls from hand to hand.

'I want to go back to school,' he said. 'Not the old one, obviously, because that sucked. But I've found the perfect place for me. It's time, Mom. No more homeschooling. I want to get out on my own. And I think we need to tell Leo.'

Fundamental

His knuckles were white from the tension. He felt broken. Shattered. It wasn't so much that Albert wanted to go back to school. *That* was inevitable and also the goal he'd set for himself. To get Albert to that better place where he would be independent.

No, it was all about Alice.

The way she was turning her back on him like he had never mattered. He had been in love before, it was true, but this had been different for him. Fundamental. Now it seemed she had turned in on herself, chalking her children within an invisible circle and left him beyond it, unable to pass through.

~PART V - A YEAR LATER~

The return

When he walked past the automatic doors of the airport, he was expecting to see his mother. But Luisa stood there instead, a pushchair in front of her, and Faye seated cutely with a bottle held between both hands.

'Welcome back, little brother!' Luisa said, tiptoeing to kiss him on the cheek.

He smiled, then bent to tickle the little girl's chin. She beamed.

'Well you still have an effect on the ladies,' Luisa said.

'I don't know so much about that. Where's Mamma?'

'She sends apologies. Her car wouldn't start. I'm the back-up.'

'That damn car. I don't know why she keeps it.'

Luisa shrugged. 'Sentimental. Let's go. I'm in the free half-hour parking zone.'

As they pulled off onto the highway, Luisa studied Leo in her peripheral vision. 'So?'

'So what?'

'Well, how was it? Did you find love? Did you find your calling?'

'Love? No. My calling? Maybe. I'm not even sure about that.'

'You've been in Florence for a year, Leo. You're not exactly selling it.'

'It was good. Really good. But I'm glad to be home.'

***

He parked the car at Common Ground Church. It was his first Park Run and he'd signed up online for his barcode. It was Luisa who'd convinced him.

'Get back into Cape Town life,' she'd said. 'I go every Saturday with the pram, and afterwards I have a coffee at the café. If Frans is in town, he

318

comes too. Faye loves seeing the people. You might bump into someone you know. Start reconnecting with people.'

'I've only been gone a year, Luisa.'

'Well, it feels like longer. We missed you! Faye missed her Fairy Godfather.'

'I'm not a fairy.'

'Really? From what I heard you could have been. Not a woman in sight.'

'There were a few women,' he retorted. 'Just nobody special, alright?'

'Nobody like Alice, you mean?'

Leo was silent for a moment. 'I guess so.'

'It's a new time for you now, though. A fresh start. And the exercise will be good for you.'

'Are you trying to tell me something?'

She shrugged. 'Florence,' she said cryptically, her eyes on his waist.

So here he was, in a new pair of Nikes and running shorts, a wife-beater. He overheated running in a T-shirt. Two times round the Common would be easy enough. And of course Luisa was right. He needed to set up some routines now that he'd established his practice in a small community of mental health professionals just off Main Road.

His own office. His first few patients. Teenagers. Boys mostly. He was good at striking up a rapport with them, like he had with Albert. He thought about the boy. Thirteen now.

At first Albert had written to Leo – short emails with poor spelling, despite the fact that Leo knew Albert could spell. Shortcuts always. And Leo had responded. But the longer he was away and Albert was in school, the less Albert communicated. He had friends now. Real ones. And not just Rascal, who Alice had reluctantly agreed to let Albert babysit, but which they all knew meant 'adopt'.

Now his friends were kids, flesh-and-blood kids who understood him and spoke his language. Albert had found his niche. And Leo knew this was a good thing.

But it hurt a little. Leo had felt … abandoned. And not just by Alice. Which was silly. But still genuine.

A car parked a few spaces down from where Leo was emerging, its engine roaring.

'Hey brother, help me with the pram.' Luisa's hair was piled high on her head, her fringe pinned out of her face. It made her look younger. Less harried. She was pregnant again and not exactly thrilled about it. Frans's contract had been extended just before they'd found out. Another two years of single motherhood. But now that Leo was back …

The pram was specifically designed for running, a single wheel in the front, two large wheels at the back. Luisa flipped the pram out with one hand while holding her daughter. She made it look easy. But Luisa was always competent; she made *everything* seem easy. Bending over, she clipped Faye into the seat, then tugged on the cover to protect the toddler from the sun. Faye studied Leo from her perch. And when he bent over to touch her pram mobile, he tugged on a bunny, which whooshed down and jiggered back up. She began to smile.

'She likes you,' Luisa said.

'She should. I helped get her out of you. One of the craziest and best moments of my life.' The comment, once more, made him think of Alice. A year on, and everything did.

Still.

He hadn't believed in soulmates before Alice, but now, without her, despite the elapsed time, he still felt incomplete. He wondered if she ever thought about him the way he did about her.

'Let's go, Leo,' Luisa said. 'It's only going to get more crowded.'

He followed her to the robots. They crossed as soon as the cars stopped completely and walked towards the start of the run.

Family bonding

They parked opposite the TLC, where Albert had spent those months after his suicide attempt. It was going to close, apparently, the building condemned. She wasn't surprised really. It was an old structure, and needed work. It used to smell of despair.

Sometimes she wondered if three months in that place had been good for Albert, but then she looked at him. He smiled now, without reservation and for the first time in years, he seemed to fit into his own skin. Of course, he wasn't exactly typical. The large piercing in his right eyebrow (she'd felt at the time, this was better than a tattoo, at least a piercing could close up, and she'd drawn the line at his original request for a large ring in his nose – like a cow – not that he'd described it like that).

The Park Runs had been Enjoy's idea. They needed some level of family bonding. The last year had been incredibly hard, with each of them dealing with Bruce's loss in their own unique ways.

Enjoy had taken it worst of all. She'd woken with nightmares, struggling from her blankets. Usually more independent than Albert, she now moved about in the night and Alice sometimes woke with her daughter in her bed, her tears wetting her pillow. Yet Enjoy's presence was a comfort to her too. The bed seemed too big without Bruce. Even now that Malawi had decided Bruce's spot was hers, spooning against Alice's back regardless of the temperature. And though she missed Bruce, which she did, it was Leo Alice thought of when she wondered about happiness. If she'd find it again for herself and not just through her children.

But he gone; she'd sent him away. The trauma of that conversation still stung. She recalled it clearly. His face falling. Her heartbeat in her ears. The dull thud of detachment. Her kids *needed* her. They were her responsibility. So much more important than her own happiness. And maybe she deserved to be punished for her betrayal.

But however much she might regret it now, it was still on *her*. She just had to get on with it.

Alice clipped Malawi's harness. Attached the leash. It was ironic really, she'd have to carry that mutt for most of the way. Malawi was no longer a sports model. One time around the Common and she'd be exhausted. It was the beginning of Legg-Calvé-Perthes disease, a disintegration of the head of her femur in her left hind leg. Malawi had begun to limp, sometimes walking with three legs instead of all of them. And if anyone bumped against her, she lashed out, teeth exposed. It was hard to see her dog age; it made Alice feel old too. But for now, Malawi was beaming a happy-dog grin, sniffing at the grass and tree stumps as they walked to the start of the race, following the streams of people. Even better, of course, if they encountered another dog.

'Come on, Mom,' Enjoy hustled. 'We don't want to start right at the back.'

Alice didn't really know why Enjoy was so concerned. By the time they joined the throng, Enjoy and Albert would be far ahead and would probably lap her *and* the dog. But start as you mean to continue, she supposed.

'I'm coming,' Alice said, and tugged on Malawi's leash to urge her forward.

One hundred percent

He was surprised by how fast his sister could run with the pram and her very slightly showing belly. Also people tended to move out her way, which was useful in a crowd. Faye beamed with the speed and giggled. Leo was marginally ahead, finding it difficult to match his pace with Lou's, when he heard someone call.

'Excuse me, excuse me! You dropped this.'

Both he and Luisa stopped. As he turned, he saw a familiar figure holding a misshapen off-white bunny that Faye always had with her.

He was taller. With a deeper voice. And half his hair white, the other pitch black, like a honey badger.

'Albert?' Leo said smiling broadly.

'Al now. Always Al.'

'Al? Really? I like it.' It did sound cooler, Albert was right.

Albert smiled.

'So, WTF,' the boy replied. 'You're back! And look at Faye! She's huge!'

Albert moved forward and without the faintest trace of shyness put his arms around Leo. Leo hugged him back, unused to the clumsy boyish angles and pubescent-boy smell.

'Look how you've grown!' Luisa said.

'Well,' Albert said, stepping back. 'It would be weird if I didn't, hey?'

'That was a bit obvious, wasn't it?' She laughed. 'Nice hair.'

Albert touched his head, smiling. 'Right? Are you back for good? Or just visiting from Italy?' Albert asked, looking at Leo.

Leo nodded. 'One hundred percent back.'

Albert scratched his chin. Leo noted a few stray dark hairs over his top lip, amazed at how much change a year could bring.

'You should say hello to Mom,' Albert said thoughtfully. 'She used to laugh more when you were teaching me. She's not done that much laughing this year. And she talks about you still.'

'She's here?' His heart jackhammered.

'Way behind. Malawi's holding her back. That poor dog's going to croak soon.'

Leo felt his stomach twist. Alice. He glanced at his sister, his face probably giving it all away. She grinned. 'Well, isn't this a coincidence? Why doesn't … um … Al … run with me, and you go and check on that poor dog?'

'What do you think, buddy?'

'Oh definitely. Go for it.' Albert thrust the bunny at Faye, who grabbed it between both chubby hands and beamed at him. 'Hello, Faye,' Albert said, bending down. 'I've missed you!'

Needed

'Come on, girl.' She tugged on the leash but not too hard. Just enough to get her attention. Alice wondered if perhaps Malawi was going deaf as well as being a bit crippled. *Could you even use that word or was it also un-PC for a dog? And where were those damn kids?*

So much for family bonding.

Triggered by the yank, Malawi trotted forward, her little nose to the ground, her tail pointed up. Despite being abandoned by her children, Alice was glad to be out. With all the studying she'd been doing to complete her architectural degree abandoned years before, she was starting to look ghostly, invisible even. She certainly felt invisible. Gillian, of course, told her she was being ridiculous. But her children didn't need her as much as she thought they were going to. She longed to feel needed.

At least she didn't have to worry about the building project Bruce had left half-done on his death. Martini had stepped into the gap, finishing everything up and leaving her and the children with a healthy profit. How he achieved this, she had no clue. She also hadn't known Bruce's friend had had that sort of philanthropy in him, but people could surprise you in a crisis – the ones who helped and the ones who backed away as though misfortune was contagious.

He'd stepped up to the plate.

Alice picked up her pace, hoping Malawi would at least run a little, so she could get their heart rates up. And as she did, she noticed a person running in completely the wrong direction. *Typical Millennial, breaking even the simplest of rules.*

And then she saw who it was.

He was coming straight towards her.

More times

She was wearing shorts, short ones. Her perfect legs moving along the path. Her hair was obviously longer, tied back at the nape. Alice's T-shirt was bright pink, her tackies with touches of the same colour. But mostly, he could see that she had seen him, and that her face had burst into a smile. It was illuminating. More than that.

Incandescent.

'Leo!'

She picked up her pace, running towards him as though pulled by an invisible cord. When they reached each other, she lifted her arms without hesitation to pull him into a hug. As he felt her body against his, all his senses sung. Nothing had changed for him.

Nothing.

A year now was a second.

A millisecond.

He could hear her laughing. It was the best sound. It wrapped him like a gift. He took her face in his hands, seeing the morning light reflect in the corners of her eyes. That face. Her emotions overwhelming. He could feel them in his gut.

'But you told me to leave,' he said softly, wiping a tear away. 'You said I must go.'

She laughed, almost mockingly. 'I was so damn stupid. I didn't know what the hell I was doing.'

'I really wish you'd said so.'

'My kids really needed me. And I thought–'

'What did you think, Allie?'

'I thought that I owed them my complete attention. And you deserved a chance,' she said.

'A chance for what?'

'To be. Independence from my dramas. Bruce's death. To find someone better.'

'You really hurt me,' Leo said. 'You didn't trust me enough to be there.'

She shook her head. 'That wasn't it at all. I didn't trust myself. I was spreading myself so thin. I couldn't be enough for you. *I* wasn't enough.'

'You were more than enough. You always were. I told you that then and nothing has changed.'

The relief broke through her face. 'Thank God. Because I've missed you. Every single day. I've regretted telling you to go more times than I've breathed.'

'That's a *lot* of times,' he quipped, his heart surging with joy.

She laughed. 'You're back.' She traced his face, her finger rounding his slightly stubbled jaw.

Her touch brought him home.

Power

'I'm not going anywhere,' Leo told her.

It was everything she needed to hear right now. Though she'd prided herself on managing the last year, adjusting, and on some levels even thriving, it wasn't the same as *living*.

Leo leant down. Tall, beautiful. His body bronzed by the Florentine sun. The tattoos curling around his arm, exposed by the cut-away shirt.

How had she ever encouraged him to leave? What had she been thinking?

As the crowds surged around them and Malawi tugged on the leash, he kissed her as if for the first time. Tentative then all-consuming.

After all these months, she was finally recharged.

And he was her power bank.

~PART VI - BEFORE~

Gravity

He didn't know how Nyembe had done it. Lured Bruce onto the mountain and dealt with the problem. Because the last time he'd been in contact with Nyembe, he was in the freezer – trying his damndest to get out. Those desperate cries! Begging, really.

Oliver had worn gloves the whole time.

In retrospect, when he thought about arriving at that horrible industrial estate, he was just going to talk to the man. Reason with him to cut Bruce some slack. It was the right thing to do and God help him, he'd made some truly terrible mistakes. Affairs. The accident.

He had a lot to do penance for.

But Nyembe's attitude bothered him. They would *never* cleave themselves from him.

What he did was completely necessary. He didn't doubt it, or even regret it.

But maybe now he was responsible for Bruce's death too. Perhaps he could have undone Nyembe's instruction.

If only he'd known.

Asked more before that wrench to Nyembe's head, then blocking off that door and extracting the documents he needed from the cabinet he unlocked using a key from Nyembe's desk.

The thought of his own complicity would keep him awake at night. The guilt eating at his insides, nibbling away little holes, but by bit. He'd lose several kilograms. It might have looked good on him but really he would just look haggard.

Grey.

Old.

If he could turn it all back, un-put everything in motion, he would. But it was just like gravity – he wouldn't be able to stop it.

The fix

She put the emergency phone on the shelf next to the television, where she found it. Her mother was still sleeping. Late for her. Very late. But it was stressful in their house. It made her insides hurt a bit. A whole lot, actually. And her mother was so very, very tired. The fighting just never seemed to stop.

Through Albert's open door, she could see his curtains were still closed. Maybe he was asleep too. It didn't matter. She would be back soon. If she moved quickly.

Wheeling her bike out the garage, she buzzed the gate. It would close automatically behind her, and when she was on the road, she'd pedal fast to catch up with him. He wasn't expecting her and that was okay. Good, actually. It might make their conversation easier. He couldn't write emails like that to Albert. Or tell him he was worthless. It just wasn't right. She would reason with him. He was their father but he was breaking them. It couldn't go on.

And she could fix it.

She just needed to speak to him, explain how he was wrong. He usually listened to her. Maybe he would this time too? Anyway, she was going to try.

She would do her best.

When she reached Newlands Forest parking, she chained her bike to a tree, waving at the car guard at the other side of the parking. He looked at her a moment, lifting his hand to wave at her. But he didn't stop her. Enjoy was very tall for her age. *Legs that go on forever*, her dad sometimes said. Although she was just eleven, she looked about fifteen. And people treated her as older than she was. It gave her an edge.

Today, especially, she would need it.

There was no time now to hesitate. He could be far ahead of her by now and like her, he was fit. Fitter than most people his age. Fitter than people younger than him, even. Her mind was made up; she was finally going to be brave and confront him.

Enjoy adjusted the yellow Nike cap on her head, and picking up her pace, began to ascend the mountain.

ACKNOWLEDGEMENTS

Many thanks to Brent Jennings, Vice Chairman (Search & Rescue) of the Mountain Club of South Africa (https://www.mcsacapetown.co.za) who generously shared his fascinating knowledge of mountain rescue procedures, with Table Mountain being the main focus. Thank you to www.thebowencenter.org for the quote relating to disconnect in families in this novel. To Maya Fowler-Sutherland for her editing insights. To Kara Peters for her design flair and support. To Sue Nyathi, for advice and friendship. To my mother, for being my ideal reader. To Bina, my right-hand woman and friend. And to my family, Dave, Jed and Cole, for everything.

EXCERPT FROM SHADOW SELF

HOW TO PLEAD

I'm sitting on a bench in some small room, a cramped musty space. *They're coming for you*, I hear and I look around. I can't see properly. It's like being asleep and feeling that you need to open your eyes but you can't. The more you try to focus, the more you panic, and the more out of touch you feel. I want to scratch the cataracts from my eyes, but even if I squint it's like the room is moving up and down.

A wave of room. A wave of noise.

Clattering.

Jangling.

I sit still, putting my head down between my knees.

"It's okay, Thea, I said I was here, didn't I?"

Robbie. My heart is bulging with voices, and my brother sounds exactly the same as ever. I feel seasick, leaning in a glass-bottomed boat, with fish floating around below me all dead and bloodied.

A shark dropping below me, its fin cut off, crimson and spinning.

A top, going round and round. And round and round.

Lights on. Lights off.

Lights on. Lights off.

"Ma'am, you've got to come now," and I'm not sure if it's the shark talking, but I feel a grip on my elbow, and I push it away. There's a squealing noise, like a piglet, a kettle whistle. Then I'm being lifted,

floating in a balloon.

Weeeeeeeeeeeeeeeeeeeeeeeeeeeeeeee . . .

"This is the courthouse, *mevrou*," that voice says. "You need to stand up now. We're going up the stairs."

"Don't want to," I say. "I need to sleep."

"Lady, after what you did, you've got a lifetime to sleep. Not much else to do in Worcester."

Worcester? What are they talking about? I'm not in Worcester – I'm supposed to be asleep with my kids and with Robbie. Didn't he promise?

"Leave me alone," I say. "I don't like you."

"Lady, I don't like you either."

I peer at him, and his face appears as though through mist.

Fat nose. Stubby eyelashes. Coffee eyes. A peaked hat.

"We're going to have to cuff you, ma'am," someone says, but I don't think it's him because his lips don't move.

"As in *hand*cuffs?" I ask Robbie.

"I think so," Robbie says. "What else could he mean? Just go, Thea. Remember how we used to play with handcuffs in the tree house? Cops and robbers?"

But that was fun and this hurts.

"No need to push me," I say, sounding like Mother.

"Listen, lady, just get a move on now. This magistrate don't like to wait."

So I walk. I don't like waiting either. And it irritates me when Clay is late. Clay, my husband. I always check my watch a thousand times and wonder why he can't respect me by arriving on time. Always another emergency at one of his coffee shops.

As I walk, each step is heavy as if my legs are in water. I wade the stairs.

Up, up.

The chains clank behind me where the policemen are standing. They're talking.

"So she told me that my son stole my car when I was attending an accident scene. *Dronk, jy weet.* And only sixteen. I found him at Muizenberg Beach. And he thought he was too old for a klap."

Mother specialised in those. My first husband was more like her than she would ever have admitted.

Violence. Bodies on bodies.

I shiver. What's that saying again? Like someone's walking over my grave.

At the top of the stairs, I walk into a uniform. The man holds me back.

"Steady on, wait until we're ready."

Go. Wait. Walk. Stop. Go. I wish they'd just make up their damn minds. Below me, the other cops chat on.

"And the car? What about it? No problems with the car? A dent in the front, *jong*. He's going to rake leaves for a year to pay for it."

Rake. My Zen garden relaxed me. Patterns in the sand. Swirls. Twirls.

Until Joe tipped the sand on the lounge carpet and Clay said, *Enough of this. I don't like the grit under my feet.*

337

At the top, it's buzzing. Voices up and down. And the lights are so bright.

I blink, blink, blink.

There's a hand coming towards me, and then it goes away. Someone's shouting, "Keep away from the prisoner!"

"That's you," says Robbie.

"I know," I say back. "I can feel my wrists."

My oldest daughter, Sanusha, is there, I think, with her hot olive eyes shouting, *why, why, why?* And I wish Robbie would just explain it to her. It's better. For Joe. For baby Caitie. For me. Even for Sanusha.

She has her father and he'll care for her. She doesn't need *me* to save her.

The policeman's pushing me; I could feel his fingers in my ribs.

"Ouch," I say, massaging my side.

"There," he says. "Stand over there."

I'm in front of a microphone with the sound turned off. The judge – is that what he is? – is whispering to me. And I look at him, concentrating, trying hard to hear.

"Madam," he says to me.

There's my defence attorney, Tom Harper. I know *him*, have for a long time. He's smiling at me, nodding gently. But Tom's not gentle and he's confusing me. He says something to the judge and comes closer.

"Just answer the questions, Thea," he says.

"What questions? I can't hear him."

"He asked you for your full name."

"Doesn't he know it? He needs to speak up."

"Your Worship, the prisoner says she can't hear you properly."

Then the judge booms at me and he sounds like God, like Ganesha: "Madam, please state your full name for the court."

"Just do it," says Robbie. "Do what he says, and say 'sir'. Show him some respect."

"Thea June Middleton . . . sir."

"And your full address, please?"

"28c Jamieson Road, Rondebosch." (Currently incarcerated elsewhere.)

"Now I do this for the purpose of confirming you are the correct accused, and from the records in front of me, you are."

I realise Tom is standing still in front of me, facing the judge. He has his hands folded at his waist, like a contrite schoolboy. But he turns once or twice to look at me, as though I'm supposed to understand him. As I watch the judge, his mouth opens like someone blowing smoke rings at the bar.

338

I sniff. The room smells of hate and despair. The judge shrugs and I want to step away, step back and float on a cloud, catch a smoke ring like a Bentley Belt.

"Does the accused speak English? Why isn't she answering me?" calls the red man, man in red piping.

"Yes, Your Worship. She understands you."

"Plead, Mom!" I hear a voice and it sounds like Sanusha. Sanusha under the water I'm drowning in.

"Not guilty," I say. I think I sound firm, solid, but then the big man, Mr Law, says, "Can you repeat that please."

"Louder," says Sanusha.

"Silence, miss, this is a court. We can't have interjections from the observers."

So I clamp my mouth, like Joe used to when he didn't want to lie but didn't want to tell the truth either.

"Not you," says Tom, and now I recognise his voice.

"Oh, there you are, Tom," I say.

"Yes," he says, flint-eyed. "The plea, please, Thea."

"Not guilty," I say again.

The lawyers and prosecutors and policemen and judge all jump.

They heard me this time and I laugh.

Panty boys.

Before long, the cops are escorting me down the stairs and I see Clay. Lovely Clay looking grey.

He shakes his head at me, but all the time his eyes don't leave me, as though he can't believe it's me in front of him. I wave. Kiss-kiss.

Now I can finally go back to sleep.

To continue reading *Shadow Self*click here.

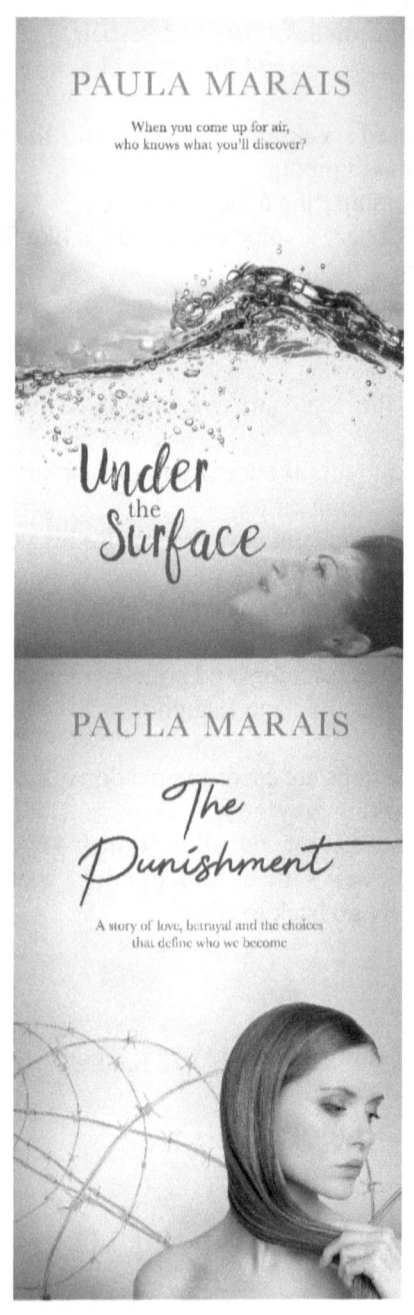

A NOTE TO MY READERS

THANK YOU SO much for supporting me by reading *A Nuclear Family*. I am so grateful for my readers - without them I don't get to do what I love best. If you enjoyed *A Nuclear Family*, please do take the time to review it on Goodreads or Amazon, so that other readers can enjoy it as well. You can also contact me directly on paula@paulamarais.com. Thank you so much.

Paula